1969

Prentice Hall Studies in Writing and Culture

——— *Series Editor* ———
Nancy Sommers
Harvard University

PRENTICE HALL STUDIES IN WRITING AND CULTURE captures the excitement of an emerging discipline that is finally coming into its own. The writers in this series are challenging basic assumptions, asking new questions, trying to broaden the inquiry about writing and the teaching of writing. They not only raise challenging questions about the classroom—about teaching and building communities of writers—they also investigate subjects as far ranging as the nature of knowledge and the role that culture plays in shaping pedagogy. Writers in the series are particularly concerned about the interplay between language and culture, about how considerations of gender, race, and audience shape our writing and our teaching. Early volumes will be devoted to the essay, audience, autobiography, and how writers teach writing. Other studies will appear over time as we explore matters that are critical to teaching writing.

Nancy Sommers is Associate Director of the Expository Writing Program at Harvard. She has also directed the composition program at the University of Oklahoma and has taught in the English Department of Rutgers University where she was a Henry Rutgers research fellow. She has published widely on the theory and practice of teaching writing. She has received the National Council of Teachers of English Promising Research Award for her work on revision and the Richard Braddock Award for her work on responding to student writing.

Books in this Series

Nancy Kline, *How Writers Teach Writing*
Kurt Spellmeyer, *Common Ground: Dialogue, Understanding,
and the Teaching of Composition*

🐦 *Audience and Rhetoric*

An Archaeological Composition of the Discourse Community

James E. Porter
Purdue University

Prentice Hall, Englewood Cliffs, New Jersey 07632

Library of Congress Cataloging-in-Publication Data

Porter, James E.,
    Audience and rhetoric / James E. Porter.
        p.   cm. -- (Prentice Hall studies in writing and culture)
    Includes bibliographical references and index.
    ISBN 0-13-050667-2 (case)   -- ISBN 0-13-050675-3 (paper)

    1. Rhetoric.   2. Audiences.   3. Reader-response criticism.
    4. Authors and readers.   5. Deconstruction.   I. Title.   II. Series.
    PN175.P6   1992
    808'.001--dc20   91-15166
                                                            CIP

Acquisitions Editor: Tracy Augustine
Editorial/production supervisor and interior design: Penelope Linskey
Copyeditor: Joyce Perkins
Cover Designer: Marianne Frasco
Prepress Buyer: Herb Klein
Manufacturing Buyer: Patrice Fraccio

© 1992 by Prentice-Hall, Inc.
A Simon & Schuster Company
Englewood Cliffs, New Jersey 07632

Printed in the United States of America
10 9 8 7 6 5 4 3 2 1

ISBN   0-13-050667-2   C

ISBN   0-13-050675-3   P

9 780130 506672

90000>

Prentice-Hall International (UK) Limited, *London*
Prentice-Hall of Australia Pty. Limited, *Sydney*
Prentice-Hall Canada Inc., *Toronto*
Prentice-Hall Hispanoamericana, S.A., *Mexico*
Prentice-Hall of India Private Limited, *New Delhi*
Prentice-Hall of Japan, Inc., *Tokyo*
Simon & Schuster Asia Pte. Ltd., *Singapore*
Editora Prentice-Hall do Brasil, Ltda., *Rio de Janeiro*

To

Gail, Jaime, and Kathleen,
With love and appreciation

ॐ *Contents*

Preface ix

Chapter 1 Introduction: The Problem of Audience 1

Chapter 2 The Theoretical Heritage of Classical Rhetoric 15

Chapter 3 Traditional Rhetoric and the Disappearance of Audience 29

Chapter 4 The New Rhetoric and the Recovery of Audience 51

Chapter 5 Reader-Response Criticism and Audience as Implied Reader 63

Chapter 6 Poststructuralism, Social Constructionism, and Audience as Community 79

Chapter 7 Composing the Discourse Community 105

Chapter 8 Conclusion: The Ethical Implications of a Social Vision of Audience 119

Appendix I Audience in Professional Writing   *127*

Appendix II Teaching a Community View of Audience   *137*

Bibliographies of Audience   *156*

Bibliography   *157*

Author Index   *177*

ॐ *Preface*

Audience has been a central concept in rhetoric at least since the fifth century B.C. and a key concern of composition since the formal emergence of that discipline in the late nineteenth century. Composition and rhetoric texts have long advised writers and speakers to "consider your audience"; and more recently, composition researchers have investigated the degree to which writers at various levels can, do, and should consider their audiences during the writing process.

My study attempts to answer some basic questions about audience, questions we need to ponder when as researchers we design studies treating audience, when as teachers we advise students to write for audiences, and when as writers we ourselves consider audiences: What do we mean by the term "audience"? What does the term refer to? What does the signifier "audience" actually signify? What exactly *is* an audience, and what does it mean to "consider" one?

These are basic questions—but not simple ones. Rhetoric and composition has long assumed the importance of audience, but has only occasionally paused to reflect on its meaning. In this study, I ponder these questions by tracing various and selected references to "audience" (and related terms, like "reader") in rhetoric and composition research and in writing texts. This study focuses mainly on contemporary treatments, on those theoretical discussions of audience appearing within the last 20 or so years within the field. But I also consider references to audience through the history of rhetoric, noting especially those key figures, such as Aristotle and George Campbell, whose treatment of audience fixed its use in rhetoric and composition—or at least directed our thinking down certain lines. Thanks to Aristotle and Campbell (discussed in Chapters 2 and 3), but even more so thanks to the rhetoric tradition of which they are simply representatives, we tend to imagine audiences as real people and as the congregated listeners of an oral discourse. We think of representatives packed into a legislative assembly, of parents in a school auditorium, of the congregation of a church. And of course we think of the "general public"—that great mass of credit-card carrying consumers addressed by the public media and targeted by advertising and marketing interests. These "real" audiences are passive, more or less, receivers of the message framed by the rhetor.

In communication studies, audience is often invoked, along with "writer" and "topic," as one of the three key spokes of the communication triangle. Though considered central to communication studies, these three concepts had not been considered theoretically problematic, at least not until the advent of poststructuralist theory. Conventionally, the writer is simply the *person* who writes. The topic is the subject matter, external to the rhetor, that serves as the referent of the discourse. The audience is the *person* or *persons* who receive the message and who are persuaded, entertained, or informed (or not, as the case may be) by the message.

But things aren't quite so simple. When we start to study individual treatments of audience, we see that "audience" is a floating, perhaps an empty, signifier. We hear people say "audience"—but mean very different things by it. The term refers to different concepts (or senses of "audience") in different contexts. Though those in rhetoric and composition have preferred the simpler sense of audience represented by the communication triangle, contemporary theorists have recognized that audiences are very often more than simply "real people." Audiences also exist in texts, in the writer's imagination, in the general culture, as well as "out there" in the assembly hall. The question rhetoric theory asks is, Where is the audience located? In the text? Outside the text? Or somewhere in between? The answer is all of the above and, at the same time, none of the above. We talk about audiences in different, sometimes contradictory, ways. Indeed, we cannot help but do so, for the term is one of those, like "writer" and "style," that defies our efforts to pinpoint its meaning.

The emergence of poststructuralist, particularly deconstructionist, theory has led us to question the basic terms that serve as the foundation for communication theory. What exactly is a writer or author? Theorists like Roland Barthes, Michel Foucault, and Sharon Crowley have asked this essential question. Generally, poststructuralist theory challenges the assumption that there can be a simple, one-to-one correspondence between signifier

Preface xi

and signified. It is simplistic, misleading, and limiting to assume that "writer" refers simply and only to the *person* producing the discourse, or to a single and stable signified, or that there can be a simple correspondence between this person and the "voice" of a given discourse. In similar fashion we can question the simple understanding of "audience" as real people. The reader-response critics (such as Norman Holland, Wolfgang Iser, Stanley Fish, and Jonathan Culler) have asked the question, What exactly is a reader or audience, and are they the same thing? Their work (discussed in Chapter 5) has been applied chiefly to literary criticism, but it has important implications for rhetoric and composition as well.

This study is partly a deconstruction of the conventional conceptions of audience, a deconstruction aimed at liberating the concept from its fixed position at the end of the assembly line of discourse production and from the east point of the communication triangle. This study reveals the complex and shifting nature of a term that compositionists have used to stabilize discursive situations. What I do, in effect, is to read rhetoric and composition's treatment of audience *through* poststructuralist critical theory. In particular, I call on the archaeological method of Michel Foucault, as he articulates it in several of his works but most clearly and explicitly in *The Archaeology of Knowledge*. Foucault's method (discussed in Chapters 1 and 6) forces its user to ask disruptive, at times rude, questions about the ordering practices of a discipline. Archaeological analysis is a useful method for entering a discipline and exploring its foundational terminology—those concepts that are accepted as given, as the grounding terms or principles for the operation of the discipline. An application of the archaeological method reveals how unstable rhetoric's foundational concepts (e.g., writer, reader, text) actually are: they do not refer to clear and stable signifiers but rather to a *range* of possibilities. The result of such an analysis is an understanding—not a definition—of the notion of audience that will, I hope, inform and enlighten research on audience and readers.

The study examines how those in rhetoric and composition have located and described audience. As I proceed, I argue that locating the audience "out there" by defining it as real people, as actual readers, while at times a useful fiction, is theoretically and pedagogically incomplete, and ideologically and politically problematic as well. Such a conception isolates rhetor from audience, thereby creating a political division that privileges the rhetor with access to knowledge (and hence, truth and power) and that places the audience in a nonparticipatory subordinate role. This view sees composing as primarily a *managerial* activity: in this model, audience is the passive receptor of a truth that is discovered separately by the writer.

To counter this limiting perspective, it is necessary to recognize the many senses of "audience" and the many senses in which audiences function. Audience can be seen as a textual property, as an ethos (or set of attitudes and conventions located in sets of texts), or as a community or discourse field. This manifold perspective is not at all alien to rhetoric and composition; in fact, it is *in* rhetoric and composition, though not dominant in it. Many rhetoric theorists acknowledge the multiple senses of audience.

In Chapter 6, I note the effect of poststructuralist and social constructionist theory, which encourages us to see the writer not as a lone agent impressing a prediscovered truth on a largely ignorant and passive audience but as "identified with" audience, as influenced by audience. Audience represents a field or community out of which the writer arises. From this view, the audience can be said to "write the writer." This view is "social epistemic," seeing composing as essentially *participatory* or *communal* in some form; audience is, thus, involved in the discovery process. This conception re-situates audience at the beginning of the composing process, imagining an audience that participates in invention, perhaps in the sense of collaboration, but definitely through existing discourse, in the social settings that provide an occasion for that discourse, and in the genres and conventions which those discourses establish. It imagines an audience that participates dialogically, through existing discursive practices, in the shaping of meaning. This "social view" of audience is by no means recent. Douglas Park, Art Walzer, and Richard Young have been encouraging us in this direction for some time—but also, for a longer time though in different ways, Chaim Perelman and Kenneth Burke. Others, like Janice Lauer and James Berlin, have been promoting a social epistemic view of rhetoric. This view has been around, though I think that poststructuralist theory is reviving it in a new way.

In Chapters 6 and 7 particularly—but implicitly thoughout the entire study—I argue that seeing the audience from the field perspective, as a "discourse community" if you like, encompasses the other conceptions of audience. I see the notion of audience as community as a more comprehensive, flexible, and coherent notion for our field than the competing conceptions. I conclude, then, by attempting to *reconstruct* a notion of audience for the discipline—by attempting to articulate a social vision of audience, and by attempting to compose the discourse community.

James E. Porter

Acknowledgements

As is customary within the community of academic publishing, my theoretical and intellectual predecessors are acknowledged mainly in the bibliography. However, I want to credit four influences in particular: Michel Foucault, James Kinneavy, Janice Lauer, and Jim Berlin, people whose methodologies, critical practices, and, especially, views of rhetoric contributed significantly to my understanding of audience and of rhetoric. I am especially grateful to Janice Lauer for introducing me to rhetoric and for her encouragement and support.

This work received support from several grants over the years. The Research and Instructional Development Support Program at Indiana University–Purdue University at Fort Wayne provided help in the form of summer grants in 1984 and 1986. Most of Chapter 2 was written during the summer of 1987, while I was a participant in an NEH Summer Seminar on "Rhetoric as Public Discourse," held at Ohio State University. I am thankful to the National Endowment for the Humanities and to Edward P. J. Corbett and to the members of that seminar for their help. A President's Council on the Humanities Grant from Indiana University in 1986 helped defray costs for supplies and other expenses.

Numerous colleagues reviewed various versions of this study and provided helpful criticisms. I want to thank in particular Dave Russell, Avon Crismore, Fred Kirchhoff, Everett Devine, Bill Karis, and Nancy DeJoy. Special thanks and appreciation go to my uncle Thomas E. Porter for his critical perspective and wise counsel.

My reviewers—Jim Berlin, Patricia Bizzell, and Douglas Park—provided valuable input and suggestions. Series editor Nancy Sommers was very patient and supportive. And I want to thank the editors at Prentice Hall for their assistance, especially Phil Miller, Tracy Augustine, Fran Falk, and Penny Linskey.

Most importantly, I want to thank my family—particularly my wife Gail and my daughters Jaime and Kathleen—for their understanding and support and love.

James E. Porter
West Lafayette, IN

I acknowledge with gratitude permission to use excerpts from the following works:

Aristotle, *The Rhetoric and Poetics of Aristotle*, intro. Edward P. J. Corbett (New York: Modern Library-Random, 1984). Reprinted by permission of Oxford University Press.

Kenneth A. Bruffee, "Social Construction, Language, and the Authority of Knowledge: A Bibliographical Essay, "*College English* 48 (1986): 773–790. Reprinted by permission.

Kenneth Burke, *A Rhetoric of Motives* (Berkeley, CA: U of California P, 1969). Copyright © 1969 The Regents of the University of California. Reprinted by permission.

Kenneth Burke, *The Philosophy of Literary Form* (New York: Random, 1961).

———— *Credits* ————

Chapter 1

✌ *Introduction: The Problem of Audience*

> The supreme orator is the one whose speech
> instructs, delights, and moves the minds of the
> audience.[1]
>
> *Cicero*

This study calls attention to, examines closely, traces an unappreciated rhetorical concept: audience. Is it really unappreciated? Perhaps not so much *neglected* as *reduced* to a simple univocity and so rendered impotent. Audience has been deconceptualized and, thus, deproblematized by some researchers and practitioners in composition. The audience is regarded primarily—and in some cases, exclusively—as "the person or persons with whom one communicates through writing or speech" or "the decoder (receiver) of the encoder's message." Audience has come to mean, in effect, real people—and there is nothing more concrete, more definable, or more "real."

Look at two handbooks defining rhetorical terms: Lanham's *A Handlist of Rhetorical Terms* and Woodson's *A Handbook of Modern Rhetorical Terms.*[2] Lanham's handbook contains entries for "polyptoton," "invention," "syncope," and six different types of definition—but none for "au-

1

dience," or "reader," or for any related term (e.g., "receiver," "addressee") that might indicate that rhetoric concerns itself with address to another. Woodson defines "anaphora," "tagmemic invention," "sentence-combining," and "cognitive domain." But there is no entry for "audience."[3] Why not? Presumably because the term is unproblematic. The audience is fixed, a given in the linear model of communication. We *know* what an audience is.

We also know how important audience is. Aristotle grants audience ultimate status by claiming that "of the three elements in speech-making—speaker, subject, and person addressed—it is the last one, the hearer, that determines the speech's end and object" (*Rhetoric* 1.3).[4] Most contemporary composition textbooks include a section on audience, usually close to the front, and proclaim audience a vital concern. These texts usually concentrate on the flesh-and-blood reader, assuming that writers will produce more effective prose if they systematically "consider" or "be aware of" the values, background, and knowledge of the receiver to ensure successful communication.[5] Many composition texts—like Richard Young, Alton Becker, and Kenneth Pike's *Rhetoric: Discovery and Change* (1970), Janice Lauer and Gene Montague's *Four Worlds of Writing* (1981), and Frank D'Angelo's *Process and Thought in Composition* (1985)[6]—stress the importance of the reader and suggest heuristics for identifying and examining readers. Writers are supposed to apply these questions to determine what they know (and do not know) about their audiences. These textbooks assume that audience analysis will make the writer more aware of audience and that this awareness will be reflected in improved writing. These audience heuristics do perform an important (though incomplete) pedagogical function in helping writers regard their readers more seriously and systematically than they might otherwise.

Generally these audience heuristics aim at analysis of the actual readership whose presence is assumed to be external to the text. For instance, a standard audience analysis question like "What is the educational level of the audience?" assumes a static and homogenous readership apart from the text. Even questions like "How much does my audience already know about my topic?" and "How many examples and illustrations do I need to get my point across?,"[7] though aimed at exploring the collective audience's relationship to topic and to text, nevertheless focus on actual readers external to the text, or what reader-response critics have termed the "real reader."[8] The writer's task vis-à-vis this real reader is thus quite work-a-day: "consider" this audience (as "real reader") and shape the text appropriately.

If any tenet in rhetoric and composition is axiomatic, it is this one: the audience is a primary factor, perhaps *the* primary factor, influencing discourse. Audience determines—or ought to determine (the principle describes an ideal world)—the writer's or speaker's subject matter and inventional method, as well as argumentative strategy, arrangement, and style. This principle translates into a simple composing direction—consider your audience—which composition texts intone dutifully, many by suggesting specific strategies for audience analysis. This principle, straight from Aristotle, is accepted by all. It is, in short, a truism.

The Problem of Locating the Audience

"Consider your audience"—a common dictum in composition and rhetoric. "Consider"? Think about, analyze, regard, study demographically. The writer finds out who her audience is and then writes the text to suit that audience. But where, exactly, *is* this audience that the writer should consider? What exactly does "consider" mean? And how does "considering" audience lead to better communication? What is most obvious and accepted about audience may be the most theoretically troublesome. The task of considering one's audience is not quite as simple as it first looks. *Locating* the audience is the first problem.

Typically, we think of audience as referring to the actual people existing apart from and prior to the discourse: the public readership of the *New York Times*; the parents the principal will address in the school gymnasium; lawyers consulting law review articles; Aunt Jane in the act of reading Johnny's thank-you note; *and* Aunt Jane before she has received Johnny's thank-you note; *and* Aunt Jane even before Johnny has written it. Here's the problem. We can certainly think of "Aunt Jane" as an audience for Johnny, but she certainly can't be an audience in the same sense at each different moment. When Johnny is in the act of composing the letter, the signifier "Aunt Jane" refers to an imaginative construction—an image of an Aunt Jane reader that Johnny conjures to produce his letter. This imaginative construction we can easily enough call the *audience*. (We might ask at this point how the writer conjures and evaluates the efficacy of this image.)

On the other hand, Aunt Jane in the act of reading is reacting to and interacting with Johnny's letter—interpreting it, misinterpreting it, feeling good or bad about it perhaps, but bringing it to a fulfillment, perhaps composing her own response to Johnny as she reads. This second "Aunt Jane" we might call the reader.

The commonsense approach treats the audience as one thing—an actual person or actual persons—and does not distinguish between the person-in-the-act-of-reading (the reader?), and the prior idea or imaginative construction that the writer develops of this reader and, to a greater or lesser extent, embodies in a discourse (the audience?). It might be convenient to force a distinction between "reader" and "audience," but it would not be consistent with previous discussions, because by and large in rhetoric and composition the two terms are treated as synonymous and interchangeable. "Reader" and "audience" are the same thing.

We can examine what one handbook says about audience, for it represents a standard treatment, from Aristotle to the present. Our representative handbook begins its discussion with this advice to writers:

> Although it often gets the least concentrated attention, your audience—the people you expect to read what you write—ought to be a most deliberate consideration as you work out a strategy for a writing task. Keep your readers in mind as you write, because they influence what you write, the way you write, even why you write. Always try to picture a specific reader or some specific group or type of reader. Then ask yourself whether the best presentation for this specific audience is likely to be simple or complex, casual or formal, general or specialized. In order to communicate, you must adjust your subject matter, your point of view, the kind of detail and explanation you use, even the words you choose, to the audience you are writing for.[9]

This passage articulates the generic, commonsense notion about the importance of audience, echoing Aristotle's advice: audience is an important consideration, influencing topic, style, point of view, development, and purpose—in other words the entire discourse. Audience is portrayed as actual readers, "the people you expect to read what you write"—that is, "audience" and "readers" are synonymous.

Not much more is said about audience in the handbook. Occasionally, "the reader" is invoked to justify a usage dictum, as in "The more remote the antecedent [of the pronoun], the more difficulty readers will have in understanding the reference."[10] But as in most treatments, audience is announced as important—but not treated in any detail.

This sample audience passage instructs writers to "keep your readers in mind." Thus, this audience is clearly an imaginative construct of the writer: the audience is in the writer's mind, it is a "picture" of the group of persons the writer expects will read the work. But where does this picture come from? How does the writer produce it? Presumably, the imaginative construct arises from the writer's prior experiences, if not with that particular audience, then with others like it. But don't we have a problem if Johnny's imaginative construction of Aunt Jane is built from observing Aunt Jane at the dinner table, Aunt Jane at family picnics, and Aunt Jane watching TV? How does Johnny discover what Aunt Jane is like *as a reader*?

If the audience has not yet convened, in any sense, as readers, how can the writer picture it? Where is the writer supposed to look for answers to audience analysis questions like "Do they have traits in common, such as level of education, similar experiences, familiarity with or interest in the topic?"[11] If the picture in the writer's head is the audience, or the readers, then what do we call those who actually do the reading? Is there ever an exact correspondence between imagined audience and real reader? The image of Aunt Jane in Johnny's head is one thing (an imaginative construct); Aunt Jane in the act of reading Johnny's letter is something else. Johnny may have a stereotyped or grossly inaccurate image of Aunt Jane. By what procedure does he check the accuracy or efficacy of his stereotype of the reader?

The commonsense treatment relies on a speech communication model that views audience as the physically real receptors of the *speaker's* discourse. The model views audience as physically present (i.e., in the flesh), and as the processors of a message. Of course, in the traditional oratory, the audience was a physically present body of real people: the citizens in the Athenian assembly, for instance. The problem with such a model is that while it may adequately describe interpretive activities (e.g., reading, voting), and be suitable for speech occasions, it does not describe audience from the point of view of the writer or speaker producing discourse. For the writer or speaker in the act of composing, the physical audience *has not yet convened*. The speaker in the act of composing is not yet facing a body of real people, and in most cases the writer never faces one. For the writer in the act of composing, the "real reader" may not exist or, even if it does, it may be irrelevant to the composing act. The idea of the "real reader" is a convenient fiction, an abstraction, ar imaginative construct that the writer calls upon or creates.[12] But an imaginative construction of what? And from what sources does this construction arise?

There is a problem of locating the audience, or of describing it, when one is holding to the generic and commonsense notion of audience as "real readers." The idea of the real reader is useful, and I am not suggesting that we should throw out real-reader analysis. What I am suggesting is that real-reader analysis is insufficient by itself as a heuristic strategy; it simply does not provide writers with enough practical help or imaginative guidance, as Douglas Park and other audience researchers have pointed out.[13] Even treatments calling upon elaborate psychological and sociological theories and models to analyze the real audience have their limitations.[14]

Many contemporary composition texts assume that the construction of the image of the audience is an imaginative activity, and they propose audience analysis questions to guide this activity. Such approaches assume that the writer has considerable imaginative capability to begin with—that, in effect, the writer already possesses the image of the audience that the questions are designed to help the writer reconstruct. To put it another way, the questions are only answerable by writers who already know the answers. Chiefly, I see such questions as serving a mnemonic function: they can help writers recall or arrange prior knowledge. The problem is that such questions will not help a writer generate new knowledge about an unknown or misconceived audience. In teaching freshman composition, for instance, I have assigned real-reader heuristics to my classes but have not found them to be very helpful to audience understanding. Students dutifully answer the questions—but the quality of those "answers" is only as good as their prior understanding of the audience. Such an exercise may even have the counterproductive effect of reinforcing audience misconceptions.

Another problem the writer faces with conventional real-reader analysis is deciding how the information collected should affect the composed product: How should information about the general educational level of an audience influence my composing decisions? For example, as a writer of computer documentation, I may know that I am writing for a "college-educated" audience. But how do I *use* this information? How does it or should it guide my composing decisions? Information about an audience has to be interpreted and *applied:* the mere data itself will not tell me how to compose or relieve me of the necessity of exercising rhetorical judgment. In fact, there can be a *gap* between the data collected about the audience (as "real" but abstracted entity) and the constructed text (which the audience will encounter as "readers").

Most real-reader analysis guides help writers discover what they already know about readers—and that's the problem. These heuristics rely on tapping a prior knowledge that may be nothing more than an inaccurate or irrelevant set of qualities attributed to the reader. The types writers call upon to define their audiences may be inadequate for their rhetorical purposes; they may not be adequate *reader* types, in other words. In addition, the commonsense treatment of audience as actual readers presupposes a speech communication model in which the audience is actually, physically present as listeners of an oral discourse. For written (and for that matter speech) *composition,* a different kind of model is necessary.

Considering audience is not a simple task. The standard treatment relies on a commonsense and empirical point of view: audience = actual people. The irony here is that this commonsense perspective violates the ground rules of its own empirical epistemology: the reader is assumed to exist during the composing process, but of course from the purely empirical view of the writer in the act of composing, no reader yet exists.

The Problem of Talking About Audience

Audience is more than simply an aggregate of individuals—though it may sometimes be useful for writers to imagine them as such. "Audience" is, first, a rhetorical concept, representing a problem and a challenge to rhetoricians and writers. It is, among other things, a composed abstraction, a textual presence. The reader-response critics were perhaps the first to appreciate the multiplicity and complexity of the concept of audience and its relevance to the interpretation of literary works. But rhetoric and composition researchers like Douglas Park, James Berlin, Chaim Perelman, James Kinneavy, Lisa Ede, Andrea Lunsford, and others have also recognized the complexity of the notion of audience and have demonstrated its importance to composition and to writing instruction.

Because the term is ubiquitous and so important, it is both interesting and problematic—especially problematic when we assume that it has a fixed meaning or if we ourselves fix the meaning in the way we teach or write about audience. The commonsense view treats "audience" and "reader" as synonymous terms and regards both as the actual persons receiving the writer's message. But despite the apparent univocity of the term, the meaning of "audience" varies, often widely, from treatment to treatment. Almost always, audiences are seen as actual people; but often they are described in terms of stereotyped characters or inventional or stylistic properties. Audience is also treated as a principle, an abstraction—sometimes as the presuppositions of a single discourse, other times as the entire set of conventions defining a discipline. "Audience" in rhetoric and composition means many things and serves many purposes. The term floats and slides, means one thing here, another there. The more it is used the less we are capable of *seeing* it: the term sometimes becomes transparent. In fact, there is no clear, simple, or single connection between the signifier "audience" and the signified.

That there are different senses of the term has been noticed by reader-response critics.[15] That audience is a concept with multiple meanings is not a new idea to rhetoric and composition either.[16] In the early 1980s, there was a flurry of critical commentary exploring the different senses of audience and attempting to mediate between them. This dialogue, begun in research by Douglas Park and Russell Long,[17] culminated in a special audience issue of *College Composition and Communication* (Volume 35, May 1984). In this issue, three separate research articles noted the complexity of the concept.[18] Such work would lead one to expect that what would ensue would be a substantial discussion of the problematics of audience. What seemed to result instead, ironically, was a virtual silence on the topic: discussion of audience all but ceased, though there are some signs that it is again being taken up.[19]

We should revive dialogue on audience, taking up the issues raised by Park, Ede, and Lunsford, and others. We need to examine, and challenge, the commonsense treatment that imagines the audience as the actual, physically present receptors of discourse, assuming that the audience occupies a fixed position in the composing process (i.e., at the end of the "assembly line" in the linear communication model) and has a certain fixed and determinable status relative to writer and text. Not only is the meaning of the term "audience" problematic, but the presence of *the* audience in the composing process is anything but fixed and stable. We need to re-examine the various ways audiences are imagined.

Researchers working from the assumptions of classical and contemporary rhetoric theory (e.g., Chaim Perelman) tend to treat audience in terms of inventional or stylistic principles; audience is, in other words, an abstract entity constructed *by* rhetoric. Some reader-response critics treat the audience as the collected assumptions of a particular text—as the "implied reader." Others argue that the field view of audience—seeing audience as "discourse community," located in a self-defining set of texts—provides a more comprehensive perspective, accounting more satisfactorily for the presence of the audience in written communication.

There are, then, several alternate conceptions of audience, views that locate audience in "pieces of writing."[20] Locating audience within inscribed texts takes on different forms. Audience has been treated

- as a property of style
- as a set of inventional principles
- as stereotyped characters or psychological types
- as a textual fiction
- as genre conventions
- as a field, or discourse community

Frequently, audience is treated in more than one of these senses at one time, and in actuality the approaches are not mutually exclusive, as we shall see. Rather, they represent different emphases. Any given treatment—whether a research article or a composition textbook—may combine several at once.

Audience is among the slipperiest of rhetoric notions, and it will and probably should remain that way. It belongs to that special class of terms, the foundational terms defining the field (like "writer" and "text"), which, as in any discipline, are the ones most likely to resist efforts to fix their meaning or function.[21] As soon as we claim decisively and univocally that "Audience is such and such," we are lost. If I try to tell you that the audience is only a textual fiction or an intertextual presence, you could reply, "Yes, but what about that fellow over there reading my book? Isn't he an audience?" (And, as Johnson refuted Berkeley by kicking a stone, you could challenge the textual fiction by kicking a reader.)

To add to the complexity, the notion of audience overlaps almost every other rhetorical concept. Matters of style and form involve audience. If you take up argument theory, enthymemes, or *topoi*, you encounter audience. Consider ethics, audience again. Punctuation? Audience rears its ugly collective head. In short, a study of "audience and rhetoric" must, to claim comprehensiveness, consider almost every topic dealt with in rhetoric and composition.[22]

Methodology: Archaeological Analysis

To bring some order to the chaos of the topic—or at least to dare an explanation for the chaos—is, in this book, to describe the classification grid that underlies such treatments. The method invoked here perhaps most closely resembles what Michel Foucault describes as "archaeological analysis."[23]

An archaeological exploration of the concept of audience attempts to reveal the ordering grid that supports the concept. It is an exploration, in a sense, of the discipline itself; it is an analytic that does not begin by accepting the foundational terminology of rhetoric and composition but rather begins by questioning the status of those very terms that are assumed to be its most stable ground. An archaeological exploration of audience, then, does not accept the "real" status of audience. Rather, it questions that status, asking questions about who has used the term, in what contexts it has been used, how it has been classified, what value has been assigned to it, what ideologies have collected around it, what assertions may be made about it, and what assertions have been disallowed.

What we discover is that sometimes these treatments negate their own assertions, sometimes they hide what they claim to reveal, or obscure what they attempt to explain. The greatest and most obvious irony, of course, is the practice of declaring audience to be of prime importance, central to the composing process and a powerful influencing agent, and then saying very little else about it.

In his book *Deconstructive Criticism*, Vincent Leitch characterizes archaeological analysis, and in so doing provides a set of critical questions we can ask about audience:

> [Archaeological analysis] correlates different disciplinary discourses so as to articulate the general system of rules governing the discursive practices of an era. To put matters another way, archaeology works toward answering a series of fundamental questions. What is it possible to speak of? What terms are destined to disappear? Which terms enter into current practice? Which ones are censured or repressed? Which ones are considered valid and which questionable? Which are eventually abandoned and which revived? What relations exist between present and past terms or foreign and native ones? What transformations are imposed on terms? Which individuals, groups, or classes have access to such discourse? How are their relations institutionalized? How does any struggle over a discourse operate? Throughout this inquiry, archaeology seeks to describe the rules in a given period and a particular society which define the limits and forms of expressibility, conservation, memory, reactivation, and appropriation. In constructing its history of discourse, archaeology isolates the fact and manner of appearance of discourses; it examines the field where they coexist, prevail, and disappear; and it investigates the transformations enacted there.[24]

Leitch's questions provide a critical terminology useful for exploring the concept of audience and its position within rhetoric and composition.

An archaeological exploration of audience must also consider the historical antecedents of contemporary treatments. We cannot *see* why we hold the assumptions we do about audience unless we examine those influences—and I think particularly of Aristotle and Campbell—that have constrained our thinking. We have to search for the "grid of intelligibility," that epistemological framework in which our notion of audience resides. In particular, we need to examine classical assumptions about the role of audience and the classical division between speech and writing (discussed in Chapter 2). The historical perspective is vital, then, to archaeology because it permits the archaeologist to consider in what ways past practices, articulations, and discursive moments intersect with the present. In fact, "archaeology does not necessarily refer back to the past":[25] contemporary discussions of audience *include* the past. Aristotle and Campbell insinuate themselves into almost any discussion of audience, inevitably—which is why it is so important to consider their orientation toward audience. Their orientation to a great extent accounts for ours.

My approach is mainly archaeological critique.[26] I examine how the sign "audience" functions within a body of texts constrained by the rubric "rhetoric and composition." I am chiefly interested in the structure of the knowledge system, and in examining rupture points within the system—i.e., historical moments when the meaning of "audience" shifts (which, in turn, correspond to shifts in the discipline itself).[27] Because audience is such a slippery concept, its analysis requires a methodology like Foucault's, which is, I believe, especially useful for examining a discipline's foundational terminology. Archaeological analysis aims to uncover that "diagram" that is the discipline's epistemological base—the base that supports, and keeps constrained, its notion of audience.

Let us be mindful of Roland Barthes' warning about Method:

> No surer way to kill a piece of research and send it to join the great waste of abandoned projects than Method. The danger of Method (of a fixation with Method) is to be grasped by considering the two demands to which the work of research must reply. The first is a demand for responsibility: the work must increase lucidity, manage to reveal the implications of a procedure, the alibis of a language, in short must constitute a *critique* (remember once again that to *criticize* means *to call into crisis*.) Here Method is inevitable, irreplaceable, not for its "results" but precisely—or on the contrary—because it realizes the highest degree of consciousness of a language *which is not forgetful of itself*. The second demand, however, is of a quite different order; it is that of writing, space of dispersion of desire, where Law is dismissed. *At a certain moment*, therefore, it is necessary to turn against Method, or at least to treat it without any founding privilege as one of the voices of plurality—as a *view*, a spectacle mounted in the text, the text which all in all is the only "true" result of any research.[28]

Barthes tells us that the work of research must be responsible; it must increase understanding by constituting a critique, calling something into crisis, by revealing the implications of a procedure—or, as in this case, of a concept. At the same time, it must be aware of its own ground, its own *gap*. According to Barthes, it must, at some juncture, turn against its method—and against Method. Problem: To what extent can any researcher *see* that gap, much less credit it? Can the researcher ever do more than acknowledge its presence, briefly, and then choose to ignore it in order to proceed with the project which must always have *some* ground, some ideology, some gap? Isn't the gap, after all, a place for the audience?

NOTES
Chapter 1

1 Cicero, *De Inventione—De Optimo Genere Oratorum—Topica*, trans. H. M. Hubbell (Cambridge, MA: Loeb-Harvard UP, 1949).

2 Richard A. Lanham, *A Handlist of Rhetorical Terms* (Berkeley, CA: U of California P, 1969); Linda Woodson, *A Handbook of Modern Rhetorical Terms* (Urbana, IL: NCTE, 1979).

3 Woodson does, however, invoke the Aristotelian distinction between the "addressee" ("the person being addressed in discourse") and the "interlocutor" ("a participant in a dialogue or conversation"). See Woodson, pp. 2, 32.

4 Aristotle, *The Rhetoric and Poetics of Aristotle*, intro. Edward P. J. Corbett (New York: Modern Library-Random, 1984).

5 For example, in *Successful Writing* (1981), Maxine Hairston claims that "the most common defect in the writing of nonprofessional writers . . . [is] their failure to identify a real audience and write to it." Hairston addresses this problem by providing an audience heuristic—a set of questions to ask about the reader—designed to help writers visualize their readers and produce texts appropriate for them. See Maxine C. Hairston, *Successful Writing: A Rhetoric for Advanced Composition* (New York: Norton, 1981), p. 46.

6 Richard E. Young, Alton L. Becker, and Kenneth L. Pike, *Rhetoric: Discovery and Change* (New York: Harcourt, 1970); Janice Lauer, Gene Montague, Andrea Lunsford, and Janet Emig, *Four Worlds of Writing* (New York: Harper & Row, 1981); and Frank J. D'Angelo, *Process and Thought in Composition*, 3rd ed. (Boston: Little, Brown, 1985).

7 Hairston, p. 48.

8 See W. Daniel Wilson, "Readers in Texts," *PMLA* 96 (1981): 848–863.

9 Glenn Leggett et al., eds., *Prentice-Hall Handbook for Writers*, 9th ed. (Englewood Cliffs, NJ: Prentice Hall, 1985), p. 307.

10 Leggett, p. 73.

11 Leggett, p. 309.

12 As George Dillon points out, "The real reader proves to be an elusive creature once we try to specify him in terms of knowledge, attitudes, and interests. We can of course imagine alternative kinds of readers: fat/slender readers of weight-reduction books, freshman/professors reading composition guides, and so on. But are those real readers? It is far from certain that they are anything more than an abstraction or projection, stereotypes, pieces of writing if there ever were." See George L. Dillon, *Rhetoric as Social Imagination* (Bloomington, IN: Indiana UP, 1986), pp. 147–148.

13 See Douglas Park, "Analyzing Audiences," *College Composition and Communication* 37 (1986): 478–488; Theodore Clevenger, Jr., *Audience Analysis* (India-

napolis, IN: Bobbs-Merrill, 1966); Robert G. Roth, "The Evolving Audience: Alternatives to Audience Accommodation," *College Composition and Communication* 38 (1987): 47–55; and Arthur E. Walzer, "Articles from the 'California Divorce Project': A Case Study of the Concept of Audience," *College Composition and Communication* 36 (1985): 150–159.

In "Analyzing Audiences," Park challenges conventional audience analysis techniques, arguing that approaching an audience demographically (i.e., asking sociological questions in a market-survey approach) is not the best way to understand an audience. Rather, Park argues that the writer needs to understand the social situation that brings the audience together in the first place: What shared principles, procedures, and values bring a certain group together in a rhetorical situation? Other analysts have criticized real-reader heuristics for neglecting or glossing over historical, cultural, or contextual factors that may influence and shape the communication situation. For instance, James Suchan and Ron Dulek have discussed the effects of the writer's "power position" vis-à-vis the audience in business communication contexts. See "Toward a Better Understanding of Reader Analysis," *Journal of Business Communication* 25 (1988): 29–45.

[14] For instance, in *The Psychology of Speakers' Audiences*, Paul Holtzman considers various psychological needs and sociological categories of listeners. He focuses, however, on the "listeners" as a group of "real people" coming to the text (the speech) with a pre-established set of beliefs and principles. The speaker's task is to (somehow) determine what those beliefs and principles are, so he can decide from what premises to launch an argument. Holtzman's model is a purely sociological one: the audience is presumed to exist as an actual sociological group *prior to* the production or presentation of discourse. Assessing the overall rhetorical context is less important than "direct" observation of human behaviors (based on models from cognitive psychology). The textual field is not the basis for analysis, people are. Holtzman is concerned with "characteristics of listeners" and with the questions that speakers must ask about their audiences based on those characteristics. But missing from Holtzman's book is any discussion of how the speaker might go about validating answers to those questions or of how information collected would affect construction of the text. See Paul D. Holtzman, *The Psychology of Speakers' Audiences* (Glenview, IL: Scott, Foresman, 1970).

[15] See Wilson; also Peter J. Rabinowitz, "Truth in Fiction: A Reexamination of Audiences," *Critical Inquiry* 4 (1977): 121–141.

[16] For example, in "The Meanings of 'Audience,'" Douglas Park points out that composition tends to talk about audience in two predominant ways. We talk about "assessing" an audience and "defining" an audience. When we refer to "assessing" (or "analyzing"), we assume a pre-existent audience—one that is already "out there," apart from the discourse. When we talk of "defining" an audience, we are thinking of audience as something developed or clarified through the writing process, or perhaps to attitudes implicit in the developing text. See Douglas Park, "The Meanings of 'Audience,'" *College English* 44 (1982): 247–257. See also Roth.

[17] Russell C. Long, "Writer-Audience Relationships: Analysis or Invention?," *College Composition and Communication* 31 (1980): 221–226.

[18] Lisa Ede, "Audience: An Introduction to Research," pp. 140–154; Lisa Ede

and Andrea Lunsford, "Audience Addressed/Audience Invoked: The Role of the Audience in Composition Theory and Pedagogy," pp. 155–171; and Barry M. Kroll, "Writing for Readers: Three Perspectives on Audience," pp. 172–185. All three articles appeared in *College Composition and Communication* 35 (1984).

[19] See Gesa Kirsch and Duane H. Roen, eds., *A Sense of Audience in Written Communication* (Newbury Park, CA: Sage, 1990).

[20] Dillon, *Rhetoric*, pp. 147–148.

[21] Kathleen Welch has done a similar analysis, noticing the "elasticity and flux" of the concept of *physis* in classical rhetoric. See "Keywords from Classical Rhetoric: The Example of *Physis*," *Rhetoric Society Quarterly* 17 (1987): 193–204.

[22] This study would not dare claim comprehensiveness. Rather, it considers some representative treatments of audience, focusing mainly on rhetoric and composition. Because I am interested in audience theory and practice mainly as it applies to rhetoric and composition and to activities of the writer and the writing teacher, this study excludes specific treatments of audience in the mass media areas such as film, theater, radio, television, and journalism; in those areas related exclusively to speech communication and speaking contexts (e.g., oral interpretation, debate); and in disciplines that apply theories from these domains, such as law, politics, and advertising. Though practitioners in these other fields often discuss audience and audience analysis techniques (e.g., for jury selection and product marketing), their work pertains chiefly to spoken discourse or to visual effect. Because my focus here is rhetorical theory, the study also excludes research on reading processes and behaviors of actual readers (such as is found in journals like *Reading Research Quarterly* and *Journal of Reading Behavior*). Despite these exclusions, we still have a considerable body of material left in the domain of rhetoric and composition, as bibliographies on audience attest (see "Bibliographies of Audience," p. 156). Besides, much of the excluded work relies on models and definitions developing out of, I believe, rhetoric and composition theory (particularly Aristotle). That is, the theory of audience in rhetoric and composition is to a great extent the underlying theory in these other areas as well. Though the practices of audience analysis may be quite different from community to community, the underlying theory of audience, usually resting on a linear and/or mechanistic communication model, is quite the same.

[23] See Michel Foucault, *The Archaeology of Knowledge and the Discourse on Language*, trans. A. M. Sheridan Smith (New York: Pantheon-Random, 1972).

[24] Vincent B. Leitch, *Deconstructive Criticism: An Advanced Introduction* (New York: Columbia UP, 1981), pp. 151–152.

[25] Gilles Deleuze, *Foucault*, trans. and ed. Séan Hand (Minneapolis, MN: U of Minnesota P, 1983), p. 50.

[26] Archaeological analysis refers to the examination of "systems of knowledge," and, according to most Foucault critics, has a different emphasis than Foucault's genealogical approach, which focuses on "modalities of power." Archaeology, the subject of which is the construction of knowledge, is in fact only the first of two analytics taken up by Foucault, the other two being *genealogy*, which focuses on power, and *ethics*, which focuses on the self's

relationship to the self. For a discussion of the differences between Foucault's three analytics, see Arnold I. Davidson, "Archaeology, Genealogy, Ethics," in *Foucault: A Critical Reader*, ed. David Couzens Hoy (Oxford: Basil Blackwell, 1986), 221–233.

My focus is mainly archaeological, but at times I do defer to the genealogical approach to consider how the position and value of the concept of audience within the knowledge system manifests certain power relationships. In Foucault's work, knowledge always intersects with power; the two are inseparable in Foucault, though it was more in his later work that the power component became prominent. This project moves cautiously beyond archaeology to genealogy to examine the ideologies which are always coterminous with the knowledge system. Though some critics see Foucault's genealogy as a sharp break from, almost a repudiation of, archaeology (for example, Dreyfus and Rabinow), I see genealogy more as a logical development and extension of archaeology, a recognition of the implications of archaeology, and generally consistent with it—a position Deleuze concurs with (Deleuze 74).

One can certainly extend archaeology into genealogy and, beyond, into ethics. One analytic is tied to the others. (In Chapter 8, I briefly consider the explicit connections between treatments of audience and ethics; however, I hope to explore this relationship to a greater depth in a subsequent study.) In this study, I occasionally point to implications in these other dimensions: the treatment of audience in rhetoric and composition presupposes a "diagram of forces" (Deleuze 74) that intersects with a sense of power and an understanding of self, which the genealogical and ethical analytics expose.

For further discussion, see Charles C. Lemert and Garth Gillan, *Michel Foucault: Social Theory as Transgression* (New York: Columbia UP, 1982), pp. 34, 58; and Hubert C. Dreyfus and Paul Rabinow, *Michel Foucault: Beyond Structuralism and Hermeneutics*, 2nd ed. (Chicago: The U of Chicago P, 1983).

[27] Primarily, this book is a study of documents (many of them *monuments*, like Aristotle's *Rhetoric*, Campbell's *Philosophy of Rhetoric*, and Burke's *Rhetoric of Motives*), not of social institutions. However, a comprehensive study of social institutions and their relation to audience (for instance, a study of how audience treatments intersect with university disciplinarity) would certainly be valuable. I have chosen to focus on documents within the discipline, however, and to examine their classifying grid, the characterizing epistemology(ies) developed in these documents. We must remember, too, that documents themselves represent a social gathering and can be viewed as a basis for a social institution of a sort—i.e., rhetoric and composition, a field that is a knowledge system and therefore a system for power and control.

[28] Roland Barthes, "Writers, Intellectuals, Teachers," in *Image—Music—Text*, trans. Stephen Heath (New York: Hill and Wang, 1977), p. 201.

Chapter 2

⅔ *The Theoretical Heritage of Classical Rhetoric*

> For of the three elements in speech-making—
> speaker, subject, and person addressed—it is
> the last one, the hearer, that determines the
> speech's end and object.[1]

> *Aristotle*

In a strictly chronological tracing of the history of audience, one would begin with the sophists. I start my discussion of classical rhetoric with Aristotle simply because Aristotle's rhetoric, or a truncated version of it, came to be Rhetoric, or conventional rhetoric, as we know it today. I trace the line of the mainstream history of rhetoric from Aristotle, who expanded some of Plato's ideas about rhetoric into a formalized system— a system that situates the audience at the end of an assembly line of discourse production: the audience is treated as the passive receptor of the meaning discovered by the rhetor. This system burdens the rhetor— and perhaps permanently disables the writer—with responsibility for discovering truth (or meaning) and "packaging" it in discourse.

The "other classical rhetoric," the rhetoric of the sophists, was/is the silenced rhetoric. I do not consider sophistic rhetoric in this chapter. First, because in one sense sophistic rhetoric is not "classical": it was the dismissed practice that never became predominant, or rather its presence through the history of rhetoric was marginal and tentative. Second, because this entire study is an effort to revive a sophistic notion of audience, to counter the prevailing senses of audience with an alternative, one that posits audience in a different framework. This study argues, finally, for a sophistic approach to audience to supplant the classical and traditional notion, whose evolution and dominance are traced in this chapter and the next. (A sophistic sense of audience is discussed in Chapter 6.)

Classical rhetoric—that is to say, the dominant classical rhetoric of Aristotle and Cicero (particularly the early Cicero of *De Inventione*)—views the audience as the actual (i.e., physically present) listeners of the speaker's discourse. That is, classical rhetoric envisions an oral situation. This audience is a passive, acted-upon agent, the *dociles auditores*, susceptible to emotion and prone to prejudice. By no means do classical rhetoricians neglect audience. They recognize the importance of adapting the speech to fit audience disposition and the important role the audience plays in formulating public policy and in determining justice. However, as Kenneth Burke points out "both Aristotle and Cicero consider audience purely as something *given*."[2]

Aristotle's Rhetoric

In Aristotle's *Rhetoric* audience is a vital concern. To produce the desired effect on hearers, the orator must carefully choose among inventive strategies to construct a speech appropriate to the personality or disposition of the listeners. Consideration of audience personalities and emotions is a necessary step in composing a speech. Much of Book 2 is taken up with the nature of various emotions, different audience types, and argumentative forms. Aristotle acknowledges the importance of the emotional state of the listeners, claiming that the orator must understand the nature of the audience's emotional state in order to affect the audience state of mind (2.1).

Though most of Aristotle's explicit discussion of audience is contained in Book 2, the entire *Rhetoric* is concerned with audience. The matters of *logos*, *pathos*, and *ethos* discussed in Book 2 are certainly closely related to audience, but the particular topics discussed in Book 1 and the stylistic and organizational matters considered in Book 3 are also related. In fact, the entire *Rhetoric* can be seen as a compilation of discourse conventions, a set of standards that public speakers in Athens should use because listeners will recognize them, at least tacitly.[3]

It is in Book 2, however, that Aristotle explicitly considers the various emotional states of listeners and formulates a psychology of types that the rhetor should be familiar with (2.2–2.11), in effect linking psychology and rhetoric. Aristotle discusses emotions such as anger, shame, pity, indignation, and envy, as well as their opposites, and connects these emotional states with various types of human character (2.12–2.18). Aristotle divides human character—by which he means *male* character—according to age and fortune. He distinguishes between young men, old men, and "men in their prime" (2.12–2.14). Young men, he says, have strong passions, are idealistic, and are overly trustful. Elderly men are by and large cynical, skeptical, distrustful, and small-minded. Men in their prime have the proper balance of characteristics; they have, for instance, the proper balance of trust and mistrust. The rhetor must also consider "gifts of fortune" (2.15–2.17)—what we might think of as "social class" or "professional status." Aristotle notes that one's birth or family background and station in life affect one's outlook: for example, the well-born man looks down upon others; the wealthy man is more arrogant; and the man with power is more ambitious.

Aristotle discusses these audience characteristics without saying much about how knowledge of audience character might aid the speaker in preparing the speech.[4] And we are likely to see these simplistic generalizations about audience types as *not* the high point of Aristotle's thought, as archaic if not downright silly. However, the purpose, not the substance, of Aristotle's message is the point here. Aristotle has a keen sense of occasion and an awareness of the differences between audiences. He does not imagine a universal or general audience but sees audiences as having distinctive characters that should influence the speaker's approach.[5]

Description of audiences occupies a significant portion of Aristotle's *Rhetoric*—chapters one through eighteen of Book 2—a much more significant treatment than in most subsequent rhetorics. The flaw, if we can call it that, in Aristotle's treatment is in not connecting audience very closely to the construction of the speech. His psychological theory is abstracted from speaker and speech and so is susceptible to separation. In fact, the psychology of audience came to be seen as something separate from the art of rhetoric.[6]

Aristotle, in consort with Plato, also created a distinction—an insidious and enduring one—between two types of audiences.[7] There was the intelligent and philosophical individual listener with whom one engaged in dialectic. This participant/peer audience, envisioned in *Organon*, was different from the audience-as-general-public, which Aristotle describes in *Rhetoric*.[8] What Plato and Aristotle do, in effect, is to elevate the status of philosophy and, in so doing, privilege one type of discourse (dialectic, philosophy discourse) over another (rhetoric, public discourse). The distinction drawn, then, a not-so-subtle *divisio*, is between the participant audience of the dialectic and the passive mass audience of rhetoric. This division of course corresponds to the division between philosophy (the search for truth) and rhetoric (the practical art), a division that Cicero regretted.[9]

We live today with this distinction. The rhetorician considers variability in audience disposition; the dialectician (who goes by various names—philosopher, logician, scientist) does not need to, since the discourse of the dialectician will be judged by intelligent respondents (we can hardly use the term "audience") according to logical soundness. The dialectic peer audience is not assumed to be a prisoner of the emotions that dominate the larger public audience.[10]

With Aristotle's *Rhetoric* we see a formal enunciation of the notion of "the general audience" or "the general public." This very notion itself posits an ethical dilemma for any speaker whose aim is to change the beliefs of an ignorant, emotional, and prejudiced mass. Is it ethical to change an audience's beliefs without providing them sound reasons and a basis in fact for changing their beliefs? In part, the dilemma itself is created by the managerial communication situation Aristotle envisions in *Rhetoric:* a knowledgeable orator facing an ignorant audience is placed in the position of (possibly) manipulating his audience. Within this framework, audience analysis can easily deteriorate into a kind of market survey to determine exactly what prejudices and emotions the audience holds, or to determine what the audience does not know, in order to better persuade them. The process is not aimed at determining what knowledge the audience can *contribute* (as in dialectic).

This distinction drawn by Aristotle became a central assumption in rhetoric: the rhetorical situation involves a knowledgeable rhetor more or less in possession of "the truth" and an ignorant audience. And of course in such a situation, the rhetorician has nothing to learn *from* the audience; she only learns *about* the audience, through audience analysis, in order to better manage their responses. In this view, the rhetor is the privileged entity whose search for knowledge and truth is accomplished prior to the rhetorical act (in dialectic or scientific method), not through it or in conjunction with an audience.

But there are alternative readings of Aristotle's work. Andrea Lunsford and Lisa Ede have attempted to sanitize Aristotle by arguing that Aristotle's view of audience is much more a dialogic view, which recognizes that the audience contributes to the construction of the speech.[11] And in his discussion of the enthymeme Aristotle does acknowledge that the first premise—the belief or probable truth from which the speaker develops a position—must come from the audience.[12] Thus, Aristotle certainly acknowledges the importance of the audience's contribution. However, the enthymeme as an important concept soon disappeared, along with audience, from most rhetoric discussions. And we should remember that the premise of the enthymeme was not necessarily a "truth" or knowledge in

Aristotle's sense, but might be a public opinion, even a misconception or prejudice. That is, the rhetor could play upon audience misconceptions and false beliefs as long as it suited the rhetor's ends—i.e., the good of the *polis*—and the "trained thinkers" took on complete responsibility for determining what this "good" was. Aristotle may have appreciated the audience's contribution, but his division created a rift (i.e., between rhetoric and dialetic) that subsequent rhetorics widened.

In sum, I believe that we must credit Aristotle's *Rhetoric*, as Lunsford and Ede do, for appreciating the contribution of audience: Aristotle is more aware of and sensitive to audience than most subsequent rhetorics, including most contemporary ones. But at the same time, we must recognize that Aristotle's theoretical framework sets up a relational role between writer and audience—i.e., putting the rhetor in a position of authority and control relative to the audience, who is a passive agent to be persuaded— that allows for the eventual neglect of audience in rhetoric.

The Roman Rhetorics

Rhetorics after Aristotle's amplify certain sections of his work, such as expanding the brief discussions of *status* and of style. But they severely subordinate or neglect other concerns. In the Roman rhetorics, discussion of audience is generally sketchy and scattered throughout. We do not see a fully developed discussion of audience types or of emotions, as in Aristotle. Often audience is discussed in terms of the *exordium:* the stock advice is that the introduction is most important; it should capture the attention of the listeners and earn their good will. In *Rhetorica ad Herennium* and *De Inventione*, the rhetor's art is confined to discussions of invention of the case (*constitutiones*) and to arrangement and style.[13] *Rhetorica ad Herennium* does preserve a sense that different contexts call for different styles, distinguishing between the grand, the middle, and the plain styles. However, these styles are not determined so much by hearer disposition as by subject matter. The concept of audience begins to become embedded in stylistic and formal conventions—and to be treated as a function of subject matter. And, as such, not a concern of rhetoric.

The Roman rhetorics that treat audience least (*De Inventione* and *Rhetorica ad Herennium*) were the ones most influential on medieval rhetoric.[14] The rhetorics that consider audience most and that tie discussion of audience to various stylistic and organizational strategies (i.e., *De Oratore* and *Institutio Oratoria*) were not nearly as influential until the Renaissance. In *De Oratore* and *Institutio*, Cicero and Quintilian note that different audiences, or audiences in different mental states, require different approaches. The speaker has to decide the relationship between his case (including his stance toward it) and the audience frame of mind to determine which stylistic or organizational approaches will work best.

In *De Oratore*, for instance, Cicero notes that jesting works only with audiences in a receptive frame of mind and only with certain types of cases (Book 2). Quintilian notes that knowing the disposition of judges is crucial to effective legal discourse; the rhetor needs to know the available strategies for exciting judges' tempers or for calming them down (*Institutio*, Book 6.2). Thus, in *De Oratore* and *Institutio* there is a sense that audience, though it does not contribute knowledge to the speaker, should influence the construction of the speech. There is also the sense that not all stylistic strategies work for all cases or for all audiences. There is not the assumption (persisting in current-traditional rhetoric) that the audience is all of one mind, a passively receptive and homogenous blank slate. In these works, the importance of variability is emphasized; but this value is not maintained by the mainstream classical tradition.

Roman rhetorics further widened the split between the intelligent-peer audience and the general audience. Cicero imagined two distinct audiences for the speaker: the public mass the orator addressed when he spoke *ad populum* and the smaller number of jurists and civic leaders who would render legal or deliberative decisions when the orator spoke *ad senatum*.[15] Thus "the masses" were imagined as being less likely to contribute knowledge than they were in Aristotle's rhetoric (in the Athenian assembly the public were at least voting masses). Today, the term "ad populum" designates a certain kind of logical fallacy where the speaker confirms a thesis on the basis of public popularity.

We must remember that classical rhetoric is a rhetoric of speech occasions—listing principles governing deliberative, epideictic, and forensic oratory. Thus, the dominant sense of audience is of a group of listeners, a physically present body of male citizens, who are collected at one time, in one place, for a specified occasion, i.e., to hear the orator's speech. Aristotle imagined as audience the Athenian assembly, citizens of Athens (500 or 501 adult males) who participated in trials (as jurors) and who involved themselves regularly in debate on questions of public policy. In the Greek judicial forum, the litigant had to plead his own case (though he might well deliver a memorized speech prepared by someone else).[16] This litigant could count on addressing a body of persons more or less known to him and could count on at least some agreement about conventions. Vivid audience reaction—in the form of booing, hissing, and voting—would be immediately apparent. Only rarely in written contexts does such simultaneous or measureable feedback occur.

For Aristotle, the function of the rhetor in this context was tied very closely to the "good" of the *polis*. That is, the rhetor and his listeners shared (ideally) the same goal—state security and stability—and so the activity of the rhetor is very closely connected to ethics and politics. Rhetoric served primarily a social purpose in other words. By Roman times, this connection of rhetoric to politics and ethics was beginning to sever.

Though Cicero considered rhetoric a branch of political science, he did not closely connect "the good of the state" to the rhetor's art, at least not to the extent Aristotle did (by discussing in some detail how the rhetor determined what "the good" actually *was*).

The speaker's relationship to audience was also beginning to change. In Cicero's time the orator rarely addressed the entire citizenry, but usually spoke to a select group: in judicial matters, the appointed or elected jury; in deliberative matters, the elected members of the assembly. Increasingly, judicial discourse in Rome became formulaic—and with this came a proportional decrease in the importance of the "impassioned speech." Knowledge of the law and of legal formulas and conventions became more important than the kind of general rhetorical skills valued by Aristotle. Of far more importance was a lawyer (patron) who knew how to assess the central issues of the case, who understood his proper role as advocate and who was able to make sound arguments within the legal framework.[17] Within this context, the art of rhetoric was by no means *un*important, but the art was beginning to become subordinate to specialized content areas (like law). Audience as a distinct set of predispositions may have been less important as the Roman legal and deliberative procedures became institutionalized and formalized. When conventions embody shared audience values and preferences, there is a lesser need for distinct treatment of audience. The danger that arises when audience is "conventionalized" like this is that the conventions will exclude certain voices from participation.

The Speech-Writing Relationship

Classical rhetoric was a rhetoric of *speech* occasions. As such, classical rhetoric may not provide us with a theory appropriate for *writing* occasions. We particularly need to question the presumed split between speech and writing. The classical theory of Plato and Aristotle assigns priority to speech, as Japser Neel points out. Classical theory also imagines a linear communication sequence: ideas (discovered by dialectician) to words (selected by rhetor) to audience. Such a model diminishes the role of the audience in the making of meaning.

Supporting this view of the role of audience is a set of Platonic assumptions about the relationship of ideas, speech, and writing, a view embraced by traditional rhetoric scholarship. Critics such as Eric Havelock and Walter Ong have made much of the shift from orality to literacy, assuming a division between speech and writing and assuming the priority of speech. They argue that speech as the primary form of discourse gave way to writing, as western culture moved from orality to literacy; and they argue that the differences between writing and speech, and between oral and written cultures, are considerable.[18] In an oral culture, Eric Havelock points out, "the limits of the powers of the human voice . . . [are] set by the size of an audience physically present."[19] With the advent of literacy, the audience potential is expanded. Conceivably a writer can address a reader (in some sense) who exists thousands of years in the future. Writing traverses time and space, and has a static nature as product. The audience in the literate society is not necessarily a group of physically present listeners.

We can think of other differences between writing and speech. In writing, "occasions" and "audience" are not usually as tangible nor do they have such clearcut parameters. Rarely do the intended readers of a discourse read at one time, in one place, with the writer present. The relationship between speaker and hearer can be physically close (as in a political assembly or a court of law), or it can be physically distant (as in a television broadcast), but the speaker-hearer-speech relationship is typically a concurrent one: all three elements exist together and interact simultaneously.

The writer-reader relationship is considerably more remote, at least in terms of physical relationship. The writer is physically separate from the written text, and, once she writes it, has little control over its context.[20] Readers can decide for themselves when, indeed if, to read the text, and can read it in the manner they choose. The effects of written discourse are not seen as readily as they were, for instance, in the Athenian assembly, or as they are in a court of law, where the effects of one's speech can be measured immediately in the form of a jury decision. The effects of written discourse are seldom as immediate, often never that tangible.

The audience for a written discourse is more remote, more diffuse, more abstract. We might say that in a speech situation, the speaker is the primary focus, more important, even, than the speech. However, in a written situation the writer is usually not physically present. The written text itself as a formal discourse, the print on the page, is what has the immediate presence to the reader, even more so than the writer. Thus, audience theory for written discourse must be, by necessity, more text-based than audience theory for speech communication.

Thus, though we may rely on classical rhetoric to provide a starting point for discussions of audience, ultimately classical rhetorical theory falls short in that it is not primarily a rhetoric of writing occasions. We must look to other quarters. Only recently (with reader-response criticism, I would argue) have we begun to develop a sense of audience specifically for written discourse, a notion of audience appropriate for the textual emphasis of writing.

And yet another argument has been made that the differences between speech and writing are themselves superficial: that, in fact, at a more essential level, there are no differences because speech and writing both partake of the same reliance on *sign*—and therefore neither deserves to be privileged. According to Jasper Neel, the classical, and conventional, communication model sees writing as tertiary:

> In the classical notion, . . . first there is thinking, then speaking serves as an instrument to represent thinking, and, finally, writing serves as an instrument to represent speaking. This means not only that writing remains exterior to and dependent on speaking and that speaking remains exterior to and dependent on thinking, but also that all systems of signification remain exterior to and dependent on whatever they signify. Language, in other words, must come after, remain outside of, and depend absolutely on meaning.[21]

Classical rhetoric, in other words, assumes a chronology of thought, language, speech, and writing—a linearity that places writing in the chronologically last and hierarchically subordinate position. This theoretical assumption underlies subsequent rhetoric and composition theory—and, of course, treatments of audience. To understand current-traditional neglect of audience, for instance, we must understand this theoretical model and its ground of assumption that supports the subordination of audience. In order to free audience from this linearity, we must examine the poststructuralist critique of the conventional division between speech and writing.

There is a sense in which speaking does not precede writing. In this sense, "writing" means much more than merely inscription (what Neel calls "writing in the narrow sense"[22]). Writing in a broader sense refers to the operation of certain rhetorical maneuvers, such as "the operation of supplement, différance, repetition, replacement, absence of presence, absence of closure, absence of the transcendental signified."[23] Thought and speech are, in other words, already thoroughly suffused by sign, and therefore share the same characteristics as writing-in-general, among these a reliance on audience (as well as other factors) for meaning.[24] We cannot assume a simple correspondence between sign and signifier (and certainly not between sign and referent). In this Derridean concept of writing, writing is by no means innocent, but it is not less innocent than speech; it does not "*befall* an innocent language."[25]

If we challenge the division between thought, speech, and writing, we see that the significance of writing changes—and by necessity its research and pedagogy. For instance, we would challenge the assumption that because a student's protocol (i.e., a speech) seems to be a chronologically prior event to writing that it is somehow "truer" or "closer to the meaning" than writing. If we disrupt the classical privileging of speech over writing and accept the notion of "writing in the larger sense," then we would be encouraged to examine how writing influences the student.

The linear communication model, arising out of a rhetorical theory of speech occasions, leads us to imagine the audience as residing at the end of the communication act. We can challenge this model on two grounds. First, the differences between speech and writing demand that we develop a separate model for written situations. Second, the differences between speech and writing are themselves exaggerated: in terms of their reliance on *sign* both speech and writing are equally "deferring."

The classical conception of rhetoric is the most comprehensive conception in western rhetoric—at least until the new rhetoric movement of the 1960s. For the classical practitioners, the art of rhetoric included as its subtopics argumentative forms and techniques, common and specialized knowledge (the necessity of it and problems associated with acquiring it), psychology, ethics, arrangement and style, and audience. It may be said that each subsequent rhetorical period diminished the scope of rhetoric, ultimately limiting it to concern for style and arrangement, what in Aristotle's *Rhetoric* is only the third of three books. The history of rhetoric is a chronicle of the diminishment, maybe the dismemberment, of the discipline.[26] Correspondent with the delimiting of rhetoric in general was an increased neglect, or at least subordination, of audience.

It is not within the scope of this study to consider how the notion of audience developed through the history of rhetoric—what concept of audience was prevalent in any particular time, how audiences were divided, or what value was assigned the audience in the communication act (e.g., to what degree the audience is considered to provide knowledge to the speaker).[27] Audience is a consideration in the later Roman works (e.g., *De Oratore, De Partitione Oratoria,* and *Institutio Oratoria*), but throughout audience is seen as physically present listeners, the *dociles auditores*—a body that the speaker acts upon.

Subsequent rhetorics tend to reduce the role of audience and emphasize instead either the *ethos* of the speaker or the construction of the speech. There are notable exceptions. In *De Doctrina Christiana,* for instance, Augustine does acknowledge the importance of considering audience, whom he imagines as the congregation of the faithful assembled for the preacher's sermon. The preacher must consider the disposition of the hearers to the scriptural message and accommodate the hearers in constructing the homily. However, the preacher does not look to the hearers for guidance in interpreting scripture, in discovering the content of the message. Invention (which in *De Doctrina* means interpretation of scriptures, Books 1–3) or discovery of scriptural truth is not a matter for rhetoric and is not be entrusted either to the (by now suspect) discipline of rhetoric or to the Christian congregation. The hearers listen to, and, ideally, are moved by, the Christian message. But they do not have a hand in discovering the truth of that message.[28]

Classical rhetoric divided the roles of rhetor and audience, and assigned the rhetor responsibility for developing truth. For Aristotle and Plato, this truth was not individually arrived at but was developed through the art of dialectic. By the seventeenth and eighteenth century, with the development of "the new science" and "the new logic" of Descartes, Arnauld, and Locke, the discovery of truth came about through the application of the scientific method by the "reasoned observing individual." In *Discourse on Method*, Descartes dismisses rhetoric and logic, empowering the *gaze*, or single observing self, as the source of truth.

In "The Subject and Power," Foucault talks about the dividing practice (*divisio*) as the chief way that an institution (or "discursive formation") exercises power over subjects.[29] The institution defines an agent that exercises power and a subject ("body") that the agent acts upon. Rhetoric developed historically as a discipline empowering the speaker at the expense of the audience. The audience became an object for analysis, worked on and shaped by the speaker. We can look to eighteenth-century "new rhetoric"—particularly the rhetoric of Campbell and Blair—to see how this notion of audience developed further and to see how and why audience finally disappeared, in current-traditional and expressivist rhetorics of the twentieth century, as a topic of rhetoric.

NOTES
Chapter 2

[1] Aristotle, *The Rhetoric and Poetics of Aristotle*, intro. Edward P. J. Corbett (New York: Modern Library-Random, 1984), Book 1.3.

[2] Kenneth Burke, *A Rhetoric of Motives* (Berkeley: U of California P, 1969), p. 64.

[3] Forms of discourse are audience-based insofar as they represent genre conventions that enable rhetor and audience to meet on familiar ground. For a further discussion of the relationship of form to audience, see David K. Rod, "Kenneth Burke and Susanne K. Langer on Drama and Its Audience," *Quarterly Journal of Speech* 89 (1986): 306–317; and Carolyn R. Miller, "Genre as Social Action," *Quarterly Journal of Speech* 70 (1984): 154–167.

[4] In passing, Aristotle does provide us with some advice about how knowledge of audience can help the speaker make composing decisions. He says that "the use of Maxims is appropriate only to elderly men" and that "one great advantage of Maxims to a speaker is due to the want of intelligence in his hearers" (because people love to hear what they already believe) (2.21). In Book 3, Aristotle talks about the stylistic quality of appropriateness in relation to audience disposition (3.7) and notes that audiences are susceptible to flat-

tery and need to be reminded to pay attention (3.14). Thus, certain organizational and stylistic devices "fit" certain audience types. But this kind of advice is rare. Aristotle does not provide many examples or describe in much detail how a speech might be adapted to suit listeners of various dispositions.

5 The idea that there are different classes of speakers is evident in Plato's work as well, and Aristotle's treatment of listeners in *Rhetoric* may be a working out of ideas implicit in Plato, as several critics have noted. See, for example, Forbes I. Hill, "The Rhetoric of Aristotle," in *A Synoptic History of Classical Rhetoric*, ed. James J. Murphy (Davis, CA: Hermagoras, 1983), pp. 45–48. In *Phaedrus*, Plato recognizes that speakers must adapt their discourses to suit various character types (271d-e). In fact, according to James Golden, Plato recognized the importance of audience to the speaker and developed the rudiments of a strategy for audience analysis. See James L. Golden, "Plato Revisited: A Theory of Discourse for All Seasons," in *Essays on Classical Rhetoric and Modern Discourse*, ed. Robert J. Connors, Lisa S. Ede, and Andrea A. Lunsford (Carbondale, IL: Southern Illinois UP, 1984), pp. 26–29; and James L. Golden, Goodwin F. Berquist, and William E. Coleman, *The Rhetoric of Western Thought* (Dubuque, IA: Kendall/Hunt, 1976), pp. 33–34.

6 James Murphy points out that during the middle ages, Aristotle's *Rhetoric* was more often than not included in collections of ethics treatises. That is, the work itself came to be seen as something other than "rhetoric" and its topics as beyond the scope of the discipline. See James J. Murphy, *Rhetoric in the Middle Ages* (Berkeley: U of California P, 1974), p. 101.

7 The discussion that follows in this section is a revised version of material that appears in James E. Porter, "*Divisio* as Em-/De-Powering Topic: A Basis for Argument in Retoric and Composition," *Rhetoric Review* 8 (1990): 191–205.

8 In *Organon*, Aristotle assumes as audience the interlocutor, a worthy opponent against whom one must employ all manner of logical techniques. But *Organon* is concerned with the development of "true" statements, not probable ones. And since Aristotle sees the search for "truth" as the discovery of valid propositions—that is, as inherent in assertions themselves, or text-based—he is not much concerned with either "the audience" or "the self" as explicit elements. (Because for Aristotle truth is neither provisional or contextual.) In *Organon* Aristotle discusses audience most in "Sophistical Refutations," where he considers techniques that may "mislead" this listener or another, such as confounding an opponent by artificially lengthening one's speech. In "Topics," significantly, he does not mention audience.

   Grimaldi notes the important distinction in Aristotle's *Rhetoric* between audience as Θεωρόσ (or "passive spectator") and audience as Κριτήσ (or "judge"). See William M. A. Grimaldi, S. J., *Aristotle, Rhetoric I: A Commentary* (New York: Fordham UP, 1980), p. 80.

9 We see an expression of Cicero's regret in *De Oratore*: "Socrates . . . separated the science of wise thinking from that of elegant speaking, though in reality they are closely linked together; and the genius and varied discourses of Socrates have been immortally enshrined in the compositions of Plato, Socrates himself not having left a single scrap of writing. This is the source from which has sprung the undoubtedly absurd and unprofitable and reprehensible severance between the tongue and the brain, leading to our having

one set of professors to teach us to think and another to teach us to speak" (*De Oratore* 3.16.60–61).

[10] James Berlin points out that "Aristotle's conception of the audience also reflects the sense of class division, offering a description of the emotional appeal that disparages the capacities of the lower ranks in a democratic gathering, while valorizing the rational powers of the 'trained thinkers' whose status has afforded them a formal education." See James Berlin, "Revisionary History: The Dialectical Method," *PRE/TEXT* 8 (1987), p. 54.

[11] See Lisa Ede and Andrea Lunsford, "Classical Rhetoric, Modern Rhetoric, and Contemporary Discourse Studies," *Written Communication* 1 (1984): 78–100; and Andrea Lunsford and Lisa Ede, "On Distinctions Between Classical and Modern Rhetoric," in *Essays on Classical Rhetoric and Modern Discourse*, ed. Robert J. Connors, Lisa S. Ede, and Andrea A. Lunsford (Carbondale, IL: Southern Illinois UP, 1984), 37–49.

[12] For a discussion of Aristotle's enthymeme, see James C. Raymond, "Enthymemes, Examples, and Rhetorical Method" (pp. 140–151) and John T. Gage, "An Adequate Epistemology for Composition: Classical and Modern Perspectives" (pp. 152–169), both in *Essays on Classical Rhetoric and Modern Discourse*, ed. Robert J. Connors, Lisa S. Ede, and Andrea A. Lunsford (Carbondale, IL: Southern Illinois UP, 1984); and Lloyd Bitzer, "Aristotle's Enthymeme Revisited," *Quarterly Journal of Speech* 45 (1959): 399–408.

[13] In *Rhetorica ad Herennium*, for instance, the discussion of style is divorced from effect (as it is in the later formalistic handbooks of the twentieth century). Style is discussed in terms of structure (e.g., *epanaphora* is repetition of an initial clause). The effect of various styles on different audience dispositions is not considered.

[14] See Murphy.

[15] See Richard Leo Enos and Jeanne L. McClaran, "Audience and Image in Ciceronian Rome: Creation and Constraints of the *Vir Bonus* Personality," *Central States Speech Journal* 29 (1978): 98–106; and Richard L. Street, Jr., "Lexical Diversity as an Indicator of Audience Adaptation in Ciceronian Orations," *Central States Speech Journal* 30 (1979): 286–288.

[16] See George Kennedy, *The Art of Persuasion in Ancient Greece* (Princeton, NJ: Princeton UP, 1963), pp. 91–92.

[17] See George Kennedy, *The Art of Rhetoric in the Roman World* (Princeton, NJ: Princeton UP, 1972), pp. 8–18.

[18] For representative discussions from this point of view about the speech-writing relationship, see Gillian Brown and George Yule, *Discourse Analysis* (Cambridge: Cambridge UP, 1983), pp. 4–19; Walter Ong, S.J., *Orality and Literacy: The Technologizing of the Word* (London: Methuen, 1982); Eric Havelock, *The Muse Learns to Write* (New Haven, CN: Yale UP, 1986); and Terence Hawkes, *Structuralism and Semiotics* (Berkeley, CA: U of California P, 1977), pp. 135–136.

[19] Havelock, p. 31.

[20] See Jacques Derrida, "Signature Event Context," *Glyph* 1 (1977): 172–197.

21 Jasper Neel, *Plato, Derrida, and Writing* (Carbondale, IL: Southern Illinois UP, 1988), p. 110.

22 Neel, p. 112.

23 Neel, p. 112.

24 For a fuller discussion, see Neel, pp. 112–119; and Jacques Derrida, *Dissemination*, trans. Barbara Johnson (Chicago: The U of Chicago P, 1981), passim.

25 Neel, p. 119.

26 See Robert J. Connors, Lisa S. Ede, and Andrea A. Lunsford, "The Revival of Rhetoric in America," in *Essays on Classical Rhetoric and Modern Discourse*, ed. Robert J. Connors, Lisa S. Ede, and Andrea A. Lunsford (Carbondale, IL: Southern Illinois UP, 1984), 1–15.

27 For a more in-depth discussion of this middle period between the classical and modern eras, see Thomas Willard and Stuart C. Brown, "The One and the Many: A Brief History of the Distinction," in *A Sense of Audience in Written Communication*, ed. Gesa Kirsch and Duane H. Roen (Newbury Park, CA: Sage, 1990), 40–57.

28 Augustine is "concerned rather with the *cajoling* of an audience than with the routing of opponents." See Kenneth Burke, *A Rhetoric of Motives* (Berkeley, CA: U of California P, 1969), p. 53. Later works of the *ars praedicandi*, like Gregory's *Cura Pastoralis*, consider audience a factor. But, again, the hearer is considered as a passive receiver of the preacher's message, not in any sense an interlocutor. See Murphy, pp. 289–297.

29 Michel Foucault, "The Subject and Power," *Critical Inquiry* 8 (1982): 777–795. For a discussion of the role of *divisio* in rhetoric and composition, see Porter, "*Divisio.*"

Chapter 3

🐦 *Traditional Rhetoric and the Disappearance of Audience*

Some elements of rhetoric, though real and valuable, are not practical, because the ability to employ them cannot be imparted by teaching. They have to exist in the writer himself, in the peculiar, individual bent of his nature.[1]

John Franklin Genung

The stylistic side of writing is, in fact, the only side that can be analyzed and learned.[2]

Sheridan Baker

It is now necessary to warn the writer that his concern for the reader must be pure: he must sympathize with the reader's plight (most readers are in trouble about half the time) but never seek to know his wants. The whole duty of a writer is to please and satisfy himself, and the true writer always plays to an audience of one. Let him start sniffing the air, or glancing at the Trend Machine, and he is as good as dead, although he may make a nice living.[3]

E. B. White

29

Peter Ramus and his student Omer Talon are usually blamed for delimiting the scope of rhetoric in the sixteenth century to matters of style and arrangement and for consigning invention to the discipline of philosophy. What is known today as current-traditional rhetoric is in part the heritage of the Ramistic notion of rhetoric: a limiting of rhetoric to matters of style and organization, to the virtual exclusion of other concerns such as invention and audience.

In twentieth-century composition instruction, at least two distinct rhetorics stress style: current-traditional, which has its roots in the faculty psychology of George Campbell's *The Philosophy of Rhetoric*; and expressivist, a romanticized version of faculty psychology promoted in Hugh Blair's *Lectures on Rhetoric and Belle Lettres*. These approaches have in common the diminution of three of the elements of the communication triangle (writer, reality, audience), emphasizing instead principles of textual construction, chiefly those of style. They also share the predominant assumption that invention, or the discovery of possible arguments, is prior to the art of rhetoric. Rhetoric is concerned only with the presentation of ideas already formed, and the audience is the passive receptor of those ideas.

To understand why current-traditional and expressivist rhetorics neglect audience, we need to examine several key antecedents—especially Aristotle's *Rhetoric* (discussed in Chapter 2) and George Campbell's *The Philosophy of Rhetoric*. These antecedents represent key moments in rhetoric history when a value and meaning for the signifier "audience" was firmly established in the epistemological framework of the discipline. To a great extent, these works account for current conceptions—for general beliefs about what constitutes an audience and how we ought to approach one. To understand current beliefs, we must examine their historical precedents and, especially, the theoretical assumptions upon which much current pedagogy still rests.

We face a problem, first, in circumscribing "traditional rhetoric," an elusive concept. It may be more useful to begin by identifying contemporary practices that have been influenced by competing historical traditions. James Berlin identifies four rhetorics directing contemporary practices.[4] These four—current-traditional, expressivist, neo-Aristotelian, and new rhetorical—are characterized by differing traditions and epistemologies, that is, by differing assumptions about how knowledge and truth are discovered and about how knowledge is disseminated (or created) through communication. These four rhetorics privilege competing notions of audience.

In what Richard Young and Berlin have, separately, described as the "current-traditional" and "expressivist" approaches, explicit references to audience are few.[5] In current-traditional rhetoric, "audience" usually refers to actual readers, but not much is said about it. Audience concerns are embodied in usage principles: that is, the assumption of current-traditional rhetoric is that the best way to deal with an audience is to adhere to accepted stylistic principles, which represent the standards of "the general audience," a notion of audience having its origins in Aristotle's *Rhetoric* and reaching full articulation in George Campbell's *The Philosophy of Rhetoric*.

Expressivist rhetoric, as described by Berlin, is a 1960s offshoot of, and reaction against, current-traditional rhetoric. Expressivist rhetoric can be traced from Hugh Blair's *Lectures on Rhetoric and Belle Lettres* and is associated with such people as E. B. White, James Miller, Peter Elbow, Donald Murray, and Ken Macrorie. In expressivist rhetoric, the audience is sometimes discussed, but frequently in disparaging terms. In both current-traditional and expressivist rhetoric, audience is generally not a primary focus of instruction, partly because the writer is expected to "be true" to style in current-traditional rhetoric and to self in expressivist rhetoric. To the extent that audience is treated in either, it is treated implicitly as a property of style.

This chapter traces two of the four contemporary rhetorics discussed by Berlin—current-traditional and expressivist rhetoric—focusing in particular on their roots in Hugh Blair's and George Campbell's rhetorics and on their twentieth-century manifestations, chiefly in composition textbooks and handbooks.[6] (Neo-Aristotelian and new rhetoric are discussed in Chapter 4.) I see these two rhetorics as together comprising "traditional rhetoric": these two together are still, I believe, the main forces influencing composition instruction in the United States.[7]

These two rhetorics hold two key assumptions about audience. First, they tend to accept Aristotle's notion of audience as the physically present listeners of the speech, a version of audience that privileges speech over writing. Second, they adopt George Campbell's managerial communication model: the rhetor's text "works upon" the audience, not the other way around. These two positions of course subordinate the role of audience; and when these views are coupled with a belief that the art of discovery (or invention) cannot be taught, then the result is that audience becomes an unnecessary adjunct. Eventually, audience disappears altogether as a distinct topic. It is *not* of particular importance to regard audience because audience needs are best met by attention to other concerns.

Hugh Blair and George Campbell

The most influential rhetoric text in the early nineteenth century, particularly in the United States, was Hugh Blair's *Lectures on Rhetoric and Belle Lettres*, first published in 1785 and printed in over 120 editions by 1930.[8] Generally, Blair neglects audience. When he does consider it, he regards audience as hearers, as the physically present listeners of the speaker's oration. The speaker (at the bar, at the pulpit, or in the public assembly) must determine the disposition of the audience and must make "the minds of the hearers" (a key phrase in Blair) receptive to the message. The speaker moves the audience by exposing it to images, impressing these images upon "the minds of the hearers." The minds of the hearers are, to Blair, a *tabula rasa* (or if they are not, then they should first be made "blank") upon which the rhetor sketches his message.

Blair does not say much about audience in the *Lectures*. Primarily, Blair views rhetoric as concerned with the development of taste, which is reflected in one's use of language. (He considers language the "dress" of thought.) Invention in the classical sense, he believes, is beyond the scope of the art. Blair says that the *topoi* are useless for developing arguments. Rather, the speaker should look to the subject and, *"ex visceribus causae,"* find content therein. Thus, for Blair, it is through careful attention to subject and style that one becomes an effective speaker. "Genius," which accounts for success in speaking, can be cultivated (though not created or manufactured) by exposure to eloquent works and through developing skills of critical analysis—a pedagogical assumption that later became a supporting tenet of expressivism. In Blair's belletristic pedagogy, the audience does not contribute to the discovery of knowledge and does not provide the rhetor with content. Taste, the aim of Blair's pedagogy, is a universal—it does not change from community to community—and therefore the rhetor does not have to worry about the diversity of audiences.[9]

In George Campbell's rhetoric, audience plays a more prominent role.[10] However, like Blair, Campbell viewed audience not as a contributor of knowledge, arguments, or topics, but as a body that the speaker acts upon. Campbell takes a managerial view, in other words.[11] In fact, he views the orator in terms of absolute despotism: the ideal speaker attains a kind of mastery over the body and soul of the audience.[12] Campbell differs from Blair in recognizing the complexity of audiences.

According to Campbell, rhetoric is the "art by which the discourse is adapted to its end."[13] This articulation itself presupposes that "the discourse" exists prior to the art of rhetoric and, further, that rhetoric concerns itself with manipulation (or revision, if you prefer) of a proto-text already in existence. Thus, Campbell excludes invention from rhetoric's purview. In *The Philosophy of Rhetoric*, he recognizes that audience is an important factor in rhetoric and provides the fullest discussion of audience emotions since Aristotle. However, for Campbell the rhetor does not look to audience for arguments, for content, or for the contribution of knowledge. Rather, the rhetor considers audience in order to judge how best to shape the discourse to produce the desired effect.

Campbell discusses audience explicitly under the headings "men in general" and "men in particular" (Books 1.7 and 1.8). He acknowledges that the orator must use all the powers of the mind in convincing audiences. The rhetor must appeal to all four of the mental faculties—understanding, imagination, passion, and will—and take into account what his hearers know and understand. Here, Campbell remarks that understanding varies widely from group to group, and he refers his reader to the discussion of men in particular. To affect the hearer's imagination, Campbell suggests that the rhetor use the principle of resemblance, stimulating the imagination by representing a known entity in a new, original way. The rhetor does this by employing one of several types of comparisons (either literal or figurative ones, such as simile, allegory, or metaphor). To aid the memory, the speaker must adhere to principles of coherence and order, and use repetition. To invoke the passions, the rhetor must attend to the principle of vivacity, appealing to the senses by using concrete, vivid imagery.

Under "men in particular" (Book 1.8), Campbell has little to say. He notes that the differences between audiences may be great, especially in terms of their understanding. Since "characters of audiences may be infinitely diversified,"[14] not much can be said about particular audiences. Campbell's treatment of particular audiences in Book 1.8 sets the tone for subsequent works that make a similar distinction between general and particular audiences (e.g., Brooks and Warren's *Modern Rhetoric*[15]). Because audiences are so diverse, rhetoric is unable to account for the particular and so is excused from doing so.[16]

However, in Book 1.10 (Section 2), Campbell discusses in some detail the problem of the diverse audience, a problem that few rhetoricians have been willing to tackle. He suggests that the Christian congregation would be "of all audiences the most promiscuous."[17] Admittedly, the orator cannot hope to construct a speech appropriate for each listener. The orator should, though, make sure the speech is "within the reach of every class of hearers," except, of course, "mere children, fools, and a few others who, through the total neglect of parents or guardians in their education, are grossly ignorant."[18]

Two important stylistic traits emphasized in Campbell's *Rhetoric* and connected closely to concern for audience are vivacity and perspicuity. These stylistic qualities appeal to the distinct mental faculties—the understanding, the fancy (imagination), the passions, and the will—which in turn correspond to the four purposes of discourse (to inform, to please, to move, and to convince). Perspicuity and vivacity are tied to the theory of faculty psychology. Perspicuity—or denotative starkness—corresponds to the capacity for understanding. Vivacity appeals to the imagination. By using lively imagery, the rhetor can appeal to every natural audience's craving for the new and lively. Vivacity as a principle seems to have been lost to composition (having been reborn perhaps as "emphasis"?). Perspicuity became, of course, clarity, which was considered in current-traditional rhetoric as a one-to-one, denotative correspondence between the signifier and the signified (and perhaps even the referent as well). Though the stylistic qualities are tied to Campbell's psychological model, by the end of the nineteenth century these qualities (and the so-called static abstractions—unity, coherence, and emphasis) became disconnected from the *effect* on the hearer (and their basis in faculty psychology) and became stylistic dicta. Though Campbell associates particular emotional effects with certain stylistic strategies, later rhetoricians (like Barrett Wendell and Adams Sherman Hill) abstracted the techniques and dissociated them from effects.[19] Coherence, for instance, became an inherent quality of a prose passage, not a technique that attached itself to a particular mental effect.

Campbell's view of audience is very much a product of eighteenth-century faculty psychology.[20] Faculty psychology allows that the hearers have a complex mental state, that the cognitive functioning of the individual involves an interaction between understanding, passion, will, and imagination. However, the doctrine still posits the hearer in a subordinate position relative to the speaker. In Campbell's rhetoric the hearer, more than a mere *tabula rasa*, is a complex of mental faculties and prior experiences. Nevertheless, the hearer is still the passive acted-upon. The speaker's discovery of truth is, for Campbell, prior to the art of rhetoric. Rhetoric concerns itself with eloquence, with the *adaptation* of discourse; the content is developed prior to rhetoric. Cambell appreciates that audiences come to speech situations with various degrees of understanding and with a wide range of emotional dispositions. The effective speaker understands which techniques to use to affect certain faculties of mind. Campbell deals quite thoroughly with the general faculties that all persons possess but says relatively little about particular differences, which, he says, "must be obvious to a person of discernment."[21]

Campbell's treatment of audience is the most comprehensive treatment in rhetoric since Aristotle. Like Aristotle, Campbell considers the nature and diversity of the human character and throughout *Philosophy* attempts to press the faculty psychology of Hume into the service of rhetoric. As a topic, audience permeates the book. Campbell also considers questions of motivation that previous rhetoricians did not much concern themselves with, for instance taking up the question of why hearers enjoy "exhibitions of human misery" and why audiences are swayed by pathetic appeals (Book 1.11). For Campbell, the consideration of human character and motivation and audience disposition is central to rhetoric; rhetoric involves the working out of a suitable match between the style of the discourse and the audience type one wishes to affect.[22]

Current-Traditional Rhetoric

Resting on the assumptions of faculty psychology, Campbell's rhetoric emphasizes that certain stylistic strategies have certain fixed effects. The writer's task is to create the appropriate effect on the audience by employing the appropriate stylistic strategy. Later disciples of Campbell—the early current-traditionalists such as Alexander Bain, Adams Sherman Hill, John Franklin Genung, and Barrett Wendell[23]—adopted the faculty psychology approach. But it seems that each subsequent treatment reduced the role of audience in the production of discourse (with a few exceptions, such as Fred Newton Scott).

What happened was that the principles of style that had derived from a theory of audience psychology developed their own inherent value. The rhetorician did not need the notion of audience if she followed the recommended principles, because by adhering to the recommended stylistic principles the rhetor could achieve the desired effect on the audience without recourse to "extra-stylistic" guidelines. All audiences would be moved by coherent and perspicuous prose. The few psychological distinctions that George Campbell developed became outmoded; current-traditional rhetoric makes no audience distinctions.

For example, in a more "current" current-traditional textbook, the third edition of James McCrimmon's *Writing With a Purpose* (1963), the terms "audience" and "reader" are not to be found. [24] There is no chapter heading, subheading, or index entry for "reader" or for "audience." Audience is a hidden, obscured presence in the text. The text focuses on paragraphing skills, on parts of speech, on grammar and punctuation conventions, on the formal features of discourse—all of which, the text says, are the proper "purpose" of the writer. The aim of writing is thus "formal": the writer aims to produce a formally acceptable product (which presumably *pleases*, in some sense, the reader). The specialized vocabulary developed in the text relates to formal features of discourse. In places where one might expect to see a reference to "the reader," McCrimmon adopts passive voice: "Those arguments . . . are not necessarily convincing."[25] The assumption is that adherence to formal standards will result in a discourse that will affect the "general" reader in the desired manner.

By the early twentieth century, the notion of audience was disappearing. Or, rather, it was being swallowed up and becoming something else in composition instruction. A new kind of text appeared to replace the "rhetoric": the "handbook" became the ultimate arbiter. And though the handbook's roots are certainly in current-traditional rhetoric, the handbook evolved into something even more narrowly focused.

"Formalist rhetoric" has its roots in current-traditional rhetoric and is its logical extension in the twentieth century. Formalist rhetoric is manifested in the style and grammar handbooks so prevalent in the 1950s and still common today; but many composition texts of this era are formalist in their assumptions about the composing process. The formalist text maintains the stylistic principles espoused by current-traditionalism (clarity, emphasis, unity, coherence) but loses track of their connection to audience altogether. Thus, "clarity" is not "clarity to somebody"; "clarity" becomes an objective standard—that is, it is inherent in language itself.[26] The standards are legislated by the one reader who really matters and who "understands how language works"—the English teacher—and it is not variable from audience to audience.

A piece of writing is seen as a formal product primarily or exclusively—only secondarily, if at all, as a communication. As a product, the writing should conform to particular structural principles (i.e., the modes—description, narration, classification, etc.), which represent the standards of the general audience, and conform to the theory laid down by Campbell, though the handbooks rarely mention audience and never mention Campbell. Over a period of time, the principles came to develop their own independent significance. The theory justifying their existence, based in faculty psychology and on an associationalist theory of language acquisition, was lost.[27]

Current-traditional rhetoric assumes that the writer has a privileged view of an experience that the audience does not have. It assumes that the audience has a real presence outside the discourse and is the passive receptor of the writer's "truth."[28] It assumes that adherence to stylistic principles will result in appropriateness to audience. Thus, audience is important, but only as a function of style; as Berlin points out, "the audience has no part in the shaping of meaning."[29] Since audiences can be divided into two simple categories—according to Campbell, "men in general" and "men in specific"—audience analysis is not important.

Audience thus becomes subsumed under a set of organizational and stylistic strictures. Formalist handbooks refer to "the reader" but only infrequently in handbooks of the 1950s and 1960s. Handbooks of the 1970s and 1980s perhaps include a separate section entitled "audience." Usually no more than one page or so in length, this section will remind students to "consider audience" before writing; but rarely do such sections provide techniques or suggestions for how to consider audience. The bulk of any formalist handbook contains rules governing usage, and exercises. Audience is treated implicitly and generically, the assumption being that one meets the needs of audience by adhering to conventional standards (or conversely, by avoiding error) and by exercising certain rote organizational and stylistic patterns (such as the modes), not by any supplementary market survey approach to audience analysis. The legislator of these stylistic principles is, of course, the English teacher, the really real reader who represents "the intelligent and reasonable reader."[30]

The interesting feature of formalist handbooks is their enduring quality. Formalist handbooks continue to thrive, even to flourish, particularly in the middle and high schools.[31] This is testimony to the fact that they represent a view of rhetoric that is still the publically accepted view—a view that accepts the priority of thought over writing (seeing writing as simply the process of "packaging" thought) and that sees the audience as the passive receptor of the packaged message. Formalist rhetoric, despite its rhetorical narrowness, is by no means an outmoded pedagogical approach. It certainly represents the common attitude toward composition—and it is probably still the prevailing form of composition instruction.

Expressivist Rhetoric

The expressivist rhetorics produced in the 1960s and 1970s were in part a reaction against what were regarded as the excessive restrictions of current-traditional rhetoric. Expressivists like Ken Macrorie, James Miller, and Peter Elbow stressed classroom activities that centered on the student's newly developing self (instead of the teacher's old lecture notes). The aim of writing was to develop an honest, genuine voice rather than to master stylistic and grammatical conventions. The expressivists deemphasized, indeed spoke out against, what they saw as the excessive formalism of current-traditional rhetoric. And attention to audience was more often than not considered a flaw in—or at least an obstacle to—expressive writing .

We can see some evidence of distrust of audience, certainly, in classical rhetoric.[32] But composition texts in the expressivist tradition take an even more sour view of audience. The only safe audience, says E. B. White in *The Elements of Style,* is the self:

> Many references have been made in this book to "the reader"—he has been much in the news. It is now necessary to warn the writer that his concern for the reader must be pure: he must sympathize with the reader's plight (most readers are in trouble about half the time) but never seek to know his wants. The whole duty of a writer is to please and satisfy himself, and the true writer always plays to an audience of one. Let him start sniffing the air, or glancing at the Trend Machine, and he is as good as dead, although he may make a nice living.[33]

To White, the audience can be a threat to the writer's personal integrity. "Considering audience" is dangerous because it might lead to pandering, to selling the integrity of one's voice or message to "the Trend Machine"—to, literally in this passage, spiritual death. To preserve his integrity, the writer must deliberately *not* do audience analysis. Ignorance of audience insures integrity and ethical superiority. "Disdain for audience" is the preferred stance.[34]

No doubt Strunk and White are thinking of audience as "the general public"—the ignorant masses who read pulp fiction and the *National Enquirer* and watch TV. I doubt that they would object to a writer considering the position of "the intelligent reader" as threatening—but the point is that they do not associate the term "audience" with the intelligent reader, who represents the stylistic standards they themselves promote.

Richard Young has discussed the assumptions of expressivist rhetoric and has located it in composition texts as early as Genung's *The Working Principles of Rhetoric* (1900). What characterizes expressivist (as well as current-traditional) rhetoric, according to Young, is the insistence that the creative act of discovery cannot be taught. The expressivist assumption is that "the ability to write with skill requires both a creative gift and a mastery of the craft, but the discipline of rhetoric is of necessity concerned only with craft since only craft can be taught."[35]

If the creative act of discovery, or invention, cannot be taught, then what can be? In one pedagogical direction, this conviction leads to formalism, the focus of which is style and usage, the formal features of discourse—the word, the sentence, the paragraph, conventional correctness. (And formalist instruction is often defended on the basis of minimal competency arguments: since teaching invention and the complexities of audience are too difficult for the ignorant masses, our goal should be to simply get them to write correct, competent prose.)

In the other direction, however, this conviction leads to expressivism, which in the 1960s developed into a pedagogical style. In the expressivist view, invention is not teachable. Rather, as James Berlin says, expressionists

> all stress that truth is conceived as a result of a private vision that must be constantly consulted in writing. They thus emphasize that writing is a personal activity, an expression of a unique voice. The writer must be loyal to his private sense of things, not surrender to the vision of someone else.[36]

This "someone else" the writer must not "surrender to" is, of course, the audience—who represents a threat to the writer's self-integrity.[37]

Expressivist, or romantic, rhetoric emphasizes that the writer's most important audience is the self and that successful writing comes about through the writer's careful working on style to discover a "genuine" or "true" voice. Expressivist rhetoric shares at least one trait with current-traditional rhetoric in privileging style above other concerns. It is unique in that, while formalist rhetoric emphasizes conventional correctness, expressivism emphasizes personal and original voice. It also has an uncommon interest in the writer's habits and sees practice as more important to writing development than imitation or "theory." For Kenneth Macrorie, for example, the art of writing is the art of breaking free from the constraining bonds of "traditional approaches" and discovering "your own voice," "your true voice," a "distinctive tone." As Macrorie says, "all good writers speak in honest voices and tell the truth."[38]

Expressivist rhetoric has its roots in Romantic theories of art and writing and receives its strongest curricular support in departments of English (e.g., in creative writing classes), which have, historically, defended and promoted expressivist approaches to rhetoric (all the while denying that these approaches are even "rhetoric"). According to M. H. Abrams, in the poetic theory of nineteenth-century English Romanticism, the audience (understood to mean "the common reader") was not an important factor. In fact, the nineteenth century "displaced" the audience with the focus on the author.[39] Abrams notes the neglect of, ambivalence toward, and at times hostility for the audience in the poetic theory of Wordsworth, Keats, Shelley, Carlyle, and John Stuart Mill.[40] According to Wayne Booth, this poetic theory evolved into one of the general rules of modern criticism:

> True art ignores the audience; [and] true artists write only for them-
> selves. . . . Suspicion of the reader has usually been based on theories of
> pure art or pure poetry which demand that this, that, or the other element
> be purged in order that what remains might consist of nothing but pure
> elements fused in an intrinsic, internal relationship.[41]

The whole movement was, according to Booth, designed to rescue literature from the intrusion of the author and from the wicked influence of rhetoric: in short, to purify literature. Literature, and literary criticism, was to focus on the text and through it on the internal operation of the mind, the ingenious mind of the poet.[42] The distrust of audience became an ethos of the modern writer and eventually became a central aesthetic principle in New Criticism. It is no wonder then that expressivist rhetoric thrived—and still thrives—in departments of English nor that there continues to be conflict between the rhetoric and literature components of many departments of English.

Audience as Managed

During this era from just after the Civil War until the 1960s—an era referred to by some as the "dark ages" of composition[43]—there were few noticed voices of protest. Generally, this was an age marked by neglect of some of the main topics promoted by classical rhetoric—including audience. The pedagogies described here may not have been the only approaches prevalent, but they were certainly the dominant ones. We might say a word about another approach, though, distinctly in the minority, advanced by teachers such as Fred Newton Scott, Joseph Villiers Denney, and Gertrude Buck. As James Berlin points out, these rhetoricians viewed audience and social situation as a vital part of the composing process.[44]

Scott, Denney, and Buck recognized that the writer or speaker must adapt the text to the particular needs of the audience. In their text *Elementary English Composition* (1900), Scott and Denney provide separate chapters on "The Hearer" and "The Reader" (thus acknowledging a distinction between oral and written contexts).[45] They also provide writing assignments with a strong contextual base: "Try to convince a classmate that he should take up the study of Latin or German.''[46] They stressed the importance of having something to say and someone to say it to.[47] Yet even in this context-conscious text, the main emphasis is on formal correctness—on sentence construction, spelling, punctuation, and paragraph structure. And even though they are cognizant of audience, Scott and Denney accept the managerial communication model. The writer must consider audience but need not look to the audience for inventional guidance.

Traditional rhetorics share the view that considering audience means *managing* audience. The audience imagined is generally the "commonsense audience"—the real readers "out there" existing apart from the text. This view extends from the linear communication model, in which writing is tertiary to thought and to speech.[48] Meaning originates in the thoughts of the rhetor; is represented, however perfectly or imperfectly, in speech or writing; and is then transmitted to an audience. Writing is merely inscription of speech, and speech is merely articulation of thought. In this model, the audience is perceived as flesh-and-blood, actual persons, who sit passively as consumers at the end of an assembly line of discourse production. The writer might consider audience to determine the most efficient means of framing the message—but concern for audience is a secondary activity that has more to do with "packaging" than with "discovery."

Traditional rhetorics ignore audience, proceeding, I think, from something like this line of reasoning: if analyzing audience means managing it, better we should *ignore* the audience. And this argument can be defended on moral grounds. If we accept the linear, managerial communication model as *the* model, then, yes, analysis of audience could be seen as a suspicious activity (i.e., the notion of rhetoric as deceptive or manipulative, something akin to advertising). Within the assumptions of this model, ignoring the audience may be the most ethical choice.

This line of thinking spins out several different approaches to audience. Current-traditional rhetoric treats audience generically, assuming that the writer can best attend to the wants of "the general reader" simply by attending to other compositional matters, such as style and organization, coherence and unity, and the standard rhetorical patterns (the modes). In other words, audience needs are best met by adherence to formalistic principles. Such a view can also be defended on pedagogical grounds: since we cannot teach unskilled writers the art of writing to every particular audience, as a reasonable minimal goal we should teach them a kind of general literacy that will be acceptable for most occasions.[49]

But there are some approaches, neither current-traditional or expressive, that nonetheless subscribe to a managerial philosophy of composing. Most 1980s composition texts consider audience analysis an appropriate strategy, and yet most textbooks and the theories supporting them are based on a managerial treatment. For instance, the cognitive-process model of Linda Flower and John Hayes certainly represents a theoretical advance in terms of exploring how the writer's thought processes are exercised during composing—and yet its treatment of audience is still managerial. Both because the model has been so influential and because the model *does* consider audience an important component, its treatment of audience is worth examining in detail.

The Flower-Hayes model, based on Herbert Simon's model of psychological functions, isolates the cognitive operations that writers activate during the composing process. In the model, the audience is consigned to the realm of the "external" or, in Flower and Hayes' terminology, the "task environment"—but is by no means neglected. The first thing one notices about Linda Flower's textbook *Problem-Solving Strategies for Writing* is that "the reader" is invoked often throughout the text to justify particular inventional, organizational, or stylistic practices.[50] "Audience" as a topic pervades the work. Several sections deal extensively with readers, and there is an entire chapter on how writers should analyze readers (Chapter 9).

The central principle of Chapter 9 stresses audience:

> KNOW the needs of your reader. The first step in designing your writing to be read is to understand the needs, attitudes, and knowledge of your particular reader, and to help that reader turn your written message into the meaning *you* intended.[51]

The refrain "designing your writing to be read" recalls George Campbell's definition of rhetoric as "the art of adapting a discourse to its end."[52] Campbell's definition and Flower's treatment both assume that the discourse is created at some particular stage and then "designed" or "adapted" to fit a reader at another stage. In Campbell's *The Philosophy of Rhetoric*, the invention of content is not a matter to be taken up by rhetoric. In Flower's work it is, but creation of content is a cognitive activity separate from and prior to consideration of reader. In other words, the audience is not a participator in the development of content or knowledge. Content is a private affair between writer and "subject"; the reader enters the picture later, in the design phase.

This advice assumes that "the meaning you intended" exists apart from the "written message": in other words, intention exists prior to and apart from the text, though an effective text apparently captures the intention perfectly, that is, so the reader can then process the text to recreate the meaning intended by the writer. The description assumes a linear and mechanical communication process: writer has meaning, writer puts meaning in text, reader gets meaning. In fact, this model is explicitly and unabashedly identified as the operative theoretical model for the book.[53] Flower provides a lengthy discussion entitled "The Creative Reader," which describes the cognitive nature of the reading activity; thus, we are given more than the usual amount of attention to the reader. But, again, this knowledge of the reader is pressed into the service of the design phase (or revision).

The textbook includes samples of audience analysis, written by students who have developed fairly detailed pictures of their expected readers, using the audience analysis questions that Flower suggests.[54] The image of the audience in the samples is of a real reader (e.g., "Dot Schwartz, the bookstore manager"). Flower offers a real-reader heuristic, but it suffers from the same limitations as real-reader heuristics generally (as discussed in Chapter 1): How will information about Dot the bookstore manager *as person* help me form a reading role for *Dot the reader?* (Because Dot the reader of my document does not yet exist.) The discussion assumes an unproblematic, one-to-one correspondence between person and reader.

The discussion of audience analysis is certainly more developed than in most composition texts, but the essential problem remains the same: We have audience analysis questions, but, presuming that the audience is not the same as "the person," where do we find this audience? If the exercise relies on imagination, then we run into a practical pedagogical problem: How does the writer understand the person as a reader? How does the writer measure the accuracy or efficacy of her imaginative construction? What if the writer lacks the imagination to develop a picture of an audience? Though providing a more detailed discussion of audience, *Problem-Solving Strategies* ends up limiting itself by equating audience with real readers.

To understand the theory on which this audience pedagogy rests, we must turn to Flower and Hayes's article describing the cognitive-process model. In "A Cognitive Process Theory of Writing," Flower and Hayes directly challenge new rhetoric's focus on situation.[55] They acknowledge the influence of purpose and exigence, admitting that both "have a hand in guiding the writer's process," but they question the nature of that influence: "it is not at all clear how they do so or how they interact."[56] Flower and Hayes believe that it is far more useful to "turn our attention to the writing process itself"—that is, to engage in what they suggest is "direct observation" of the writer's cognitive processes (through protocol analysis).

Actually, Flower and Hayes do not reject theory per se. They simply substitute one theory for another, preferring the theoretical models describing thinking processes. These models are of course no more or less empirically derived than models and principles from rhetoric theory. But they certainly provide a different emphasis, an emphasis that Flower and Hayes suggest is more appropriate for composition than rhetorical models.

The cognitive-process model itself consists of three parts: the "task environment," "the writer's long-term memory," and "writing processes." The model isolates those immediate and conscious activities of the individual writer as "writing processes," which refer to cognitive activities (e.g., planning, translating, reviewing, monitoring) that writers activate during composing. In this model, audience occupies two places. Audience resides in the "rhetorical problem," which is part of task environment— that is, outside the writer, as real reader. And it resides in the writer's long-term memory. Audience then is not considered part of the immediate, conscious portion of the writer's process. It is, rather, a subsystem accessed by writers.

The audience referred to here is, of course, two different audiences, though no distinction is drawn. One audience is the real reader and the other is the writer's experiences of other audiences (stored in long-term memory). The writer collects information about the reader in the task environment (collected through real-reader analysis) and accesses memory of prior experiences with (other) audiences, presumably to build a new reader image for the document being written. The model does not provide a place for what might be, for the writer in the act of composing, the most important reader: the intended reader, or that new reader image that the writer constructs based on knowledge of real reader and of prior readers. The model also does not allow a place for the reading role assigned in a given text (the implied or presupposed reader).

Flower and Hayes' cognitive process model provides an interesting perspective on the composing process, and I do not want to suggest that it is not a useful model. It has been especially useful in drawing distinctions between cognitive operations—for instance, in noting the importance of the planning function. Its weakness is that it focuses primarily on the presumed-to-be internal cognitive operations and their connection to textual strategies. It does not tell us much about "outside," and often messier, factors. The model simply does not account for the influence of the social. The model obscures lager social and cultural concerns, as well as concerns of rhetorical context.[57]

We can examine, too, the model's assumptions about the generation of knowledge and the audience's role in generating that knowledge. Epistemologically, the cognitive-process model and the faculty psychology of George Campbell (and David Hume) are quite similar: both recognize the complexity of audience psychology (though there are differences in the way this psychology is modeled, and the cognitive-process model is clearly more specific to writing); and both recognize that the rhetor must be aware of the complexities in order to best manage the audience's responses. The model does not ignore audience—but it regards audience as a passive receptor, to be worked on by the writer, whose knowledge of audience is applied to "adapt" an already established position, to dress up, or make more accessible, material already determined.

Current-traditional and expressivist rhetorics, despite their pedagogical differences, share essentially the same philosophy of composing and the same epistemology of audience: *the audience is the "acted upon," the passive receptor of the message of the writer.* The writer's discovery of truth, or insight, or content for writing occurs outside of and prior to the realm of rhetoric. The proper purview of rhetoric is the presentation of message.

Current-traditional rhetoric, in its late-nineteenth-century manifestations, acknowledged the influence of audience at least on the writer's creation of style; formalist rhetoric ignores or denies the audience's relevance to the framing of the message. Expressivist rhetoric does not just ignore the audience, it identifies the audience as a danger, an occasion for sin. Audience is identified with the "market" or "popular opinion," and so is something every writer should strive to avoid. These assumptions about rhetoric and audience, in particular formalist and expressivist ones, held sway in composition instruction, at least until "the realm of rhetoric" was expanded by the new rhetoricians and new rhetorical theories partially adopted by composition in the 1970s and 1980s.

From classical, current-traditional, and expressivist rhetoric we inherit several ideas. Audience refers to actual, flesh-and-blood readers who are relatively stupid, relatively homogenous, and relatively emotional. Contemporary practice now reaffirms, for the most part, the importance of considering this reader and acknowledges that there are audience differences that may affect the written text. Proponents of expressivism are nervous about this: audience concern is related to "advertising" and "persuasion" (immoral genres). If "considering audience" means managing or manipulating readers, then we would be better off morally simply ignoring audience. Writer/author integrity should take precedence over the audience. For proponents of current-traditionalism, concerns of form (structure and style) and subject take precedence. Overall, what I have chosen to term "traditional rhetoric" obscures audience, both strategically and ethically. Thanks to a series of epistemological shifts at several key moments in rhetorical history (classical rhetoric, eighteenth-century new rhetoric, twentieth-century current-traditionalism), the audience effectively disappears.

NOTES
Chapter 3

[1] John Franklin Genung, *The Practical Elements of Rhetoric.* (Boston: Ginn, 1892), p. xi.

[2] Sheridan Baker, *The Practical Stylist*, 4th ed. (New York: Crowell, 1977), p. 1.

[3] William Strunk, Jr., and E. B. White, *The Elements of Style*, revised edition (New York: Macmillan, 1962), pp. 70–71.

[4] James A. Berlin, "Contemporary Composition: The Major Pedagoical Theories," *College English* 44 (1982): 765–777.

[5] Richard Young, "Paradigms and Problems: Needed Research in Rhetorical Invention," in *Research in Composing*, ed. Charles Cooper and Lee Odell (Urbana, IL: NCTE, 1978), 29–47; James A. Berlin and Robert P. Inkster, "Current-Traditional Rhetoric: Paradigm and Practice," *Freshman English News* 8 (1980): 1–4, 13–14. The oxymoronic term "current-traditional rhetoric" was first coined by Daniel Fogarty, in *Roots for a New Rhetoric* (New York: Russell and Russell, 1959), p. 118.

[6] For a full discussion of the development of nineteenth-century current-traditional and expressivist rhetorics and their influence on composition instruction in the United States, see James Berlin, *Writing Instruction in Nineteenth-Century American Colleges* (Carbondale, IL: Southern Illinois UP, 1984).

[7] Donald Stewart provides some evidence supporting this claim in "Textbooks Revisited" in *Research in Composition and Rhetoric: A Bibliographic Sourcebook*, ed. Michael G. Moran and Ronald F. Lunsford (Westport, CN: Greenwood, 1984), 453–468.

[8] Hugh Blair, *Lectures on Rhetoric and Belle Lettres*, 2 vols., ed. Harold F. Harding (Carbondale, IL: Southern Illinois UP, 1965).

[9] For a discussion of Blair's treatment of audience, see John C. McDonald, "Taste and the Shaping of Audience in Hugh Blair," in *Visions of Rhetoric*, ed. Charles W. Kneupper (Arlington, TX: Rhetoric Society of America, 1987), 22–29.

[10] George Campbell, *The Philosophy of Rhetoric*, ed. Lloyd F. Bitzer (Carbondale, IL: Southern Illinois UP, 1963). For a discussion of George Campbell's theory of audience, see Stuart C. Brown and Thomas Willard, "George Campbell's Audience: Historical and Theoretical Considerations," in *A Sense of Audience in Written Communication*, ed. Gesa Kirsch and Duane H. Roen (Newbury Park, CA: Sage, 1990), 58–72.

[11] See John Hagaman, "George Campbell and the Creative Management of Audience," *Rhetoric Society Quarterly* 13 (1983): 21–24.

[12] Campbell, Book 1.1, pp. 4–5.

[13] Campbell, Book 1.1, p. 1.

[14] Campbell, Book 1.8, p. 96.

[15] Cleanth Brooks and Robert Penn Warren, *Modern Rhetoric* 2nd. ed. (New York: Harcourt, 1958).

[16] We see a more recent version of the idea that writers cannot account for individual audiences in Sheridan Baker's *The Complete Stylist and Handbook* (3rd ed., 1984): "The notion of adjusting your writing to a whole scale of audiences, though attractive in theory, hardly works out in practice. You are

writing, and the written word presupposes a literate norm that immediately eliminates all the lower ranges of mere talk" (New York: Harper & Row, 1984, p. 6).

17 Campbell, Book 1.10, p. 102.

18 Campbell, Book 1.10, p. 102. Elsewhere, Campbell remarks that the more "gross" the audience, and the "least improved" in knowledge and discernment, the easier it is to work upon their passions.

19 See Sharon Crowley, "The Current-Traditional Theory of Style: An Informal History," *Rhetoric Society Quarterly* 16 (1986): 233–250.

20 For a discussion of Campbell's theory of faculty psychology (and its origins in the philosophy of David Hume), see Lloyd F. Bitzer, 'Introduction,' *The Philosophy of Rhetoric*, by George Campbell (Carbondale, IL: Southern Illinois UP, 1963), ix–xxxvii; Lloyd F. Bitzer, "Hume's Philosophy in George Campbell's Philosophy of Rhetoric," *Philosophy and Rhetoric* 2 (1969): 139–166; and Vincent M. Bevilacqua, "Philosophical Origins of George Campbell's *Philosophy of Rhetoric*," *Speech Monographs* 32 (1965): 1–12.

21 Campbell, Book 1.8, p. 96.

22 This approach to audience has its roots in Aristotle, who also identified audience types. Where Aristotle's approach differs significantly is in elevating the importance of the *topoi* as devices for affecting audiences. By Campbell's time the *topoi* had been dismissed as a viable strategy, helped no doubt by the remonstrances of John Locke (*Essay on Human Understanding*) and Antoine Arnauld (*Port-Royal Logic*). In Campbell's work the rhetor does not consider how to affect audience by reasoning strategies; rhetoric attends to stylistic strategies only.

23 Alexander Bain, *English Composition and Rhetoric*, Enlarged Edition (New York: Appleton, 1887); Barrett Wendell, *English Composition* (New York: Scribner's, 1912); Adams Sherman Hill, *The Principles of Rhetoric*, New Edition (New York: Harper and Brothers, 1895); John Franklin Genung, *The Working Principles of Rhetoric* (Boston: Ginn, 1900). James Berlin discusses these figures in *Writing Instruction*, p. 7.

24 James McCrimmon, *Writing with a Purpose*, 3rd ed. (Boston: Houghton Mifflin, 1963).

25 McCrimmon, p. 315.

26 Current-traditional rhetoric, as it evolved into the handbook genre, is, according to Richard Young, characterized by "emphasis on the composed product rather than the composing process; the analysis of discourse into words, sentences, and paragraphs; the classification of discourse into description, narration, exposition, and argument; the strong concern with usage (syntax, spelling, punctuation) and with style (economy, clarity, emphasis)." See Young, "Paradigms," p. 31.

27 See Berlin, *Writing Instruction*. For an application of associationalist theory to composition, see Bain.

28 See Berlin and Inkster, p. 4; Berlin, "Contemporary Composition," p. 775.

29 Berlin, *Writing Instruction*, p. 64.

[30] Sheridan Baker, *The Complete Stylist and Handbook*, 3rd ed. (New York: Harper & Row, 1984), pp. 6–7.

[31] See Stewart.

[32] Quintilian warns the ideal orator that "above all it is important that he . . . never, like so many, be led by a desire to win applause to neglect the interest of the actual case," (*Institutio Oratoria*, 12.8.1).

[33] Strunk and White, p. 71.

[34] As Joyce Wexler points out, showing disdain for audience is a distinct *ethos* of modern writers. She argues, however, that this is sometimes a public, but not especially a private, *ethos*: "While modernists' public condemnations of rhetoric are well known, their private confessions of longing for fame are often forgotten. In addition to the material rewards of fame, they wanted their work to have specific effects on a wide audience, not just a coterie. . . . Modernist writers may have felt alienated from society but not from their potential readers" (286, 288). Perhaps there is a kind of belletristic discourse where it is best to develop a detachment from, even a disdain, for audience. Not caring (or at least adopting the mask of not caring) about your readers can be a powerful and profitable persuasive strategy. See Joyce Wexler, "Modernist Writers and Publishers," *Studies in the Novel* 17 (1985): 286–295.

[35] Richard E. Young, "Concepts of Art and the Teaching of Writing," in *The Rhetorical Tradition and Modern Writing*, ed. James J. Murphy (New York: MLA, 1982), p. 131.

[36] Berlin, *Writing Instruction*, p. 89. According to Berlin, expressionistic (or "subjective") rhetoric is characterized by "the conviction that reality is a personal and private construct . . . For the expressionist, truth is always discovered within, through an internal glimpse, an examination of the private inner world." See James A. Berlin, *Rhetoric and Reality: Writing Instruction in American Colleges, 1900–1985* (Carbondale, IL: Southern Illinois UP, 1987), p. 145. Berlin also points out there are various degrees of expressionism, ranging from "anarchists, arguing for complete and uninhibited freedom in writing" to "transactionalists," who "see reality as arising out of the interaction of the private vision of the individual and the language used to express this vision" (*Rhetoric and Reality*, pp. 145–146).

[37] Peter Elbow discusses how concern for audience can also threaten the effectiveness of the writer's composing process in "Closing My Eyes as I Speak: An Argument for Ignoring Audience," *College English* 49 (1987): 50–69.

[38] Ken Macrorie, *Telling Writing*, 2nd ed. (Rochelle Park, NJ: Hayden, 1976), p. 5. See also Ken Macrorie, *Uptaught* (New York: Hayden, 1970). Perhaps the most comprehensive and explicit articulation of expressivist principles can be found in James E. Miller, Jr., *Word, Self, Reality* (New York: Harper & Row, 1972). For further discussion of the expressivist view of audience, see Donald M. Murray, "Teaching the Other Self: The Writer's First Reader," *College Composition and Communication* 33 (1982): 140–147.

[39] M. H. Abrams, *The Mirror and the Lamp* (London: Oxford UP, 1953), p. 72.

[40] Abrams, pp. 25–26.

[41] Wayne Booth, *The Rhetoric of Fiction* (Chicago: The U of Chicago P, 1961), pp 89, 91.

[42] Abrams, p. 22.

[43] See Robert J. Connors, "Textbooks and the Evolution of the Discipline," *College Composition and Communication* 37 (1986), p. 189.

[44] Berlin, *Writing Instruction*, pp. 77–84.

[45] Fred Newton Scott and Joseph Villiers Denney, *Elementary English Composition* (Boston: Allyn and Bacon, 1900; rev. 1908).

[46] Scott and Denney, p. 224.

[47] See Gertrude Buck, "Recent Tendencies in the Teaching of English Composition," *Education Review* 22 (1901): 371–383.

[48] See Jasper Neel, *Plato, Derrida, and Writing* (Carbondale, IL: Southern Illinois UP, 1988).

[49] Such a view has a good deal of popular support. E. D. Hirsch's argument for a minimal standard of cultural literacy arises out of a formalist approach to audience, or what he calls "the common reader": "When we address a general audience we must assume that we are addressing a 'common reader,' that is, a literate person who shares with us a common body of knowledge and associations." See E. D. Hirsch, Jr., *Cultural Literacy: What Every American Needs to Know* (New York: Vintage-Random, 1988), p. 135.

[50] Linda Flower, *Problem-Solving Strategies for Writing*, 2nd ed. (New York: Harcourt, 1985).

[51] Flower, *Problem-Solving Strategies*, p. 129.

[52] Campbell, *The Philosophy of Rhetoric*, p. 1.

[53] Flower, *Problem-Solving Strategies*, pp. 136–137.

[54] Flower, *Problem-Solving Strategies*, pp. 133–135.

[55] Linda Flower and John R. Hayes, "A Cognitive Process Theory of Writing," *College Composition and Communication* 32 (1981): 365–387.

[56] Flower and Hayes, "Cognitive Process Theory," p. 366.

[57] In later work, Linda Flower recognizes the *gap* in the cognitive-process model: "The Hayes/Flower cognitive process model is a case in point. Although this model suggests key *places where* social and contextual knowledge operate within a cognitive framework, that early research did little more than specify that the 'task environment' was an important element in the process; it failed to account for *how* the situation in which the writer operates might shape composing, and it had little to say about the specific conventions, schemata, or commonplaces that might inform the writer's 'long-term memory.' " See Linda Flower, "Cognition, Context, and Theory Building," *College Composition and Communication* 40 (1989), p. 283.

In another article, Flower and Hayes concede that the rhetorical problem (which includes audience) is an important part of the writing process. However audience, as an external factor in the task environment, is difficult to account for. In what forms does the writer receive information about audience? How does the writer construct an image of audience? Assuming that an image can be constructed, how does the writer connect this image to textual strategies? While the cognitive-process model is a useful tool for understanding parts of the writer's composing process, it does not very well describe the relationship of social context (task environment) to the individual writer. See Linda Flower and John R. Hayes, "The Dynamics of Composing: Making Plans and Juggling Constraints," in *Cognitive Processes in Writing*, ed. Lee W. Gregg and Erwin R. Steinberg (Hillsdale, NJ: Erlbaum, 1980), p. 40.

Chapter 4

The New Rhetoric and the Recovery of Audience

> The orator indeed is obliged to adapt himself to his audience if he wishes to have any effect on it and we can easily understand that the discourse which is most efficacious on an incompetent audience is not necessarily that which would win the assent of a philosopher. But why not allow that argumentations can be addressed to every kind of audience? . . . We believe then that audiences are not independent of one another, that particular concrete audiences are capable of validating a concept of the universal audience which characterizes them.[1]
>
> *Chaim Perelman and L. Olbrechts-Tyteca*

Until the 1960s current-traditional and expressivist rhetorics dominated composition instruction in the United States—and perhaps still do[2]— chiefly because composition instruction was consigned to departments of English, where approaches emphasizing the formal features of discourse and the creative intentions of the author were favored. (The bond between English departments and romantic theories of art and criticism is a strong one.)

In the 1960s, however, we see the beginnings of what was later termed a "paradigm shift" within rhetoric and composition.[3] Between 1960 and 1975—a period James Berlin refers to as the "renaissance of rhetoric"[4]—current-traditional and expressivist approaches were challenged by the rediscovery of classical rhetoric and the emergence of "the new rhetoric." Later, in the 1970s and into the early 1980s, developing cognitive and empirical approaches to composition also challenged the authority of the traditional rhetorics. These new rhetorics, and various applications of these rhetorics in composition, all played a role in "recovering" audience as a key concept, though their notions of audience were quite different. This chapter touches upon some key developments in the new rhetoric, focusing in particular on figures such as Chaim Perelman, James Kinneavy, and Richard Young, whose theories have directed and expanded our understanding of audience.

The New Rhetoric

Throughout the history of rhetoric there have been several self-proclaimed "new" rhetorics. As used here, the term "new rhetoric" refers both to a theoretical shift and to its subsequent effects on composition curricula. The new rhetoric started as a post-Second World War movement in rhetorical theory that developed out of the principles of classical rhetoric. The new rhetoric developed beyond classical rhetoric, however, to envision an even broader concept of rhetoric, borrowing from (and, at time, disagreeing with) contemporary philosophy, cognitive and developmental psychology, linguistics, and literary theory. Kenneth Burke and Richard Weaver were perhaps the earliest to appreciate this fuller notion of rhetoric, but the movement achieved formal identity in Daniel Fogarty's *Roots for a New Rhetoric* (1959) and Chaim Perelman and L. Olbrechts-Tyteca's *The New Rhetoric* (1958; trans. 1969).

In *Roots for a New Rhetoric,* Daniel Fogarty sounded the call for a new, more expansive rhetoric, one that would resurrect the principles of classical rhetoric but that would fuse them with insights from contemporary linguistics, semantics, and communication theory.[5] Identifying the roots of this new rhetoric in Kenneth Burke, I. A. Richards, and contemporary semanticists, Fogarty called for a return to the philosophical basis of rhetoric, to replace the stale and narrow approach to rhetoric fostered by current-traditionalism.

The new rhetoric revived the notion of audience, making it once again an important concern of rhetoric and composition instruction and a primary focus of invention. The conception of audience tends to be an abstract one, such as Perelman's "universal audience." Unlike the universal audience of current-traditional rhetoric (an abstraction defined primarily by stylistic conventions), the universal audience of the new rhetoric is defined more by principles of invention, chiefly of informal logic. The new rhetoricians also reestablish the Aristotelian link between audience, situation, and invention. Especially important is situational or rhetorical context.

A number of new rhetoricians—most prominently, Wayne Booth, Lloyd Bitzer, and James Kinneavy—identify "situational context" or "rhetorical situation" as the significant perspective for rhetoric.[6] Lloyd Bitzer, for instance, sees rhetorical situation as the controlling and fundamental concern of rhetorical theory; and he sees all rhetoric as situational.[7] For Bitzer, the three constituents of the rhetorical situation are exigence, constraints, and audience. The audience is that group of real hearers that the rhetor has some chance of affecting: in other words, not the entire body of "real readers" (or hearers) but a select group of real readers—those susceptible to change.[8] It is to this sub-set of all real readers that a writer addresses discourse.

Bitzer's sense of communication is chiefly linear: the writer works to change the audience (those potentially changeable). And Bitzer's epistemology is a realistic one: the rhetorical situation provides constraints and an audience that both exist prior to the discourse. The constraints and the audience are "located in reality" and "are objective and publicly observable facts in the world we experience."[9] They are not, to Bitzer, "created" by the rhetor. The exigence is the need for discourse, arising out of social situations, which the writer recognizes at the appropriate time.[10] Bitzer's contribution is in reviving the situational emphasis, though his sense of communication is still very much managerial, and his sense of audience and situation realistic.

"The new rhetoric" achieved self-definition in Fogarty's work and in another major treatise, Chaim Perelman and L. Olbrecht-Tyteca's *The New Rhetoric*. In this latter work especially, audience plays a prominent role. "The New Rhetoric," at least as Perelman articulates it, is a new or revived branch of study devoted to the analysis of informal reasoning.[11] It is a rhetoric that reinstantiates the art of dialectic (called by Aristotle "analytics") into rhetoric. Perelman sees rhetoric as including dialectic—that is, as including the concerns of Aristotle's *Organon*, as well as the *Rhetoric*. His rhetoric stresses the reasoning strategies that writers share in common with audiences and that writers must use and apply in their writing to convince audiences.

In *The New Rhetoric* Perelman and Olbrechts-Tyteca challenge the Aristotelian division between dialectic and rhetoric by arguing that all discourse aims at adherence of belief—and is thus in some sense "rhetorical." All discourse consequently involves an audience whose attitudes and beliefs must by accounted for by the rhetor. There is *not* an ontological difference between dialectic (or logic) and rhetoric; dialectic does not belong to some special realm beyond "audience." Rather, the differences between dialectic and what is commonly called rhetoric are simply differences in deployment of argumentative strategies. Rhetoric cannot neglect audience because, according to Perelman, the audience provides the basic premises from which any argument (for Perelman, any discourse) must proceed. To argue effectively, the rhetor must have a sense of audience. And all discourse *is* argument in the sense that all discourse aims to achieve the adherence of the audience.[12]

For Perelman "the audience is not necessarily made up of those the speaker expressly addresses": "If . . . we want to define the audience in a useful manner, we must regard it as *the gathering of those whom the speaker wants to influence by his or her arguments.*"[13] The audience is thus those whom the rhetor wishes to change. And every particular audience shares to some degree the characteristics of the "universal audience."

By "universal audience" Perelman means those "competent and reasonable" members of humanity[14] who share in a general sense of what is reasonable. This universal audience implicitly accepts a set of general argumentative strategies (basic premises and beliefs coupled with standard strategies of deployment, such the *topoi*) that are "universal" in the sense that all discourse partakes of them. In this idealized realm, then, there is or should be a discourse available to everyone—an "idealized philosophy discourse"[15]—that will enable all persons to come to complete consubstantiality, or agreement of mind about public policy.

Of course this is only an ideal, and Perelman recognizes that no particular audience will fit the characteristics of the universal audience. Particular audiences share some features with the universal audience, however, and the rhetor must understand in what ways the particular audience conforms and does not conform to the standards of the universal audience.[16]

This theory of the universal audience can be challenged on the grounds that it is an attempt to claim universal and absolute status for what are really local and politically motivated strategies. Perelman does posit a universal ground for argument—an ideal realm of argument theory in which resides this universal reader—though he recognizes that real audiences never achieve this ideal.[17]

Perelman recognizes that the rhetor must be aware of the sociological and psychological makeup of the audience and would benefit from having a profile of the real reader. At the same time, Perelman suggests that this concern is beyond the scope of rhetoric—or at least extratextual. Rhetoric, he suggests, ought to concern itself with the artistic proofs, with those elements of the discourse itself which produce belief, and with general argumentative strategies acceptable to the universal audience. In one sense, then, Perelman sounds very much like George Campbell: rhetoric cannot deal with particular audiences (though rhetors should); rhetoric, rather, deals with the general principles (for Campbell, of style; for Perelman, of argumentation). Perelman differs radically from Campbell in most respects, though. For instance, he explicitly rejects Campbell's psychologically based theory, insisting that rhetors "do not address what we call 'faculties,' such as intellect, emotion, or will; they address the whole person."[18]

New Rhetoric Theory and Composition

The phrase "the new rhetoric" has also been used within composition to refer to the curricular movement in the late 1960s and 1970s that applied new rhetoric principles to writing instruction, chiefly within departments of English. The "renaissance" in composition studies perhaps begins with those whom James Berlin calls the neo-Aristotelians. Neo-Aristotelian rhetoric refers to the work of a few scholars—particularly Edward Corbett, Richard Hughes, and P. Albert Duhamel—who rediscovered the importance of classical rhetoric and applied it to composition instruction.[19] As Berlin describes them, the neo-Aristotelians hold firmly to the vision of rhetoric espoused by Aristotle. Thus, they view audience as an important factor, but as less important than the inventive strategies (in particular, the *topoi*) that the writer employs to discover means of persuading audiences. Their contribution to the new rhetoric was in reinstating invention as a topic of composition and applying the principles of classical rhetoric for use in freshman composition.

Later, scholars like Richard Young, James Kinneavy, W. Ross Winterowd, William Irmscher, Frank D'Angelo, and Janice Lauer recognized the relevance and value of the new rhetoric to composition and brought these principles into the English composition curriculum, challenging the established current-traditional and expressivist approaches. Several of the key developments in audience theory are located in what were packaged as composition textbooks: in particular, James Kinneavy's *A Theory of Discourse* and Richard Young, Alton Becker, and Kenneth Pike's *Rhetoric: Discovery and Change*—both of which were significant in synthesizing a large body of material from a variety of disciplines to develop interesting new approaches to audience.[20]

In *A Theory of Discourse* (and in a follow-up volume, *Aims and Audiences in Writing*), James Kinneavy develops a comprehensive theory for classifying discourse types.[21] Audience plays a prominent role in his theory, as his classification system is based on *aim,* or the intent of a piece of writing. By "aim," Kinneavy does not mean *intention,* at least not in the conventional sense of *author's* purpose for writing. For Kinneavy, the aim of a discourse is "embodied in the text itself—given the qualifications of situation and culture.''[22] "Aim" signifies the posture a text takes toward its audience. One can determine the aim, or communicative emphasis, of a discourse by examining the "logic" of the discourse,[23] its announced methodologies, and the information it includes (and excludes), as well as its arrangement and style. Thus, Kinneavy's program attempts to mediate between two polarized positions: that meaning "resides" in the text and that meaning is determined by context or by the reader. For Kinneavy, audience expectations are embodied in text conventions.

Kinneavy identifies four dominant aims, determined by which element of the communication triangle a discourse emphasizes: "expressive discourse" emphasizes the writer, "persuasive discourse" the reader, "reference discourse" the reality (or the external world referred to), and "literary discourse" the medium. Reference discourse is divided into three types—science, informative, and exploratory—each corresponding to a different degree of certainty about the " referent": informative discourse describes a reality that is relatively "certain"; science discourse a "probable" reality; and exploratory discourse a "possible" reality. Thus, there are a total of six aims, each with its own "logic" and conventions of form and style.

Kinneavy attempts to reestablish *purpose* as the center of rhetorical concern, while avoiding the pitfalls of the intentional and affective fallacies, which have long plagued purpose.[24] Aim is not simply what writers say they intend (the intentional fallacy), nor is it determined by whatever effect the discourse happens to have on its reader (the affective fallacy). Rather, aim is embodied in the text itself—though situational context is also factored in. Kinneavy's theory attempts to reconcile communication theory and New Criticism (in curricular terms, the departments of speech and English), by maintaining the textual emphasis of New Criticism while at the same time opening the door to admit the indisputable influence of situation.

In Kinneavy's system, audience analysis refers to the effort of understanding the "logics" of various types of discourse as they operate in different contexts. He cites several examples showing how the "logic" of the sample, as well as its form and style, presupposes certain types of audiences.[25] Kinneavy is concerned with the communicative interaction between the text (with its own logic) and the reader. The focus of Kinneavy's concern is textual analysis; and yet he is constantly checking his textual analysis against the imagined readers. In his description of informative discourse, for instance, he identifies three chief characteristics: factuality, comprehensiveness, surprise value. A social constructionist would insist that "factuality" or "comprehensiveness" depends on some social agreement about these terms; Kinneavy tries very hard to show how certain styles are inherently "factual" and certain treatments inherently "comprehensive." He runs into a more difficult problem with the characteristic of "surprise value"—since "surprise" cannot be something "in" the text alone; it is an explicit reference to an imagined audience response. In this case, and others like it, Kinneavy is stuck with the reader, or the imagined audience, as an external influence: his theory balances—perhaps harmoniously, perhaps precipitously—between text and situation.

Kinneavy's system is admirably constructed, rivaling Aristotle's in its comprehensive classification of discourse types. But his theory poses problems, especially from the poststructuralist perspective. For one, in its presentation of discourse compartments, his theory does not account very well for "messiness," for the perversity of readers or for the complexities of discourse. Kinneavy's theory poses a problem for those who see his aims as operative in every discourse. For example, literary is not necessarily a distinct discourse type: some see it as a function that is exercised, to a greater or lesser degree, in every discourse; others see it as referring to a type of reading. The inescapable fact is that aims mix. A *New York Times* article reporting on an oil spill in the Persian Gulf may simply be, to Kinneavy, "informative discourse," but the article will be persuasive in its inevitable political and cultural bias; literary in the at-least-implicit reliance on tropes and on everyday metaphors[26]; and expressive in that it works toward achieving an identity, if not for the individual writer or the newspaper, then certainly on behalf of "the nation."[27]

Kinneavy's theory also poses a problem for those (like Perelman) who see "persuasive" as an overarching category—that is, who see all discourse as essentially persuasive. Kinneavy's theory has been criticized for privileging reference discourse because it reflects "reality" (or attains "referentiality") to the highest degree. "Persuasion" as a distinct aim is treated by Kinneavy as it is in Aristotle: persuasion is how one attempts to change the ignorant, passive masses, who are too slow or impatient to tolerate dialectical (or reference) discourse—though Kinneavy does argue for the social and moral worth of persuasive discourse. Finally, Kinneavy's theory poses a problem from the social constructionist perspective, where meaning and aim are not seen as something evident "in" discourse so much as interpretive conventions established within discourse communities, agreements about how we will read discourse. Although Kinneavy's theory frequently calls on social and cultural context, his preference is clearly for the text as the primary locus of meaning and intent.[28]

Despite these criticisms, Kinneavy's theory, in its attempt to reconcile formalism and communication theory, represents an important historical point in the recovery of audience. Kinneavy reinstates aim—and his theory has had, and will probably continue to have, considerable influence on composition pedagogy. Of all the new rhetorical theories, Kinneavy's has probably been the most successful in challenging the current-traditional and expressivist stronghold on composition pedagogy—no doubt because his classification system maintains strong links to formalism and expressivism (especially in its defining "expressive" as a distinct discourse aim) while at the same time stressing the situational emphasis of the new rhetoric.

In *Rhetoric: Discovery and Change*, Richard Young, Alton Becker, and Kenneth Pike call upon the insights of linguistic theory, the new rhetoric, and cognitive psychology to develop an overall rhetoric that emphasizes the thinking processes writers must activate in rhetorical situations.[29] Their treatment of audience is complex. Though the textbook prefers the conception of readers as actual persons, the authors consider the influences of several kinds of readers. They consider especially the importance of writer-reader relationships, considering strategies writers can use to "build bridges" with readers. *Rhetoric: Discovery and Change* stresses context, defined as the social situations in which discourse operates. The authors even discuss the social situations constraining the writer—though they perhaps subordinate these concerns, privileging the writer with considerable control over rhetorical situation. The textbook focuses not so much on understanding readers demographically but on understanding the beliefs, values, and attitudes of readers, which play a far greater role in influencing the writer's composing processes. To help the writer determine reader knowledge and attitude, Young, Becker, and Pike offer a heuristic strategy for analyzing audiences based on their nine-cell tagmemic heuristic.[30] But they do not consider treatment of only the real reader. In a separate chapter, they discuss the ways in which texts address readers—or, in other terms, how texts embody reader expectations.[31]

The discussion of audience in *Rhetoric: Discovery and Change* represents a considerable advance over previous textbooks certainly, but perhaps over previous treatments generally. Young, Becker, and Pike recognize the complexity of the notion of audience; but beyond that, they manage to develop a pedagogy for reader analysis that does not sacrifice complexity and that accounts for the possibility of, and even encourages, dialogue between rhetor and reader. In its treatment of audience and in its effective integration of that treatment within an overall composing framework, *Rhetoric: Discovery and Change* represents a breakthrough—a point at which the theoretical principles of the new (and classical) rhetoric and the approaches of cognitive psychology coalesce into a single coherent and comprehensive pedagogy that most subsequent textbooks have so far not matched.[32]

Generally, the new rhetoric stresses the purposive nature of discourse, and its situational ground. A discourse is seen as more than merely a set of formal features but as existing for a communicative purpose, as an attempt to change an audience and as an action for a specified reason on a specified occasion. While formalist rhetoric emphasizes paragraph construction and formal coherence, the new rhetoric focuses on questions relating to context: for example, What strategies will change an audience who does not agree with me? Questions are addressed in terms of purpose and action, not in terms of aesthetic or formal principles. The emphasis on purpose, which of course implies an audience, is one of the key contributions of Kinneavy and a key feature of the new rhetoric.

New rhetoricians characterize audience in a number of ways: Perelman as a kind of universal presence embodied in rhetorical and logical principles; Kinneavy as implied in genre conventions; Young, Becker, and Pike in a fairly complex way—as a combination of real reader, universal reader, and implied reader. They do share a common position, though: that audience is much more than simply stylistic conventions. For the neo-Aristotelians and the new rhetoricians, audience is important as a distinct concern of invention: audience must intersect the rhetor's reasoning processes, and rhetoric must in some way account for variations among audiences because different audiences in different situations will require different strategies. Though each of these rhetoricians in some way appeals to universal principles governing discourse, they all recognize that rhetoric is situational, operating very clearly on local levels, and that audience contributes in various ways to the construction of any discourse.

Since the new rhetoric movement of the 1960s, interest in rhetoric—and in audience theory and audience analysis techniques—has revived. One sign of the recovery of audience is the increased research on the topic. Between 1969 and 1978 in the journal of *College Composition and Communication,* there was one article published with the word "audience" in the title.[33] Between 1979 and 1988, there have been ten, including three articles in a special audience issue in May of 1984. I would not want to make too much of this single bit of quantitative data, but it does reveal something that can be demonstrated by other means: in the early 1980s audience emerged as a topic worthy of a distinct program of research. To a great extent, this recovery is due to the influence of the new rhetoricians.

The new rhetoric represents a return to a more comprehensive view of rhetoric, perhaps even more so than that of classical rhetoric, because it attempts to cover a wider range of discourse types, and it attempts to generate a theory specifically for written discourse. For the new rhetoricians (including early theoreticians like Burke, Fogarty, and Perelman, as well as later ones like Corbett, Young, and Kinneavy, who applied the theory to composition instruction), rhetoric is the entire "art of effective communication,"[34] concerned with "discourse addressed to any sort of audience—a crowd in a public square or a gathering of specialists, a single being or all humanity." [35] While Aristotle conceived of rhetoric as the art of persuading ordinary, or public, audiences, the new rhetoricians view all discourse as essentially persuasive and so see rhetoric more broadly as the art of communicating with any audience. We now think of rhetoric as applying to all discourse—even academic and disciplinary discourse—

though many of our colleagues in other disciplines and certainly the public at large still tend not to think of "rhetoric" in this way.

NOTES
Chapter 4

1 Chaim Perelman and L. Olbrechts-Tyteca, *The New Rhetoric*, trans. William Kluback (Notre Dame, IN: U of Notre Dame P, 1969), pp. 7, 35.

2 See Donald C. Stewart, "Textbooks Revisited," in *Research in Composition and Rhetoric: A Bibliographic Sourcebook*, ed. Michael G. Moran and Ronald F. Lunsford (Westport, CN: Greenwood, 1984), 453–468.

3 See Maxine C. Hairston, "The Winds of Change: Thomas Kuhn and the Revolution in the Teaching of Writing," *College Composition and Communication* 33 (1982): 76–88.

4 James A. Berlin, *Rhetoric and Reality: Writing Instruction in American Colleges, 1900–1985* (Carbondale, IL: Southern Illinois UP, 1987) , p. 120.

5 Daniel J. Fogarty, S. J., *Roots for a New Rhetoric* (New York: Russell and Russell, 1959).

6 See Wayne Booth, "The Rhetorical Stance," *College Composition and Communication* 14 (1963): 139–145; and James L. Kinneavy, "The Relation of the Whole to the Part in Interpretation Theory and in the Composing Process," in *Linguistics, Stylistics, and the Teaching of Composition*, ed. Donald A. McQuade (Akron, OH: U of Akron English Department, 1979), 1–23.

7 According to Bitzer, "Rhetorical works belong to the class of things which obtain their character from the circumstances of the historic context in which they occur. . . . the situation is the source and ground of rhetorical activity." See Lloyd F. Bitzer, "The Rhetorical Situation," *Philosophy and Rhetoric* 1 (1968), pp. 3, 6.

8 Bitzer's audience must be distinguished from a body of mere hearers or readers: "Properly speaking, a rhetorical audience consists only of those persons who are capable of being influenced by discourse and of being mediators of change." Bitzer, "Rhetorical Situation," p. 8.

9 Bitzer, "Rhetorical Situation," p. 11.

10 Bitzer's "realistic" view of rhetorical situation was subsequently challenged by Richard Vatz, who argues that situations are not "located in reality" so much as they are created by discourse. That is, for Vatz, the rhetorical situation generates events, not the other way around. Scott Consigny, in a later response, attempted to reconcile these opposing views of the "reality" of

rhetorical situation. See Richard E. Vatz, "The Myth of the Rhetorical Situation," *Philosophy and Rhetoric* 6 (1973): 154–161; and Scott Consigny, "Rhetoric and Its Situations," *Philosophy and Rhetoric* 7 (1974): 175–186.

11 See James L. Golden, Goodwin F. Berquist, and William E. Coleman, *The Rhetoric of Western Thought* (Dubuque, IA: Kendall/Hunt, 1976), p. 187.

12 Douglas Park sees this point as Perelman's chief contribution to rhetoric: "Perelman's insistence on extending the rhetorical perspective to science, philosophy, and by implication to all forms of discourse that seek adherence to beliefs is, of course, the major significance of *The New Rhetoric*." See Douglas Park, "Perelman's Universal Audience," paper presented at the Conference on College Composition and Communication, St. Louis, MO, March 18, 1988.

13 Chaim Perelman, *The Realm of Rhetoric*, trans. William Kluback (Notre Dame, IN: Notre Dame UP, 1982), p. 14.

14 Perelman, *Realm*, p. 14.

15 Perelman and Olbrechts-Tyteca, p. 7.

16 For an application of Perelman's theory of the universal audience to composition instruction, see W. Ross Winterowd's *The Contemporary Writer* (New York: Harcourt, 1975), especially pp. 147 ff.

17 Douglas Park sees the universal audience as an ideal set of attitudes that speakers address. Despite the fact that no actual audience ever matches the ideal, a speaker persuades her audience by trying to get them to accept her version of the universal audience. This view of the universal audience is similar to the reader-response critics' notion of the implied reader (discussed in Chapter 5). See Park, "Universal Audience."

18 Perelman, *Realm*, p. 13.

19 See James A. Berlin, "Contemporary Composition: The Major Pedagogical Theories," *College English* 44 (1982): 765–777; Edward P. J. Corbett, *Classical Rhetoric for the Modern Student*, 2nd ed. (New York: Oxford UP, 1971); and Richard E. Hughes and P. Albert Duhamel, *Rhetoric: Principles and Usage*, 2nd ed. (Englewood Cliffs, NJ: Prentice Hall, 1967).

20 Composition textbooks that show the influence of the new rhetoric, especially in their treatment of audience, include Janice Lauer, Gene Montague, Andrea Lunsford, and Janet Emig, *Four Worlds of Writing* (New York: Harper & Row, 1981); and William F. Irmscher, *The Holt Guide to English*, 2nd ed. (New York: Holt, Rinehart, 1976).

21 James L. Kinneavy, *A Theory of Discourse: The Aims of Discourse* (Englewood Cliffs, NJ: Prentice Hall, 1971); and James L. Kinneavy, John Q. Cope, and J. W. Campbell, *Aims and Audiences in Writing* (Dubuque, IA: Kendall/Hunt, 1976).

22 Kinneavy, *Theory*, p. 49.

23 Kinneavy, *Theory*, p. 107.

24 Kinneavy, *Theory*, p. 49

[25] See, for example, Kinneavy's analysis of Stewart Alsop's *Saturday Evening Post* article, in *Theory*, pp. 135–141.

[26] See George Lakoff and Mark Johnson, *Metaphors We Live By* (Chicago: The U of Chicago P, 1980).

[27] Kinneavy agrees that aims overlap, but he argues for the theoretical and practical usefulness of his theory, insisting that most discourses have a dominant aim. He acknowledges that some discourses can have multiple aims; he cites the example of *The Diary of a Young Girl*, presumably written by Anne Frank, which has been read as referential, expressive, persuasive, *and* literary discourse. But by admitting the possibility of the multiplicity of aims, Kinneavy may be admitting the virus that proves fatal to his system. See Kinneavy, *Theory*, pp. 60–62.

[28] A text that borrows from Kinneavy's theory to develop a comprehensive discussion of audience is Jan Youga's *The Elements of Audience Analysis* (New York: Macmillan, 1989). For Youga, the audience is an easily definable entity: "audience can be defined as the intended receiver of the writer's message" (1). She then proceeds to discuss audience, as Kinneavy does, in terms of textual features, such as informational content, style, and mechanics—that is, analyzing texts to determine what kind of reader is presupposed.

[29] Richard E. Young, Alton L. Becker, and Kenneth L. Pike, *Rhetoric: Discovery and Change* (New York: Harcourt, 1970).

[30] Young, Becker, Pike, pp. 179–180.

[31] Perhaps the most well-known feature of *Rhetoric: Discovery and Change* is its application of Carl Rogers' psychology to rhetorical situations. What is now known as "Rogerian rhetoric" signifies a strategy for persuading audiences who may feel threatened by the rhetor's position. When in such situations, the writer is advised to seek strategies for reducing threat, mainly by understanding the reader's position and accommodating that position in the text. For discussions of Rogerian rhetoric, see Paul Bator, "Aristotelian and Rogerian Rhetoric," *College Composition and Communication* 31 (1980): 427–432; Lisa Ede, "Is Rogerian Rhetoric Really Rogerian?" *Rhetoric Review* 3 (1984): 40–48; Maxine C. Hairston, "Carl Rogers' Alternative to Traditional Rhetoric," *College Composition and Communication* 27 (1976): 373–377; Maxine C. Hairston, "Using Carl Rogers' Communication Theories in the Composition Classroom," *Rhetoric Review* 1 (1982): 50–55; and Andrea Lunsford, "Aristotelian vs. Rogerian Rhetoric: A Reassessment," *College Composition and Communication* 30 (1979): 146–151.

[32] Perhaps because it *does* recognize the complexities of audience, however, *Rhetoric: Discovery and Change* has not influenced composition pedagogy to the extent Kinneavy's theory has.

[33] Kenneth Jurkiewicz, "How to Begin to Win Friends and Influence People: The Role of the Audience in the Prewriting Process," *College Composition and Communication* 26 (1975): 173–176.

[34] Edward P. J. Corbett, *The Little Rhetoric and Handbook*, 2nd ed. (Glenview, IL: Scott, Foresman, 1982), p. 1.

[35] Perelman, *Realm*, p. 5.

Chapter 5

☙ *Reader-Response Criticism and Audience as Implied Reader*

> A fully elaborated view of audience . . . must balance the creativity of the writer with the different, but equally important, creativity of the reader.[1]
>
> *Lisa Ede and Andrea Lunsford*

The contribution of reader-response criticism to rhetoric is its recognition of the importance of audience to "the making of meaning," its acknowledgement of the presence (and ambiguities) of multiple senses of "audience" and "reader," and its emphasis on the "reader in the text." Reader-response criticism recognizes that "meaning" is not something locked into the language of a text but is, rather, a construction that involves text and reader in interaction. The reader contributes something to meaning—in fact, she constructs, or at least helps construct, meaning through the reading act. How and to what extent does the reader do this? That is what reader-response critics argue about.

Reader-response criticism refers to the work of an eclectic group of literary critics, including Wolfgang Iser, Judith Fetterley, Stanley Fish, Norman Holland, David Bleich, Jonathan Culler, Louise Rosenblatt, and Steven Mailloux, who share the assumption that the reader of the text plays a more prominent role in " the making of meaning" than previous critical theories acknowledged.[2] Beyond this shared focus on "reader," there is actually little agreement among reader-response critics as to how to locate the "reader" or which of several types is the key reader in interpretation. They differ in their sense of the nature and extent of the reader's contribution to textual meaning.

David Bleich, for instance, argues that "reader" refers primarily to individual reader responses (oral or written), and that all such responses are "personal"—that is, influenced chiefly by the individual experience of the real reader.[3] Norman Holland characterizes readers in terms of psychological types or attitudes that texts embody and to which real people conform.[4] For Wolfgang Iser, the reader is primarily a property of a given text; the reader exists in the gaps of the text (i.e., the scenes and attitudes circumscribed by the text).[5] Thus, Bleich looks for the reader in people's responses to literary works; Holland in psychological "forms"; and Iser practices a conservative, almost New Critical form of reader-response criticism, looking "in" the literary work itself.[6]

Still other reader-response critics trace the development of the reader within a particular literary text, looking for changes that occur in the structure of the reader through the act of reading. Steven Mailloux, for instance, argues that in Melville's *Moby Dick* Ishmael functions as a tutor, training the reader how to read the book in the first quarter of the novel; by the last quarter of the novel Ishmael disappears as narrator because "he is no longer needed as a teacher."[7] For other reader-response critics, literature comes in fact to be about the reader. For Stanley Fish, *Paradise Lost* has as its center of reference "its reader, who is also its subject.[8] Those critics associated with the German *Rezeptionästhetik* ("aesthetics of reception")—whose main figure is Hans Robert Jauss—examine how responses to literary works are shaped by attitudes and beliefs of different communities at different points in time.[9] Stanley Fish's notion of the "interpretive community" (discussed in Chapter 6) also considers the influence of the literary community's reading conventions.[10]

Feminist criticism—which some view as a development of, and others as a reaction against, reader-response criticism—has also provided a serious challenge to the traditional authority of the literary text and the focus on the author.[11] The central tenet of feminist criticism, according to Patricia Lorimer Lundberg, is "that issues of gender are of paramount importance in literary studies because the way everyone has been socialized by gender affects the way he or she writes and reads texts."[12] Feminist theory holds that gender difference is at work in both the production and interpretation of literary (or, any) texts, and that a feminist reading exposes the operation of that gender difference.[13] Lundberg, for instance, calls upon Bakhtinian dialogics as a tactic for interacting with the multiple voices of literary texts—which would include reading *against* a text if its voice is monovocal, and especially if that single voice is a hegemonic masculine one.

The work of the reader-response critics has produced a profuse, and at times seemingly redundant, vocabulary for describing the various presences of the reader in the text, outside the text, and in the writer's mind. W. Daniel Wilson has attempted to clarify some of the confusion generated by this vocabulary.[14] Combining the theory of several prominent reader-response critics and combining terms that, to Wilson, mean nearly the same thing, he isolates three distinct kinds of reading presences: the real reader, the implied reader, and the characterized reader.[15]

According to Wilson, the *real reader* refers to any actual flesh-and-blood persons outside the text who read it. This reading is observable in some kind of response, either oral or written. The *implied reader* (also called the ideal reader or fictional audience) is the abstract conception of the audience embodied in a text. The implied reader is defined by Wilson as "the behavior, attitudes, and background—presupposed or defined, usually indirectly, in the text itself."[16] The implied reader is distinct from, though related to, the real reader; it is an abstraction, an image of the real reader—or a reading role—that a text embodies. The *characterized reader* is a concrete conception of the reader embodied in a text, that is, a reader who is addressed by the text and consequently who becomes "characterized." (The characterized reader is especially important to literary analysts.) Wilson identifies a fourth kind of reader, the *intended reader*, or "the idea of the reader that forms in the author's mind."[17] But he does not see this reader as significant, perhaps because from the perspective of literary interpretation, this reader is the one least accessible to the literary critic. However, from the writer's point of view, and from the point of view of rhetoric, this reader is of considerable importance.

This distinction between readers is most commonly used in the interpretation of literary works. An analysis of Robert Browning's poem "My Last Duchess" demonstrates how these different senses of reader are involved in the interpretive process. The opening line of the poem, "That's my last duchess painted on the wall, / Looking as if she were alive," signals immediately the presence of a narrator, the Duke, who is a persona of the author. And if we have access to extratextual information about Browning and the dramatic monologue or prior knowledge about interpretive conventions in general, we may decide that there is a wide discrepancy between the speaking voice (the Duke) and Browning himself. Within the fictionalized world of the poem, the narrator (the Duke) addresses his remarks to a persona, an emissary of "the Count," who is the father of the woman the Duke hopes to marry to replace his "last" duchess. In a sense, though, the duke is only incidentally addressing the emissary; his remarks are really intended for the count, whom the emissary represents, and for his daughter. Thus, we could consider that the poem has two or three personae who function as audiences within the fictional world of the text.

The real reader of "My Last Duchess" is anyone who picks up the poem and reads it. We know this reader only insofar as we can observe this reader's response; in fact, the real reader is evidenced only through an oral or written response.

The implied reader of the poem is the reading role the poem presupposes. First and most obviously, the implied reader reads English, appreciates poetry and understands poetic conventions (in particular, the conventions of the dramatic monologue), recognizes the poem's allusions (e.g., to the Italian Renaissance, to Neptune, to Fra Pandolf) appreciates the irony of and the true reasons for the Duke's remarks, and perhaps, too, is acquainted with the historical background of the poem. The implied reader also understands the implied threat that operates at the core of the poem. The implied reader is, thus, sharp enough to see through to the duke's ulterior purposes; is capable of a certain degree of aesthetic distance; and can, to a degree, appreciate the duke's delicate malevolence. The implied reader is the aesthetic response presupposed by the poem.

The intended reader is the idea of the reader in Browning's mind, a construction that in all probability is inacessible to us except insofar as it can be gleaned from the poem itself. If we had additional textual evidence—perhaps autobiographical notes or drafts of the poem—we might attempt to reconstruct this reader.

Understanding the poem means, in part, understanding how the various reading roles intersect in the poem—and how they intersect with, and around, Browning's central persona. According to one set of reading conventions, the conventions of the literary community, if we confuse Browning with his persona (if we read the poem as autobiography), then we misread the work; we commit the biographical fallacy. Similarly, we misread the poem if we confuse ourselves as real readers with the audiences within the fictional world of the poem (e.g., the emissary). (Real readers not accustomed to the conventions of the dramatic monologue may do this.) As real readers, we may or may not be capable of adopting the implied reading role assigned in the poem. (As Wilson says, "The implied reader incorporates the reading behavior that real readers are supposed to adopt, even if they fail to do so."[18]) Even if we are capable of adopting the reading role, we may resist doing so for aesthetic or personal reasons.

That the implied reader in the poem is not the same as the real reader is made most evident by the fact that the poem is seldom anthologized without footnotes. Footnotes represent an editorial attempt to educate real readers so that they can more effectively adopt the implied reader's role;

footnotes compensate for gaps between real readers and the implied reader.

Wilson's treatment of readers offers us more distinctions than Ong's more well known notion of the "fictional audience."[19] But in essence, both Wilson and Ong support the view that writers do not write for real readers: they create fictional audiences to which real readers adapt.[20] In "The Writer's Audience Is Always a Fiction," Ong's point is precisely that the writer imagines a reader and then addresses that imaginative construct. For instance, Hemingway's *For Whom the Bell Tolls* assumes a reader who is acquainted with the history of the Spanish Civil War.[21] Similarly, the opening of Hemingway's *A Farewell to Arms* assumes a reader who has prior knowledge of the novel's context: "In the late summer of that year we lived in a house in a village that looked across the river and the plain to the mountains."[22] As Ong points out, this passage assumes reader familiarity with "that" year, "the" river," and "the" mountains; the use of the demonstrative pronoun and the definite articles presupposes familiarity.[23] Of course few real readers would be familiar with this backdrop. Most real readers would be at odds with the implied reader from the outset. The real reader is thus forced to adopt the role the novel provides, the role of a confidante in this case, or to put down the book and reject the role. The same is true of *Tristram Shandy;* in order to read Sterne's novel, the real reader must be willing to submit to certain peculiarities. The implied reader is someone agile enough to appreciate the complex reading situation and the presence of the characterized reader. Some real readers balk at reading *Tristram Shandy;* some readers loathe Hemingway— though, admittedly, not always because of the reading role assigned.

Reader-response critics apply their theory almost exclusively to fictive discourse. To them, fictive discourse is unique because it requires that its readers adopt certain implied reading roles. It is in this creation and adoption of reading roles that fictive discourse gains its aesthetic energy and strength—at least when it is successful. Literature requires that its real readers suspend their identities to engage the role of the implied reader. With some works (like *Finnegans Wake* or Pound's *Cantos,* for example), a greater degree of suspension is called for. Some works assume a more complicated implied reader and thus require a greater effort, or degree of aesthetic appreciation, from real readers.

Wilson's distinct contribution to reader-response theory—in addition to sorting out the jargon—is his isolation of the characterized reader as a distinct reading presence. (Ong, for instance, does not distinguish between implied and characterized readers.) When T. S. Eliot writes "Let us go then, you and I," he is not addressing the real or implied reader. His persona is addressing the characterized reader; the implied reader appreciates this distinction. When Matthew Arnold's persona intones "Ah, love, let us be true / To one another!," he is speaking to a characterized reader, not to the real or implied readers. Similarly, though perhaps not as obviously, when Tristram Shandy (not Sterne) refers to "Madam" or "gentle reader," he is addressing a characterized reader, a negative foil whose presence in the work the implied reader is meant to ridicule and enjoy but not identify with.[24] In each case, the degree of characterization varies widely, of course.

This distinguishing between reading presences is more than mere hermeneutic hair-splitting. For Wilson and other reader-response critics, defining the implied reader is important because "*our* relation to the implied reader is crucial to our understanding of the text."[25] The implied reader is the "textual structure *through* which communication occurs . . . an essential link in the line of communication between the author and every (real) reader, one that determines to a large extent the success and quality of the communication."[26] Theoretically, the notion of the implied reader is important because it "can potentially mediate between the two extremes of criticism": the belief that "totally objective elucidation of textual meaning" is possible and the belief that it is not."[27] The implied reader binds real reader and text together; it represents, the intersection, as it were, of real reader and text, assisting communication.

Finding the Implied Reader[28]

The key to uncovering the implied reader(s) is in discovering the intertextual base of a text—that is, the pre-texts, the knowledge base, that supports the text in question. "Intertextuality" as a concept has been associated with both structuralism and poststructuralism, with theorists Roland Barthes, Julia Kristeva, Jacques Derrida, Hayden White, Harold Bloom, Michel Foucault, and Michael Riffaterre. (Of course, the theory is most often applied in literary analysis.) The central assumption of these critics has been described by Vincent Leitch: "The text is not an autonomous or unified object, but a set of relations with other texts. Its system of language, its grammar, its lexicon, drag along numerous bits and pieces— traces—of history so that the text resembles a Cultural Salvation Army Outlet with unaccountable collections of incompatible ideas, beliefs, and sources."[29] It is these "unaccountable collections" that intertextual critics focus on, not the text as autonomous entity. In fact, these critics have redefined the notion of "text": text *is* intertext, or simply Text. The traditional notion of the text as the single work of a given author, and even the very notions of author and reader, are regarded as simply convenient fictions for domesticating discourse. The old borders that we used to rope off discourse, proclaim these critics, are no longer useful.

We can distinguish between two types of intertextuality: iterability and presupposition. Iterability refers to the "repeatability" of certain textual fragments, to citation in its broadest sense to include not only explicit allusions, references, and quotations within a discourse but also unannounced sources and influences, cliches, phrases in the air, and traditions. That is to say, every discourse is composed of "traces," pieces of other texts that help constitute its meaning. (I will discuss this aspect of intertextuality in my analysis of the Declaration of Independence.) Presupposition refers to assumptions a text makes about its referent, its readers, and its context—to portions of the text that are read but that are not explicitly "there." For example, as Jonathan Culler discusses, the phrase "John married Fred's sister" is an assertion that logically presupposes that John exists, that Fred exists, and that Fred has a sister. "Open the door" contains a practical presupposition, assuming the presence of a decoder who is capable of being addressed and who is in a better position to open the door than the encoder and/or is someone who the encoder feels *should* open the door, perhaps because of a difference in social status. "Once upon a time" is a trace rich in rhetorical presupposition, signaling to even the youngest reader the opening of a fictional narrative. Texts not only refer to but in fact *contain* other texts.[30]

An examination of three sample texts will illustrate the various facets of intertextuality. The first, the Declaration of Independence, is popularly viewed as the work of Thomas Jefferson. Yet if we examine the text closely in its rhetorical milieu, we see that Jefferson was author only in the very loosest of senses. A number of historians and at least two composition researchers have analyzed the Declaration, with interesting results.[31] Their work suggests that Jefferson was by no means an original framer or a creative genius, as some like to suppose. Jefferson was a skilled writer, to be sure, but chiefly because he was an effective borrower of traces.

To produce his original draft of the Declaration, Jefferson seems to have borrowed, either consciously or unconsciously, from his culture's Text. Much has been made of Jefferson's reliance on Locke's social contract theory.[32] Locke's theory influenced colonial political philosophy, emerging in various pamphlets and newspaper articles of the times, and served as the foundation for the opening section of the Declaration. The Declaration contains many traces that can be found in other, earlier documents. There are traces from a First Continental Congress resolution, a Massachusetts Council declaration, George Mason's "Declaration of Rights for Virginia," a political pamphlet of James Otis, and a variety of other sources, including a colonial play. Ironically, the overall form of the Declaration (theoretical argument followed by list of grievances) strongly resembles the English Bill of Rights of 1689, in which Parliament lists the abuses of James II and declares new powers for itself. Several of the abuses in the Declaration seem to have been taken, more or less verbatim, from a *Pennsylvania Evening Post* article. And the most memorable phrases in the Declaration seem to be least Jefferson's: "That all men are created equal" is a sentiment from Euripides that Jefferson copied in his literary commonplace book as a boy; "Life, Liberty, and the pursuit of Happiness" was a cliche of the times, appearing in numerous political documents.[33]

Thus, the Declaration is constructed out of and contributes to a textual field that is accessible to its real readers. The implied audience recognizes the sources and intertextual connections; real readers may recognize some of them, or perhaps only experience a vague feeling of familiarity. The point is that the text of the Declaration of Independence was constructed from bits and pieces of other texts—which come, in a sense, from the very audience the Declaration addresses.

Intertextuality can be seen working similarly in contemporary forums. Recall this scene from a Pepsi commercial: a young boy in jeans jacket, accompanied by dog, stands in some desolate plains crossroads next to a gas station, next to which is a soft drink machine. An alien spacecraft, resembling one from Spielberg's *Close Encounters of the Third Kind*, appears overhead. To the boy's joyful amazement, the spaceship hovers over the vending machine and begins sucking Pepsi cans into the ship. It takes *only* Pepsi, then eventually takes the entire machine. The ad closes with a graphic: "Pepsi. The Choice of a New Generation."

Clearly, the commercial presupposes familiarity with Spielberg's movie—or at least with his pacific vision of alien spacecraft. To put it another way, the implied reader of this commercial understands the textual connotations. We see several American cliches, well-worn signs from the depression era: the desolate plains, the general store, the pop machine, the country boy with dog. These distinctively American traces are juxtaposed against images from science fiction and the 1960s catchphrase "new generation" in the coda. In this array of signs, we have tradition and countertradition harmonized. Pepsi squeezes itself in the middle and thus becomes the great American conciliator. The ad's use of irony may serve to distract viewers momentarily from noticing how Pepsi achieves its purpose by assigning itself an exalted role through use of the intertext.

We find an interesting example of practical presupposition in John Kifner's *New York Times* headline article reporting on the Kent State incident of 1970:

> Four students at Kent State University, two of them women, were shot to death this afternoon by a volley of National Guard gunfire. At least 8 other students were wounded.
>
> The burst of gunfire came about 20 minutes after the guardsmen broke up a noon rally on the Commons, a grassy campus gathering spot, by lobbing tear gas at a crowd of about 1,000 young people.[34]

From one perspective, the phrase "two of them women" is a simple statement of fact; however, it presupposes a certain attitude—that the event, horrible enough as it was, is more significant because two of the persons killed were women. It might be going too far to say that the phrase presupposes a sexist attitude ("women aren't supposed to be killed in protests or battles''), but can we imagine the phrase "two of them men" in this context? Though equally factual, "two of them men" would have been considered odd in 1970 (and would be today as well) because it presupposes a cultural mindset alien from the one dominant at the time. "Two of them women" is shocking (and hence it was reported) because it upsets the conventional sense of order of the readers, in this case the readers of *The New York Times*.

Additionally (and more than a little ironically), the text contains a number of traces that have the effect of blunting the shock of the event. Notice that Kifner does not say directly that the students were shot by National Guardsmen. Rather they were shot "by a volley of . . . gunfire." The tear gas was "lobbed," and the event occurred at a "grassy campus gathering spot." "Volley" and "lobbed" are military terms but with connections to sport as well. "Grassy campus gathering spot" suggests a picnic. "Burst" can recall the glorious sight of bombs "bursting" in "The Star Spangled Banner." This pastiche of signs casts the text into a certain context, making it distinctively American. Or we might say that the turbulent milieu of the sixties provided a distinctive array of signs from which John Kifner borrowed to produce his article.

Each of the three texts examined contains phrases or images familiar to the implied reading presence and presupposes certain audience attitudes. Thus, the intertext exerts its influence partly in the form of audience expectation. All of these texts rely on real readers to have some of the characteristics, or at least a few of the essential ones, of the implied readers presupposed by these texts. We might then say that the audience of each of these texts is as responsible for its production as the writer. We might exaggerate this position somewhat by saying that readers, not writers, create discourse—which is precisely the central point of the reader-response critics.

The Implied Reader in Composition Research

It should be clear from the foregoing discussion that the insights of the reader-response critics apply to nonfictive writing as well as to fictive discourse.[35] In fact, all discourse presupposes a knowledge base, contains "pre-texts," and rests on a textual field. We can refer to all of this as the "implied reader," but rhetoric provides us with another term—"audience." "Audience" can refer to the presupposed attitude—in Wilson's words, "the behavior, attitudes, and background—presupposed or defined, usually indirectly, in the text itself."[36] If we take "text" to mean the entire "textual field" supporting the (individual) text or discourse, then we will have a decidedly poststructural notion of audience, which will prove compatible with—though unquestionably different from—both traditional and contemporary criticism alike.

This distinction between real and implied reader (or, perhaps, between audience and reader) has important implications for rhetoric and composition, as Douglas Park and Jeffrey Porter have pointed out.[37] When writers produce prose they embody in the prose a reading role—an implied reader—which may or may not resemble the real reader. Thus, it is useful for writers to be able to identify this presupposed implied reader, so they can judge whether their text has produced a role that the real reader will willingly adopt. Reader-response criticism challenges the notion that there can ever be a one-to-one, linear correspondence between the reader in the writer's mind, the reader in the text, and the real reader. It is, in fact, the dissonance between these "reading presences" that makes reading and writing interesting activities and that both enables and prevents the exchange of ideas through communication.

For instance, in writing a persuasive essay a writer might well decide to write for the real reader by creating in the text an idealized characterized reader, one who is logical, ethical, intelligent, concerned, honest—in effect, an image that the real reader will find acceptable precisely because it is *not* an exact image of the real reader. The writer makes in effect what Young, Becker, and Pike call the "assumption of familiarity": "The reader is addressed as if he were intelligent, curious, honest, sincere—in short, as if he possessed the same qualities that the writer attributes to himself."[38] The implied reader, of course, will recognize this characterized reader as a foil, as a persuasive strategy. With some real readers, such a technique may backfire (the real reader may feel manipulated). In other cases, the real reader may admire the strategy and appreciate the writer's effort to communicate. In such scenarios, the writer is "considering" his audience; but the nature and use of that analysis are much more complex than the writer's simply sketching a reader profile and then producing a text to match the profile. The managerial communication model simply does not account for these types of complex or interactive writer-reader relations.

According to William Ross, Martin Luther King achieves a powerful persuasive effect in "Letter from Birmingham Jail" precisely because he addresses an ethical, moral, concerned, and fair-minded reader, one who is distinct from at least some of the real readers King addressed. King creates a characterized reader—the "men of good will"—which, according to Ross, traps the "audience in a role they would rather not have played."[39] The implied reader, however, recognizes the strategy and in fact may appreciate the implicit irony in King's characterization. Thus, King's characterization cuts two ways and works to his advantage with two very different reader types. The characterization provides an ethical model that King wants all people to adopt—it is a positive model for those willing to embrace it. But the characterization also works as a criticism of those readers who do not fit it and who are reluctant to embrace it. King's characterized reader places those real readers who are his critics in a forced dilemma.

Chaim Perelman reports seeing this notice in a French cafe: *"Brave toutou, ne grimpe pas sur la banquette."* ("Nice doggie, don't climb on the bench.")[40] As Perelman points out, such directions do "not imply that all the dogs let in the cafe can read and comprehend French."[41] Rather, the notice employs a comic characterized reader—the literate doggie—as a way to persuade real readers (presumably, dog owners) to keep their animals off cafe benches. Such a discourse is probably a tacit admission that many real readers ignore plain, blunt discourse (e.g., "Dogs are not allowed on cafe benches"). The notice also gives real readers credit for some intelligence and a sense of humor as well. The targeted real readers are at least likely to notice and appreciate the directive—whether or not they heed it.

Reader-response critics have focused almost exclusively on reading responses to literary texts and with problems associated with the reader role in literary criticism—in other words, with what happens *after* the text has been written. Composition and rhetoric theorists have applied their theories to the study of nonliterary discourse, specifically to questions involving audience analysis in the inventive phase. They have tended to conflate the many notions of audience into two simple types, or into one simple distinction between "the reader outside the text" and "the reader in the text."

Such discussions of audience often take the form of (or begin by assuming) a disparity between two "audience camps." On one side are those who concentrate on the reader outside the text, the real readers who pick up a text and read it. This group emphasizes the importance of "collecting information" about the audience, of defining the actual readers' needs as precisely as possible, or of making the prose reader-based. This group assumes that the important reader is the empirically observable one outside the text; the writer's job is to understand this reader by collecting demographic data and then to write a text that somehow addresses this reader's needs.

On the other side are those influenced by reader-response criticism. This group concentrates on the reader in the text, what has been called at different times by different critics the implied reader, the ideal reader, the authorial reader, the reading role, and the fictional audience. The debate has been whether the real reader or the implied reader is more critical from the writer's point of view. Which is the more useful audience to focus on? Do writers primarily *address* readers or *create* them?

Lisa Ede and Andrea Lunsford have pointed out that such a "debate" actually resolves itself: both positions have validity; neither position is sufficient alone. In their Braddock-Award-winning article "Audience Addressed/Audience Invoked: The Role of Audience in Composition Theory and Pedagogy," they discuss the two competing epistemologies of audience—one that privileges the real reader an the other that privileges the implied reader—and argue for a synthesis of views.[42] Audiences are both "addressed" and created (though Ede and Lunsford prefer "invoked"). Writers imagine an intended reader, invoke a role for that reader (perhaps in a draft stage), shift back to the real reader (sometimes actually consulting the reader by requesting feedback), and so on. The writer balances, as it were, addressing the real reader and invoking a reading role in the text, working eventually to finished product.[43]

Reader-response criticism focuses primarily on the reader, which is understood at least partly as a textual property (e.g., the implied reader) or as sets of interpretive responses to pieces of writing. The general perspective on the reader is a useful one for composition and rhetoric, but ultimately reader-response criticism alone is not a sufficient theory for rhetoric and composition. It has several limitations. For one, reader-response criticism has tended to focus on the reader or readers present in single works of fiction; that is, it has accepted the conventional borders of the lone text as fixed ground and it has, by and large, limited itself to discussion of the literary canon. It is only the later reader-response critics (e.g., Fish, Mailloux) who have moved beyond the focus on the single work to examine the intertextual field or the reading conventions of an entire literary community—but even these critics seem wedded to a literary canon. Second, the reader-response critics have been concerned largely with interpretive questions, that is, with matters relating to reader response. Thus, they have tended to subordinate or neglect discussion of the intended reader, a vital even if problematic reading presence from the point of view of rhetoric.

Nevertheless, the work of the reader-response critics has raised our consciousness to how readers complicate interpretation and to how different reading presences interact to create textual interpretations. The contribution of the reader-response critics is in emphasizing how textual and extratextual structures intersect to produce meanings. By shifting emphasis away from the text and, more importantly, away from the author, reader-response criticism de-centers criticism—and in this sense anticipates the developments of poststructuralism.

NOTES
Chapter 5

[1] Lisa Ede and Andrea Lunsford, "Audience Addressed/Audience Invoked: The Role of Audience in Composition Theory and Pedagogy," *College Composition and Communication* 35 (1984), p. 169.

2 Jane P. Tompkins, Introduction, *Reader-Response Criticism: From Formalism to Post-Structuralism*, ed. Jane P. Tompkins (Baltimore, MD: Johns Hopkins UP, 1980), ix–xxvi.

3 David Bleich, *Readings and Feelings: An Introduction to Subjective Criticism* (Urbana, IL: NCTE, 1975).

4 Norman Holland, *Five Readers Reading* (New Haven, CN: Yale UP, 1975).

5 Wolfgang Iser, *The Implied Reader* (Baltimore, MD: Johns Hopkins UP, 1974).

6 For a more detailed discussion of the development of reader-response criticism, see Tompkins; Susan R. Suleiman, "Introduction: Varieties of Audience-Oriented Criticism," in *The Reader in the Text: Essays on Audience and Interpretation*, ed. Susan R. Suleiman and Inge Crosman (Princeton, NJ: Princeton UP, 1980), 3–45; and Raman Selden, "Reader-Oriented Theories" (Chapter 5), in *A Reader's Guide to Contemporary Literary Theory* (Lexington, KY: The UP of Kentucky, 1985), 106–127.

7 Steven Mailloux, "Learning to Read: Interpretation and Reader-Response Criticism," *Studies in the Literary Imagination* 12 (1979), p. 98.

8 Mailloux, p. 102.

9 Hans Robert Jauss, *Toward an Aesthetic of Reception*, trans. Timothy Bahti (Minneapolis, MN: U of Minnesota P, 1982).

10 Stanley Fish, *Is There a Text in this Class? The Authority of Interpretive Communities* (Cambridge, MA: Harvard UP, 1980).

11 Patricia Lorimer Lundberg .views feminist theory as both an extension from and a critique of earlier work in reader-response criticism, though Patrocinio Schweickart sees them as two "parallel developments." See Patricia Lorimer Lundberg, "Dialogically Feminized Reading: A Critique of Reader-Response Criticism, *Reader* 22 (1989): 9–37; and Patrocinio P. Schweickart, "Add Gender and Stir," *Reader* 13 (1985), p. 1.

12 Lundberg, p. 19.

13 For an example of a feminist rhetorical reading of magazine advertising, see Diana George and Diane Shoos, "The Culture of the Bath: Cigarette Advertising and the Representation of Leisure," *Reader* 23 (1990): 50–66. See also Elisabeth Däumer, "Gender Bias in the Concept of Audience," *Reader* 13 (1985): 32–44.

14 W. Daniel Wilson, "Readers in Texts," *PMLA* 96 (1981): 848–863.

15 For an alternate terminology, see Peter J. Rabinowitz, "Truth in Fiction: A Reexamination of Audiences," *Critical Inquiry* 4 (1977): 121–141.

16 Wilson, p. 848.

17 Wilson, p. 849.

18 Wilson, pp. 852–853.

19 Walter Ong, S. J., "The Writer's Audience Is Always a Fiction," *PMLA* 90 (1975): 9–21.

20 Wilson and Ong disagree about the extent to which real readers are capable

of adapting to roles. Wilson finds Iser's position, that "no real reader can completely correspond to the role cut out for him or her . . . ," more "flexible" than Ong's. See Wilson, p. 853.

21 Peter J. Rabinowitz, "Assertion and Assumption: Fictional Patterns and the External World," *PMLA* 96 (1981), p. 410.

22 Ernest Hemingway, *A Farewell to Arms* (New York: Scribner's, 1929), p. 3.

23 Ong, "The Writer's Audience," p. 9.

24 Wilson, p. 855.

25 Wilson, p. 853.

26 Wilson, pp. 857, 859.

27 Wilson, p. 860.

28 The discussion in this section is a revised version of material that appears in James E. Porter, "Intertextuality and the Discourse Community," *Rhetoric Review* 5 (1986): 34–47.

29 Vincent B. Leitch, *Deconstructive Criticism: An Advanced Introduction* (New York: Columbia UP, 1983), p. 59.

30 Jonathan Culler, *The Pursuit of Signs: Semiotics, Literature, Deconstruction* (Ithaca: Cornell UP, 1981).

31 See James L. Kinneavy, *A Theory of Discourse: The Aims of Discourse* (Englewood Cliffs, NJ: Prentice Hall, 1971), pp. 393–449; and Elaine P. Maimon et al., *Readings in the Arts and Sciences* (Boston: Little, Brown, 1984), pp. 6–32.

32 Carl Becker, *The Declaration of Independence*, 2nd ed. (New York: Vintage-Random, 1942).

33 Edward Dumbauld, *The Declaration of Independence*, 2nd ed. (Norman, OK: U of Oklahoma P, 1968).

34 John Kifner, "4 Kent State Students Killed by Troops," *New York Times* 5 May 1970:1.

35 For an example of how this theory applies to nonfictive discourse, see Gay Gragson and Jack Selzer, "Fictionalizing the Readers of Scholarly Articles in Biology," *Written Communication* 7 (1990): 25–58.

36 Wilson, p. 848.

37 Douglas Park, "The Meanings of 'Audience,' " *College English* 44 (1982): 247–257; and Jeffrey Porter, "The Reasonable Reader: Knowledge and Inquiry in Freshman English," *College English* 49 (1987): 332–344.

38 Richard E. Young, Alton L. Becker, and Kenneth L. Pike, *Rhetoric: Discovery and Change* (New York: Harcourt, 1970), p. 208.

39 William T. Ross, "Self and Audience in Composition," *Freshman English News* 13 (Spring 1984), p. 15.

40 Chaim Perelman, *The Realm of Rhetoric*, trans. William Kluback (Notre Dame, IN: U of Notre Dame P, 1982), p. 14.

[41] Perelman, *Realm*, p. 14.

[42] Ede and Lunsford (see note 1). Louise Wetherbee Phelps criticizes Ede and Lunsford's approach to audience because it "does not begin to account for the vast intrusion of the social into the realm of authorship." See Louise Wetherbee Phelps, "Audience and Authorship: The Disappearing Boundary," in *A Sense of Audience in Written Communication,* ed. Gesa Kirsch and Duane H. Roen (Newbury Park, CA: Sage, 1990), p. 158.

[43] Composition textbooks that have borrowed from reader-response criticism focus especially on the relationship between the reader in the text and the reader outside the text. Thus, audience analysis can be seen to have at least two components: writers perform a real reader analysis, and they perform an "implied reader analysis" on their text, examining their draft to see what reading role it embodies. Two composition texts that include references to the implied reader or "the reading role," thus acknowledging the (at least) dual nature of audience, are Janice Lauer, Gene Montague, Andrea Lunsford, and Janet Emig, *Four Worlds of Writing,* 2nd ed. (New York: Harper & Row, 1985); and Frank J. D'Angelo, *Process and Thought in Composition,* 3rd ed. (Boston: Little, Brown, 1985). A few composition texts even include exercises in which the writer is asked to identify the implied reader in a given prose passage. See, for example, Young, Becker, and Pike, p. 183; and Kathleen Macdonald, *When Writers Write* (Englewood Cliffs, NJ: Prentice-Hall, 1983), pp. 10–11.

Chapter 6

𝕰 ## *Poststructuralism, Social Constructionism, and Audience as Community*

Imagine that you enter a parlor. You come late. When you arrive, others have long preceded you, and they are engaged in a heated discussion, a discussion too heated for them to pause and tell you exactly what it is about. In fact, the discussion had already begun long before any of them got there, so that no one present is qualified to retrace for you all the steps that had gone before. You listen for a while, until you decide that you have caught the tenor of the argument; then you put in your oar. Someone answers you; you answer him; another comes to your defense; another aligns himself against you, to either the embarrassment or gratification of your opponent, depending upon the quality of your ally's assistance. However, the discussion is interminable. The hour grows late, you must depart. And you do depart, with the discussion still vigorously in progress.[1]

Kenneth Burke

Kenneth Burke's anecdote of the parlor serves as a useful starting point for discussing the notion of "audience as community." Burke's parlor tale reminds us that discourse arises out of a social context—a context that exists before the writer or speaker encounters it and that influences the writer's or speaker's performance. Burke's parlor tale also serves as a metaphor for the composing process, though quite a different one from stage-process or cognitive-process models. Burke's model focuses on the role of the social context in the composing process and calls attention to the "field" in which the speaker's discourse resides. In this scene, Burke does not highlight either the cognitive operation of the speaker or the textual evolution of the speech. It is not that these things are unimportant; the model simply does not call attention to them.

In Burke's parlor, a single "heated discussion" is taking place. Burke may be imagining here a common public language, a universal academic discourse perhaps, that all are capable of joining. I imagine a slightly different scene, where several conversations are taking place. Allow an update, if you will, a revision of the Burke parlor . . .

Imagine a reception. You walk in the door, a little nervously, and see several groups engaged in discussion. You cruise the room and skirt several of these groups, catching bits and pieces of conversations as you go. In one conversation, several men are discussing the Cleveland Browns' most recent game. In another, a group is discussing the S & L crisis. In another an English professor is conversing with an accountant about the value of literary study. Several married couples are comparing child-rearing tales. After getting a drink and pausing a few moments you join a group, probably basing your decision on which group includes the most people you know or people you would most like to know. Or perhaps you choose based on which conversation seems, from a distance, most compatible with your interests and abilities. Or perhaps you decide based on the "look" of the group—for instance, based on the ages and dress of the conversants. Maybe someone invites you to join a group. You may make a mistake, however, and select a group you don't fit in with and have little to say to. You back out gracefully. Eventually you find a group whose interests match your own. You listen for a few minutes, pick up on the conversation and contribute. During the evening, these separate groups break up, form new groups, and develop new topics. The couples talking about children move away and join discussions about politics, the English professor presents her views on the Cleveland Browns. You become more at ease, the party gels—though all personalities do not mix with all other personalities and topics. You leave eventually, with the party still in progress.

This discoursing scene is similar to Burke's in many respects. Our speaker-character enters a defined field; our speaker's discourse is thus constrained by topics and styles already established. The key difference is that the reception is messier: there are multiple conversations defined by different speakers, different topics, different styles. Speakers may move from one conversational clique to another, in some cases with ease, in other cases with difficulty, in a few cases perhaps not at all.

Both parlor and reception scenes suggest a conception of audience: not of an audience that is a passive decoder, but an audience that is an active force ultimately shaping the character of the speaker. Notice that the composer is the silent, passive one—at least at first. Thus, these scenes provide an alternative to traditional conceptions of speaker-writer as the activator, as the prime mover of discourse, and of the audience as the passive recipient. Notice, though, that both scenes are described from the point of view of the speaker—which is, by tradition, rhetoric's viewpoint. But they stress the role the audience plays in the construction of the speech, and even, in a way, the construction of the speaker.

Notice too that the traditional distinction between composer and audience breaks down eventually. Partyers are both composers and audience. The model of communication illustrated here may thus be said to be dialogic or dialectic. We could even call it collaborative. That is, the development of discourse—and the creation of knowledge—is not the responsibility of any single discourser working in isolation (the expressivist image of the writer). Rather, discourse is developed through interaction—it is developed dialogically, through the process of the "person" moving from speaker role to audience role and back and forth. In fact, the roles of rhetor/author and audience blur. The boundaries between the two roles disappear.[2]

Focusing on the composing role, we can define the successful composer as one who picks up on conversations quickly and makes a strong contribution. To a great extent, the composer must understand and accept the given topic (e.g., know what "S & L crisis" refers to), the mode of logic, the premises, and the tone of the conversation. The composer may change the topic—but to do so too abruptly would be to disrupt the conversation—to violate speech-act conventions, or, in a different vocabulary, to be a boor. The composer may bring information, "texts," from her own experience outside the conversation—and in fact is expected to do so—but such "texts" must be made relevant to the discussion at hand.

What motivates the speaker in this model? According to Burke it is the urge to become part of the group, to achieve identification:

> The individual person, striving to form himself in accordance with the communicative norms that match the cooperative ways of his society, is by the same token concerned with the rhetoric of identification. To act upon himself persuasively, he must variously resort to images and ideas that are formative.[3]

The community provides speaking and writing roles for its members—an *ethos* in other words. The "individual person" who wishes to "identify" with the community adopts the role provided.

The view of composition implicit here—and the role of audience suggested—counters the traditional and still prevailing theories and pedagogies of audience. This view does not assume that the writing process begins with the writer. It assumes, rather, that the writer enters a "discussion already in progress," a discussion with established ground rules, certain presupposed knowledge, and accepted topics treated according to approved methods and styles.

We might call this notion of audience as community a poststructuralist notion, though this is not a very precise articulation. "Poststructuralism" is a catchall term used to describe a variety of interpretive approaches that challenge the authority of the traditional unities of discourse—chiefly writer and text, though we might also include reader—in determining meaning. Poststructural criticism is not a single, coherent critical movement with well-defined proponents and positions.[4] "Poststructuralism" is often used generally (in contexts like this one) to refer to "critical theories which challenge traditional aims, methods, and assumptions, especially the assumption that meaning resides in the text."[5] Poststructuralism as a general activity rejects critical approaches that romanticize the self or reify the text. But it also goes beyond to question the status of any foundational terminology—those concepts that disciplines and institutions accept as the unexamined and privileged ground supporting their positions and practices.

Poststructuralists, insofar as they constitute a "group," privilege the diverse influences that, as they say, "write the writer." The idea of audience as community is poststructuralist, then, only insofar as it challenges the notion of a universal ground for discourse, that is, a universal set of logical principles. This rejection of the universal audience is Derridean, according to John W. Murphy, because it holds the view that

> rhetoric is based on "common sense," but not a *sensus communis* that can be associated with a hypothetical "universal audience." The *sensus communis* that the rhetorician must envision is not based on Reason, but the logic that is linguistically "traced" to form the "domain of commitment" that a collective of persons inhabit. Derrida maintains that the only way reliable discourse can be engendered with an audience is by making an attempt to tap the concrete base of knowledge, or "biography" of a community . . . that gives a group of people a sense of solidarity or meaning.[6]

"Common sense," then, is not to be taken to mean "common to all." Rather, common sense is *local:* every community has its own "common sense," its own "biography," a set of character traits that is its "domain of commitment." To put it another way, the characters of audiences are as different as they are similar: the rhetorician should look for the distinguishing character of an audience and not "common" or universal traits.

The community approach to audience has also been termed a social constructionist view, a position Kenneth Bruffee has described as follows:

> A social constructionist position in any discipline assumes that entities we normally call reality, knowledge, thought, facts, selves, and so on are constructs generated by communities of like-minded peers. Social construction understands reality, knowledge, thought, facts, texts, selves, and so on as community-generated and community-maintained linguistic entities—or, more broadly speaking, symbolic entities—that define or "constitute" the communities that generate them, much as the language of the *United States Constitution*, the *Declaration of Independence*, and the "Gettysburg Address" in part constitutes the political, the legal, and to some extent the cultural community of Americans.[7]

From a social constructionist perspective, the genius or cognitive functioning of the individual is not the preferred perspective, nor is the text. Rather, the social view privileges "communities of discourse" and their discursive practices. This approach stresses audience. The audience in fact is seen as coauthor, as a virtual participant in the production of discourse. The sense of audience here is not the universal audience of Perelman and the new rhetoric nor the empirically observable "real reader." The social constructionist, or field view, conceives of audience as a structure embodied in the sets of texts that define a given discourse community, as a discourse field or ground from which the writer's text springs—a kind of "communal implied reader," in other words. The field view grants the audience considerable power in the production of discourse; the audience is a "discourse community" constraining, defining, and in effect creating the writer. "The writer" is a role, a subject position, constituted by community constraints.

A number of researchers in rhetoric and composition have adopted as their primary object of study the group, the community, or the discipline and in various ways have examined how the community influences the production of discourse. Patricia Bizzell has considered how the university works as a community to establish overall academic conventions.[8] Susan Peck MacDonald has compared and contrasted problem-solving methods of practitioners in the humanities with those in the social sciences.[9] Charles Bazerman has examined how the composing process of a physicist influences the construction of knowledge within the science community.[10] Greg Myers has studied the conventions of writing within the biology discourse community.[11] Karen Burke LeFevre has examined the senses in which invention occurs as a social activity.[12] Several researchers have examined the linguistic features of various types of professional writing.[13] Others have examined the nature of collaborative writing.[14]

The work of all these researchers is united by a concern for the presence of community. These researchers note the senses in which writers in various communities are influenced or constrained—either by the heuristic methods of disciplines, by the expectations of audiences, or by the linguistic conventions of genres. The focus of this research is not so much the cognitive processes of the individual writer as the relationship of the writer to the social body of which she is a part and, in some cases, the discourse conventions of the social body as a whole.

Other researchers have pointed out the relationship between the discourse community and the more traditional notion of "audience"—and have talked about the sense in which the discourse community can be viewed as an aspect of audience.[15] We might also begin to see that in the same sense the discourse community is as much the author as the audience—and it may be within the concept of discourse community that the traditionally separate roles of writer and audience come together. The division between writer and reader breaks down in the discourse community: from the social perspective the discourse community is at once the producer and consumer of its own discourse.

The notion of "discourse community" is one way to describe the influence of the audience during the composing process. The term "discourse community" refers vaguely to discursive practices out of which the writer operates. The term calls attention to the discursive field that influences writers—or constrains them, depending on your attitude about the forcefulness of this field. Despite its ambiguity, the notion of discourse community is, I believe, a particularly powerful and useful concept for discussing this field. It allows us to collect our research data and speculations around a central warrant: that writing does not occur *in vacuo* but rather is a socially constrained or guided activity. The constraints come not only from the immediate rhetorical occasion or context but from the entire social network (the discipline, the group, the society) of which the writer is inevitably a part. We may reasonably disagree as to the degree and nature of the influence on the writer—but we must acknowledge the social constraints. The term "discourse community" is useful for describing a space that was unacknowledged before because we did not have a term for it. The term realigns the traditional unities—writer, audience, text—into a new configuration. What was before largely scene, unnoticed background, becomes foreground.

The Problem of Circumscribing Discourse Communities

On an abstract level, the presence and influence of the discourse community seem indisputable. We run into difficulties, though, when we start to look for actual discourse communities and attempt to gauge their degree of influence. We find that researchers do not agree on how to "look at" them, where to find them, or how to circumscribe them. We do not seem to know, really, where particular discourse communities begin and end. At best, they seem to have fuzzy boundaries.

What exactly is a discourse community? some ask.[16] Perhaps the question is badly phrased: "exactness" and "discourse community" may not function together as a meaningful coordination. Writing-across-the-curriculum researchers have tended to view discourse communities in terms of academic disciplines (e.g., philosophy, literature, history, engineering, science) or institutional or organizational borders (e.g., "the corporation").[17] But are these academic disciplines and institutions the same as discourse communities? Or are discourse communities defined at more specific levels? Are all scientists members of the same discourse community? Or do particle physicists and DNA researchers make up distinct discourse communities? Is the group of researchers working on readability in technical writing a discourse community? Or are the parameters larger (e.g., "tech writing researchers," "writing instructors")? And how do we account for the fact that some researchers on readability in technical writing take a linguistic perspective, while others do cognitive or rhetorical analysis? Should discourse communities be defined in terms of object of study, in terms of research methodology, in terms of frequency of communication, or in terms of genre and stylistic conventions?

A court case I was involved in illustrates the difficulty of locating discourse communities.[18] As an expert witness—a rhetorical analyst—in an insurance fraud lawsuit, I was asked to study a set of insurance ads and informational brochures to determine their meaning and to analyze an insurance policy for overall readability. The insurance company was being sued by some ex-policyholders for alleged misleading advertising and unreadable policies. The policyholders claimed that they enrolled in what was advertised as a noncancellable insurance policy. The advertisements published by the insurance company suggest as much; however, the actual policy contains a cancellability clause that gives the company the right to cancel. The problem with the clause is that it is written at such a low level of readability that the intended readers (new policyholders) would be unlikely to fathom the meaning intended by the insurance company.[19]

But the insurance company argued that the cancellability clause was written in legally correct form, or to put it another way, that it satisfied the conventions and standards of the legal/insurance discourse community. Speaking for the plaintiffs, I tried to argue for something like a "public discourse community," whose readability standards and cognitive capacity were embodied in readability and document design principles found in technical writing research. I even suggested a revision of the cancellability clause that might satisfy these cognitive norms. I pointed out that rhetorical ethics demanded that the one discourse community (the legal/insurance community) was obligated to accommodate the larger discourse community ("the public") of which it was a part. The insurance company argued that if any "norms" applied to the documents they were legal norms.

The ads and the policy contain an odd mix of legal syntax and insurance jargon and several personal appeals aimed, obviously, at the consumer. What is the discourse community here? Is it defined by law, by insurance, or by "public conventions" (whatever those might be)? The issue becomes more complicated when we consider that even the apparently well-defined notion of "insurance writing" itself operates on several levels. We can observe the writing habits of one insurance company, we can notice what standard practices are observed by the insurance industry in general (e.g., the insurance industry publishes guidelines for advertising and policy writing), or we can see insurance writing as a subset of business writing. On what level do we look for "the discourse community"?

Discourse communities may operate a little like ecosystems. An ecosystem is a convenient ecological space defined by certain characteristics that set it off from abutting systems. But shift your perspective slightly and the borders of the original ecosystem break down, because ecosystems inevitably interact with systems abutting them. Discourse communities cannot be isolated from other discourse communities any more than the writer can be isolated as an object of study from his social field.[20] In other words, we need to remember that discourse communities overlap—and are flexible and locally constituted. They may cross academic and institutional boundaries, and they may exist only momentarily.

The Sociological Notion of Discourse Community

We may need to clarify what we are doing when we "look at" discourse communities. "Looking at" seems to mean different things to different researchers. There seem to be at least two different (and perhaps competing) theoretical sources of discourse community informing contemporary research. First, there is the sociological and linguistic notion of the "speech community,"[21] a realist perspective that presumes the existence of the sociological group (blacks, Hopi, scientists, student writers) and investigates the discourse from the perspective, often, of linguistic analysis[22] or ethnography.[23] This perspective is markedly different from—and not to be confused with—the poststructural perspective that sees the discourse community not as an a priori sociological group but as a set of local practices or paradigms defined by discourse.

Much social constructionist research relies on the linguistic and anthropological notion of the "speech community."[24] Some who do research on "speech communities" examine cultures and agencies that communicate primarily through oral discourse and examine those agencies sociologically, relying on a notion of social construction similar to that developed by Berger and Luckmann.[25] Researchers operating out of this epistemology assume the priority of the sociological group. For example, they would tend not to consider that the concept of "the poor" is a rhetorically situated ordering principle (i.e., an abstraction situated in a political context), but as an actual collection of people whose characteristics make them "poor."[26]

This approach creates a problem for rhetorical analysis—in fact, the sociological categories may not be the most significant or helpful boundaries for circumscribing discourse communities. Consider an example. We can, conventionally, think of "the family" as a typical sociological unit. But different types of families can have different reasoning strategies and communicative patterns, as Basil Bernstein points out.[27] Bernstein illustrates this point by means of common scenarios: A child says to her mother, "I want to stay up late." One type of mother might respond, "You can't, because children should be in bed by 9." Another might say, "You can't, because I would like to go to bed early." Another might say, simply, "You can't." Another would say, "Okay." These different responses, according to Bernstein, reflect far more than individual preferences; they signify views of authority, in a sense political positions—or in another vocabulary, rhetorical postures. They presuppose certain views of authority (and an entire dynamics of power), certain attitudes about the nature of argument (at least to children), and certain principles of verification. The discourse community here can be defined in terms of argumentative approach rather than demographic character.

The common academic and sociological communities that researchers call on—family, city, humanities, social sciences, the corporation—may not be the most significant distinctions for rhetoric. Character types—old man, young woman, sanguine, "opposed"—may not work well either. It may be that for rhetoric, discourse communities are best defined in terms of rhetorical features—argumentative techniques, heuristic strategies, or research methodologies, for instance.

Social constructionist research has tended to think of discourse communities in terms of academic disciplines or professional contexts—in terms of established institutional boundaries, in other words. Written texts may be the primary object of study, but it is assumed that the social field exists prior to these texts and brings these texts into existence. The community is assumed to be historically a priori. Carl Mills has challenged this sociological notion of discourse community:

> Can socially motivated notions of discourse communities serve as the basis for rigorous theory on language use? I think not. Note first of all the circularity in the definitions of speech communities, discourse communities, interpretative communities given above. The existence of such communities is presumed, and then they are used to explain facts of language use. . . . a rigorous theory of language use should attain explanatory adequacy, that is, it should provide us with a principled basis for choosing among competing descriptively adequate theories. Socially motivated theories do not appear capable of providing such a basis for choice. In fact, the findings of socially

motivated theories, rather than explaining language use, seem to be, instead, second-order data which are themselves in need of explanation.[28]

Foucault's Discursive Formation

While the realistic notion of discourse community may be useful because it gives us clear parameters for research, I believe that it has some gaps in its orientation. In Mills's words, its data is itself "in need of explanation." These gaps can be explored more fully if we consider an alternate notion of discourse community, one extending from poststructural criticism—particularly from Thomas Kuhn ("paradigm"), Stanley Fish ("interpretive community"), and Michel Foucault ("discursive formation"). From this general direction the discourse community is less a sociological entity and more a set of principles and practices.

The advantage of this second perspective is that (1) it focuses directly on texts in terms of rhetorical principles of operation (and is, thus, closely allied to rhetoric as discipline); (2) it allows us, because of its rhetoric orientation, to tolerate, even welcome, a high degree of instability and ambiguity; (3) it takes a broad historical view of communities and examines both the changes within and between communities and the relationship of these communities to "general culture"; and, (4) it provides insight into the operation of communities, which are *not* nice neat packages but which are messy, ill-defined, and unstable.

Stanley Fish recognizes the power of regulating discourse communities in his argument that "interpretive communities" dictate reading practices, in effect determining interpretations:

> Indeed, it is interpretive communities, rather than either the text or the reader, that produce meanings and are responsible for the emergence of formal features. Interpretive communities are made up of those who share interpretive strategies not for reading but for writing texts, for constituting their properties. In other words these strategies exist prior to the act of reading and thereby determine the shape of what is read rather than, as is usually assumed, the other way around.[29]

Fish's point here is that community reading conventions "determine" textual meaning more so than "the text" (which cannot be "read" at all except through some manner of reading convention) or the individual person (who cannot be a "reader" unless constrained by some assumptions about the nature of the reading process). Most American poststructuralist and reader-response theory focuses on questions of interpretation, that is, the interest lies in describing reading behaviors and in uncovering new interpretations of the traditional canon. Thus, Fish's focus is primarily the interpretive response of the reader, and he is interested in a rather specialized reading community—the literary community. The problem with Fish's notion of interpretive community is, according to Frank Lentricchia, that it "walls off" communities, and does not account for an individual's entrance into a community or for community change and development.[30] Like Thomas Kuhn, Fish has a fairly static and inflexible notion of community—a notion that ties communities closely to, and perhaps permanently with, academic and other evident institutional boundaries.[31]

Foucault presents a more flexible and historically conscious perspective in his notion of the "discursive formation," a concept he discusses in *The Archaeology of Knowledge*—a work that can be read, interestingly enough, as a treatise on discourse communities.[32] One key feature of Foucault's treatment is that he emphasizes the "birth" of discursive formations—though he dismisses the conventional notion of "origin." Foucault argues that we cannot understand a field until we understand its birth, its emergence (e.g., the birth of the prison, of the clinic, of the concept of "sexuality"). In that historical moment lies the key to understanding the perspective and classifying orientation of the formation being studied.[33] (When social constructionist researchers look at academic disciplines as communities and study their conventions they often do so synchronically—and do not consider the birth of key concepts or important signifying shifts.) Foucault's analytical approach—called "archaeology"—is designed to reveal some of the features of the discursive formation that the traditional structural analysis does not reveal.[34]

Foucault begins *The Archaeology of Knowledge* by questioning the status of an entire set of terms that often serve as grounding concepts for historical and rhetorical studies—"author" and "text" in particular. His intent is to eliminate "a whole mass of notions, each of which, in its own way, diversifies the theme of continuity."[35] He challenges concepts such as tradition, influence, evolution, as well as the traditional "unities of discourse." We cannot accept these boundaries as fixed and inflexible foundations, says Foucault, because these boundaries are themselves the products of discursive formations. Foucault goes on to question traditional divisions and groupings between disciplines such as science, literature, philosophy, religion, and history, and between discourse genres. These boundaries, Foucault says,

> are always themselves reflexive categories, principles of classification, normative rules, institutionalized types; they in turn are facts of discourse that deserve to be analyzed beside others; of course, they also have complex relations with each other, but they are not intrinsic, autochthonous, and universally recognizable characteristics.[36]

From this perspective, discourse communities are not sociological entities. Rather, the term "discourse community" refers to sets of relations (or "articulations") defined by discourse. These sets of relations have no ultimate foundation in Foucault's treatment: the sets hold each other up, overlap, intersect, abut—but they do not refer to and are not applications of an overall determinate structure. The coherence of the community is not established a priori by the existence of its members. Rather, its coherence is established by what Foucault terms a "regularity in dispersion."[37] That is to say, there is no single nodal point of reference for the community; the discourses disperse themselves. At the same time, coherence is achieved through the principle of the dispersion of discourses. That is, the discourses themselves, as a group, cohere through their interrelationship.

We might find an analogy for this in chaos theory, a scientific model developed to account for turbulence (or "flow") in nature. Chaos theorists discovered that in plotting fluid dynamics they could not at any time predict the exact position of emerging points; the points appear randomly on a graph.[38] In other words, fluid behavior is not precisely predictable. However, they determined a kind of general order to fluid behavior: the points are constrained by a field called a "strange attractor." Thus, though individual points are neither determinate or predictable, scientists can predict the general field in which points will appear. To arrive at these conclusions, chaos theorists had to revise their Euclidean and linear thinking and their restricted sense of proof. To describe such common natural events as turbulence, they had to adopt a nonlinear, probabilistic geometry that would explain "randomness within order"—a field view of nature that sees motion and change as a kind of chaos constrained by a kind of order— or what Foucault would call a "regularity in dispersion."

Similarly, in our attempts to understand the relationships between discourses, we need to develop a field view of those discourses. We cannot privilege any particular point as determinate—the text, the author—because we will not be able to explain adequately the natural ebb and flow of discourse, the turbulence of discursive practice, through such a geometry. We need a geometry that focuses our attention on the field. With this new geometry, we will sacrifice some of the certainty of our prior commitments. But we will gain an explanatory power; we will be able to account for the interaction of discursive practices.

What is wrong with viewing discourse communities as sociological entities? Such a perspective is simply another way of privileging the writer—except that we substitute the group for the individual. Such a view leads us down the same trail of assuming the priority of the subject—now the group—with language following behind as simply the representation of thought. Such a view keeps us locked within the parameters of the linear/management communication model. We have perhaps developed our sense of the "writer" somewhat—but we have not changed our attitude toward audience much, and we still do not have a model accounting for the influence of the social on the rhetor.

The poststructural view of community does not privilege the actual group. Rather, it sees writing itself as constitutive of relations. The abutment of discourse creates relations (as well as spaces). It provides subject *positions* (but does not begin with subjects). Discourse communities function like strange attractors: they are a force field providing an interrelational coherence for discourses.

Thus, we should be wary of self-established sociological groupings. From the poststructural perspective, boundaries or divisions are not inherent in institutions or disciplines themselves but rather are "facts of discourse" that should fall under our examination. They are not fixed or real; they are rhetorical constructs (though the original moment of construction is not always, or often, evident). We cannot accept the divisions as given or assume them as a foundation because to do so would be to miss the essential framework on which the community is based. For example, in examining the traditional literary community, we can say much more than simply that literary criticism accepts the text as the significant unit for study. Rather, according to Foucault's program, we must ask certain questions: Why does literature accept "the text" as the significant unit for analysis? By what set of procedures and methods does literary criticism establish certain works as canonical and certain others not? What function does the signifier "literature" serve in this community? When and under what circumstances did the signifier "literature" come into use? How does the rubric "literary criticism" function to order knowledge—and, extending into genealogy, to apply itself as a force? In what systems (e.g., educational, social, political) does the bureaucracy overseeing "literature" reside?

If we accept rhetoric and composition's own articulations about the value of audience, we see only that the discipline *says* it regards audience as a vital concern. But to understand audience, we have to examine the place of that signifier in the discursive field of composition practice.[39] Looking at the discursive field, as we have done in this study, shows us the complications, the inconsistencies, the gaps in the treatment of audience. Thus, the archaeologist questions the foundational terminology (and its floating, unstable signifies), and does not merely accept the foundation as a starting point and solid ground for investigation.

Foucault's analysis has been applied especially to consideration of the science community.[40] Foucault's work leads us to ask such questions as, Why does "science" constitute itself as such, giving itself a separate status under the rubric "science"? What function does the signifier "science" serve for authors who claim the role of "scientist"? How is the term wielded? In what contexts and for what purposes? What is it considered to be distinct from? (The antiterm is often not stated but is presupposed.) In other words, what is the conceptual grid that supports the notion of "science"?

In short, we cannot accept the terminology of the discourse community as the stable foundation for study of the community. If we do this, we will be missing the underlying conceptual grid that, Foucault claims, is the most significant characteristic of the discursive system.[41] As Gilles Deleuze explains

> The institutions [i.e., the State, the Family, Religion, Production, the Market-place, Art, Morality, etc.] are not sources or essences, and have neither essence nor interiority. They are practices or operating mechanisms which do not explain power, since they presuppose its relations and are content to "fix" them, as part of a function that is not productive but reproductive.[42]

We should not, then, accept "science" as a stable discourse community just because science discourse uses this term for purposes of self-identification. "Science" within the discursive formation (as yet unnamed) is, rather, a signifier with a certain rhetorical purpose, exercising certain dividing strategies (science versus what? literature? humanities? culture?).[43]

We can not, according to Foucault, accept any discipline's own borders, or the borders of "the corporation" (as in business writing research), as a fixed foundation for research into the discourse community. Well, we *can*—but to do so is to miss much, the essential, of what the formation is. Neither can we accept the writer, as least as "lone consciousness," as the foundation for study. Foucault points out that "this system [i.e., the discursive formation] is not established by the synthetic activity of a consciousness identical with itself, dumb and anterior to all speech, but by the specificity of a discursive practice."[44]

We have, thus, dismissed what we *cannot* do—but what is left for us to do? What should we look for?

Foucault identifies as the characterizing center the "system of formation"—by which he means those practices, the group of relations that constitute a system of conceptual formation.[45] This system is discernible *in* the discursive practices and is not anterior to it. We might consider such a system an underlying tropical base or an ethical posture—but in Foucault's archaeology this system is comprised in a number of ways. The archaeologist searches for "surfaces of emergence,"[46] or the points at which new concepts and terms are entered and entertained. The investigator looks to discover the "authorities of delimitation"—or principles determining who is allowed to speak, with what authority and when. The researcher looks for "grids of specification"[47]—those frameworks that establish, order, and evaluate knowledge.

What does such an analysis look like? We can apply the technique to a simple sentence: "As scientists, we are obligated to maintain complete objectivity." A more traditional rhetorical analysis might conclude simply that such a sentence is intended to persuade a body of individuals (scientists) to assent to a collective principle or value (objectivity). It is an exhortation, perhaps even a prayer for this discourse community, presupposing a context in which it is deemed necessary to utter such a proclamation.

An archaeological analysis would look further, however, to expose the "grid" that supports this sentence; it would look at the presuppositions and the dividing practices. Scientists as opposed to what? (What identities are excluded in this division? What is the other half, the unnamed antagonist to the "we"?) When did such an articulation first appear, and under what circumstances?

Examine again the first sentence from the *New York Times* article reporting on the Kent State shooting of May 1970 (discussed in Chapter 5): "Four Kent State University students, two of them women, were shot to death this afternoon by a volley of National Guard gunfire."[48] The phrase "two of them women" is an aside in this sentence, but it provides a glimpse of a discursive formation. The phrase itself does not tell us much— *but the fact of its being said does.* It is the unstated enunciations bordering that sentence (e.g., two of them not men, two of them men, women being shot is more newsworthy/shocking than men being shot) and the underlying gender division (male/female) that give that sentence significance.[49] If we miss the significance of that aside, we miss understanding the ordering practices of that discursive formation. The phrase speaks volumes.

Foucault's archaeology provides other (and more detailed) discussions of the nature of discursive formations. The term "discourse community" has achieved popular status—but it is perhaps an unfortunate word choice, though it does seem to describe what many researchers are doing. The term suggests a sociological context that accepts as "real" the defining body (people, engineers, blacks, the poor, student writers, middle-class whites) and uses that terminology as the starting point and foundation for research. Foucault insists that the defining essence, or chief characteristic, is the system of formal principles, or the "enunciative modalities," and that, further, these principles are discernible from textual analysis—the kind of analysis that examines the "borders" of discourse, the presuppositions, the divisions assumed (though not always expressed), and the pretexts.[50]

What advantage would accrue from adopting Foucault's notion of the discursive formation? An archaeological analysis reveals ruptures and discontinuities in the discursive formation—and notes especially where change and birth of new concepts occur.[51] The analysis generates a sense of the *way* a discursive formation operates: we can know something about *how* it thinks (its epistemology) rather than simply *what* it thinks. We can expose the tacit methodological assumptions, rather than simply accepting the explicit founding terminology. We can better observe the political and ideological operations, which some communities attempt to disguise or are not even conscious of in their discursive practices.[52] As an example, looking at rhetoric and composition from this perspective might lead us to conclude that there is not simply one discipline—but several competing discursive formations, all arising out of competing traditions (or epistemologies) and struggling for ordering control of the discipline.[53] An archaeologist would not accept "composition" as a firm ground but would rather investigate to see if what collects under that signifier is not rather a variety of dispersed practices.

The Critique of Discourse Community

There have been several critiques of the concept of discourse community, arguments against using "community" as a theoretical basis for composition. The difficulty I have with some of these is that they assume a notion of discourse community that is not the only, or the best, possible. These criticisms of the concept are based mainly on a concern for protecting the status of the individual writer. They see the concept of discourse community—and pedagogies extending from it—as threatening to students. Jim Corder sees social constructionist thought as "engaging, sometimes exhilarating and provocative" (also as fairly obvious), but he wonders what will happen to the "solitary human" who, within the "tribe" (Corder's synonym for discourse community) has "little place and small function."[54] Kurt Spellmeyer issues a more vigorous and direct challenge to "discourse community theorists": he urges a return to "the essay in the academy" as a way to rescue the personal voice from what he sees as the threat of "discipline-specific writing."[55]

I think that these criticisms are partly justified: in emphasizing the influence of community, we cannot forget the role of the writer. Heresy resides at both extremes. But we might remember that community theories themselves are reactions to what was perceived as the overemphasis on the writer and her cognitive processes. They serve as a balancing corrective to that emphasis—though we must avoid swinging too far in either direction.

However, Corder's and Spellmeyer's criticisms presuppose a limited characterization of discourse community theory. Both equate "discourse community" with "academic discourse community": they imagine this community as a rigid set of disciplinary constraints, and they imagine pedagogies based on this community as stifling and harmful to students. Thus, their critiques are warranted by a dire view of discourse community. They do not consider that a *poststructuralist* sense of discourse community might be a very different kind of model altogether.

Corder, Spellmeyer, and Joseph Harris are all nervous about the idea of discourse community, because to them it suggests tight compartmentalization, rigidity, determinism—and the diminishment, if not the dismemberment, of the individual writer. Joseph Harris wants discourse communities to be nice and friendly and open.[56] But are all of them really like this? Harris seems to be expressing a desire for a certain ideal type of discourse community—which is not the same thing as arguing about the *model* we plan to employ. Is Harris objecting to too rigid communities or is he objecting to our having a too rigid model for communities? I am not sure.

Harris challenges the concept of "discourse community," first on grounds of ambiguity and second on the grounds that it suggests "discipline"—which he sees as defined by "consensus" (a notion that he finds troubling). Consensus is certainly a defining characteristic of discourse community—but it seems to me that a sound model, one with fuller explanatory power, would include the notion of "displacement" as well. Communities are not well defined, static entities—but are discontinuous. Discourse communities establish boundaries and power relationships that include and exclude. This is inevitable. But it is also inevitable that those boundaries are interrupted and redrawn. Those who object to discourse community theory seem to do so because it suggests "fixed regions." They are thinking of community in the sociological sense. But if we look more to Foucault's sense of discursive formation and to his notion of genealogy, we may find a model that allows for the "repositioning" and "polyphony" that Harris desires and the "heteroglossia" that Spellmeyer wants us to recognize and promote. The problem is not discourse community theory per se—but a particular, limited view of what the concept means.

This is where I find poststructuralist social theory helpful. It sees discontinuity as the "inescapable provenance." Do not imagine discourse communities as nice, neat compartments, built by the constrained accumulation of knowledge wholly from within (Kuhn's description of "normal science"). (Though some groups may perceive themselves this way—and it is certainly possible for us to construct models based on this view.) Such an approach to the discourse community does not explain nearly enough. Rather, see a discourse community as a collection of "fissures" and ruptures, of "heterogenous layers,"[57] of intersecting systems, institutions, values, and practices. A poststructural notion of discourse communities would see them as discontinuous and flexible, though nonetheless definable. Distinguish between discourse communities and *models* of discourse communities.

But how can we abide such a fuzzy notion of "discourse community"? On a practical level, says Harris, it simply won't work to have such a nebulous term.

That is where the notion of "forum" may help. A forum is a concrete locale, a physical place for a discourse activity—such as a journal (e.g., *Research in the Teaching of English*), a conference, a corporation, a department within a corporation. (I wonder how this concept might correspond to "the specific and material view of community" that Harris urges.[58]) The forum is a convenient and practical starting point for our inquiries into discourse communities: forums represent conventional, sociological boundaries, where several discourse communities may intersect. We may, in investigating a forum, discover that several competing ideologies, methodologies, principles, and stances intersect within that forum.

We could call the Conference on College Composition and Communication (CCCC) a forum, but is it *a* discourse community? We meet and establish a common terrain, but we disagree. I do not see a confining consensus or the disciplinary rigidity—much to the contrary. Rather, I see an ethical gathering, a concrete place where those of various persuasions agree to meet to address common concerns. Those who want to enter this forum must understand some of what is going on in the forum if they hope to enter it felicitously. They need to understand conventions to some degree. Does this mean that their individual personalities are diminished? View the attempt to cooperate with another not as an obliteration of the self but rather as an attempt to define the self at a more ethical level, as representing a willingness to change the self and to recognize that the idea of *the* self is itself limiting.

The problem is not whether or not there are social constraints to writing. We know that there are. The issue is to decide what models to call upon, how to describe communities in our research, and how to account for social constraints in our pedagogies. Spellmeyer's pedagogical answer is to return to the academic essay, which for him represents a genre that enables students to encounter disciplinary knowledge while at the same time preserving (or developing) a sense of individual voice. Ironically, though, the criteria for Spellmeyer's critique themselves arise out of a discourse community. He is representing the values of "the essay in the academy," a tradition with strong curricular ties to the English department and to the romantic theory that supports expressivist rhetoric—and that perceives audience as a threat to writer integrity. (A thorough forum analysis might reveal aspects of this tradition's epistemology.) This discourse community is as powerful and as constraining as any Spellmeyer criticizes. It has its own rules: for instance, students must develop honest, sincere voices—"honest and sincere" being described as use of first-person pronoun, appeal to personal experience for validation and authority, and a rebellious stance toward institutions, bureaucracies, and other social agencies and accepted authorities—in short, the "I" is privileged over the "we." While English teachers may be comfortable within such a community, students have as much trouble learning the conventions of this community as of any other. The point is that this pedagogy will not enable us to resist the influence of community. It will simply, and arbitrarily, position us within one community. It will not save us from rhetoric. It will, rather, make us subject to an unselfconscious rhetoric.

Any theory of discourse community or research on a particular community must, to achieve theoretical validity, account for change, instability, and ambiguity. It must question the basic terminology of the field under investigation, including the dividing terminology itself, because the foundational terminology provides traces of the formation's principles of operation. The researcher must be sensitive to the *asides*, the phrases tossed off, as it were, to the side of the "main" discourse. These can provide valuable clues to the discursive formation. We must examine more than we do the history of discursive formations, especially the emergence and development of their conceptual grids, and note *changes* occurring within the grounding terminology—the varying uses of key terms within the discipline.

It is of course impossible not to have some grounding for our research investigations.[59] Since we must begin somewhere, we may as well continue to work with the traditional borders, with the academic disciplines, but we would be best advised not to trust those borders very much. Foucault's program does not give us a pure critical stance from which to analyze discursive formations—because, of course, his program has its own boundaries.[60] The value of Foucault's program is that it expands the scope of our study and allows us to observe facets of discursive behavior that may be missed in a more traditional analysis.

NOTES
Chapter 6

[1] Kenneth Burke, *The Philosophy of Literary Form* 3rd ed. (Berkeley, CA: Univ. of California, 1973), pp. 110–111.

[2] See Louise Wetherbee Phelps, "Audience and Authorship: The Disappearing Boundary," in *A Sense of Audience in Written Communication*, ed. Gesa Kirsch and Duane H. Roen (Newbury Park, CA: Sage, 1990), 153–174.

[3] Kenneth Burke, *A Rhetoric of Motives* (Berkeley, CA: U of California P, 1969), p. 39.

[4] In fact, as Jonathan Culler has remarked, "The field . . . is contentiously constituted by apparently incompatible activities. . . . contemporary critical theory is confusing and confused." See Jonathan Culler, *On Deconstruction: Theory and Criticism after Structuralism* (Ithaca, NY: Cornell UP, 1982), p. 17

[5] Culler, *On Deconstruction.*

[6] John W. Murphy, "Jacques Derrida: A Rhetoric That Deconstructs Common Sense" *Diogenes* 128 (1984), p. 139.

7 Kenneth A. Bruffee, "Social Construction, Language, and the Authority of Knowledge: A Bibliographical Essay," *College English* 48 (1986), p. 774.

8 Patricia Bizzell, "College Composition: Initiation into the Academic Discourse Community," *Curriculum Inquiry* 12 (1982): 191–207.

9 Susan Peck MacDonald, "Problem Definition in Academic Writing," *College English* 49 (1987): 315–331.

10 Charles Bazerman, "The Writing of Scientific Non-Fiction: Contexts, Choices, Constraints," *PRE/TEXT* 5 (1984): 39–74.

11 Greg Myers, "The Social Construction of Two Biologists' Proposals," *Written Communication* 2 (1985): 219–245.

12 Karen Burke LeFevre, *Invention as a Social Act* (Carbondale, IL: Southern Illinois UP, 1987).

13 See, for example, John Swales and Hazem Najjar, "The Writing of Research Article Introductions," *Written Communication* 4 (1987): 175–191; and Kim Brian Lovejoy, "Discourse Communities in the Academy: A Cohesion Analysis of Texts in Three Disciplines," paper presented at the Applied Linguistics Section, Midwest MLA Conference, Columbus, OH, November 12, 1987.

14 See Ann Ruggles Gere, *Writing Groups: History, Theory, and Implications* (Carbondale, IL: Southern Illinois UP, 1987).

15 Douglas Park, "Analyzing Audiences," *College Composition and Communication* 37 (1986): 478–488; James E. Porter, "Intertextuality and the Discourse Community," *Rhetoric Review* 5 (1986): 34–47; and James E. Porter, "Reading Presences in Texts: Audience as Discourse Community," in *Oldspeak/Newspeak: Rhetorical Transformations*, ed. Charles Kneupper (Arlington, TX: Rhetoric Society of America, 1985), 241–256.

16 See James E. Porter, "The Problem of Defining Discourse Communities," paper presented at the Conference on College Composition and Communication, St. Louis, MO, March 19, 1988.

17 See, for example, Elaine P. Maimon et al., *Readings in the Arts and Sciences* (Boston: Little, Brown, 1984).

18 See James E. Porter, "Truth in Technical Advertising: A Case Study," *IEEE Transactions on Professional Communication* 30 (1987): 182–189.

19 The cancellability clause reads as follows: "This Certificate is effective as of the date shown on the Identification Card and is renewable automatically, according to the mode of payment designated, by the payment of fees by or for the Member and the acceptance thereof by The Corporations subject to such membership fees and coverage provisions in effect on the date of any such renewal." The entire cancellability section rated a 7.3, or "very difficult," on the Flesch scale (24th grade reading level on the Fog Index). The sentence is long (58 words) and syntactically complex. It is structured so that the average reader is likely to notice the phrase "and is renewable automatically"—a phrase likely to reinforce the faulty notion that the policy is noncancellable in an absolute sense. The key phrase that would correct this misconception—" and the acceptance thereof by The Corporations"—is embedded deep within the sentence. Thus the phrase cuing the reader to the

cancellability terms of the policy is syntactically buried, and, in this sentence, indirectly stated. The company has since revised the clause and improved the readability of the passage. See Porter, "Truth," p. 187.

20 Elaine Maimon suggests that we might look at specific disciplinary communities as "circles within the larger circle of the academic community which is itself encompassed by the educated world. Some of the inner circles are concentric—e.g., literature specialists are included within the larger community of English specialists. Some of the inner circles are overlapping, like Venn diagrams, with shadings and crosshatchings to show the shared territories and boundaries." See Elaine Maimon, "Knowledge, Acknowledgement, and Writing Across the Curriculum," in *The Territory of Language: Linguistics, Stylistics, and the Teaching of Composition,* ed. Donald A. McQuade (Carbondale, IL: Southern Illinois UP, 1986), p. 93. See also Patricia Bizzell, "Cognition, Convention, and Certainty: What We Need to Know about Writing," *PRE/TEXT* 3 (1982): 213–243.

21 See Carl Mills, "Linguistic Models, Research Designs, and Discourse Communities," paper presented at the Applied Linguistics Section, Midwest MLA Conference, Columbus, OH, November 12, 1987. See also Charles Arthur Willard, *Argumentation and the Social Grounds of Knowledge* (University, AL: U of Alabama P, 1983).

22 See, for example, Martin Nystrand, "Rhetoric's 'Audience' and Linguistics' 'Speech Community': Implications for Understanding Writing, Reading, and Text," in *What Writers Know,* ed. Martin Nystrand (New York: Academic Press, 1982), 1–28.

23 See, for example, Shirley Brice Heath, *Ways with Words* (New York: Cambridge UP, 1983).

24 See John J. Gumperz, "Linguistics: The Speech Community," in *International Encyclopedia of the Social Sciences,* ed. David L. Sills (New York: Macmillan, 1968), 9:381–386.

25 Peter L. Berger and Thomas Luckmann, *The Social Construction of Reality* (Garden City, NY: Doubleday, 1966).

26 There has been more recognition of the rhetorical nature of social science research and of the problematics related to language and the "reporting" of observations. See, for example, Clifford Geertz, *Local Knowledge: Further Essays in Interpretive Anthropology* (New York: Basic, 1983); and John Van Maanen, *Tales of the Field: On Writing Ethnography* (Chicago: The U of Chicago P, 1988).

27 Basil Bernstein, *Class, Codes, and Control* (New York: Schocken, 1975).

28 Mills, p. 5.

29 Stanley Fish, *Is There A Text in This Class? The Authority of Interpretive Communities* (Cambridge, MA: Harvard UP, 1980), p. 14.

30 Frank Lentricchia, *After the New Criticism* (Chicago: The U of Chicago P, 1980).

31 See Thomas Kuhn, *The Structure of Scientific Revolutions,* 2nd ed. (Chicago: The U of Chicago P, 1970).

[32] Michel Foucault, *The Archaeology of Knowledge and the Discourse on Language*, trans. A. M. Sheridan Smith (New York: Pantheon-Random, 1972).

[33] For example, in order to understand a culture's ideas about discipline and punishment, Foucault suggests, it is necessary to understand the emergence of those concepts (i.e., to isolate the *events*, like the Great Confinement, which represent divergences from past practices), and the elaborate classification system that supports or represses those ideas. Foucault has applied his archaeological method to analyze the concepts of the clinic, discipline and punishment, and sexuality. He has noticed, for instance, that the "birth of the prison" corresponded with a change in the classification of criminal offenses, specifically with a dramatic increase in the vocabulary describing criminal offenses; this change corresponded with a new architectural model of the prison, Bentham's panopticon. See Michel Foucault, *Discipline and Punish: The Birth of the Prison*, trans. Alan Sheridan (New York: Vintage-Random, 1979).

[34] Archaeology is not a structuralist methodology, because it does not attempt to uncover crosscultural or universal laws. Rather, it attempts to uncover the "local, changing rules which at a given period in a particular discursive formation define what counts as an identical meaningful statement." See Hubert C. Dreyfus and Paul Rabinow, *Michel Foucault: Beyond Structuralism and Hermeneutics*, 2nd ed. (Chicago: The U of Chicago P, 1983), p. 55.

[35] Foucault, *Archaeology*, p. 21.

[36] Foucault, *Archaeology*, p. 22.

[37] See Foucault, *Archaeology*. For a further discussion of the nature of the discursive formation, see Ernesto Laclau and Chantal Mouffe, *Hegemony and Socialist Strategy: Towards a Radical Democratic Politics*, trans. Winston Moore and Paul Cammack (Thetford, England: The Thetford Press, 1985), especially pp. 105–106.

[38] James Gleick, *Chaos: Making a New Science* (New York: Penguin, 1987), p. 150.

[39] Foucault does not accept at face value the "behavior, mentality, or set of ideas" of any age (or discipline). Rather, his analytic looks for those "visible and articulable features" that make "these things possible." (For instance, unlike most traditional historians, Foucault does not accept Enlightenment figures' own explanations and justifications for social and political behavior as a foundational ground for his analysis of social developments in eighteenth-century France.) Foucault's historical and theoretical analytic questions those foundational concepts that conventional historical analysis might accept as given and in so doing "revives" history. Foucault finds explanations for behavior in the "gaps" of discourse: through the archaeological analytic, Foucault uncovers the implicit system coordinating discursive practices, a system implied by, but not explicit in, the discursive practices.

Archaeology is chiefly a kind of *historical* analysis, then, but a very different type from conventional analysis, as Gilles Deleuze suggests: "What Foucault takes from History is that determination of visible and articulable features unique to each age which goes beyond any behaviour, mentality or set of ideas, since it makes these things possible. But History responds only because Foucault has managed to invent, no doubt in a way related to the new conceptions of certain historians, a properly philosophical form of interrogation which is itself new and which revives History." See Gilles Deleuze, *Foucault*, trans. Séan Hand (Minneapolis, MN: U of Minnesota P, 1988), pp. 48–49.

[40] Foucault has observed that our attitudes about sex and sexual behaviors are constrained by psychologists' discourse on sex. Sexual behaviors have been classified, sliced, measured, and rated according to an elaborate discursive system that tells us not only what can be said about sexuality but what cannot be said. (Foucault has studied the birth of psychology as a discipline to understand how this phenomenon occurs.) See Michel Foucault, *The History of Sexuality, Volume 1: An Introduction*, trans. Robert Hurley (New York: Vintage-Random, 1980).

[41] According to Dreyfus and Rabinow, Foucault's archaeology is an *analytic* method that "seeks to discover the *a priori* conditions that make possible the analysis practiced in each specific discipline." See Dreyfus and Rabinow, p. 56. Archaeology seeks to uncover the *dispositif*, or "grid of intelligibility," that determines what can be said within a specific discipline—that is, the grid that allows for the generation of, and controls, knowledge within a discipline.

Archaeological analysis does not have any of the traditional critical aims—determining the intent of the writer, deriving meaning from the text, or tracing cultural influences. Its aim is to reveal what Foucault has described in various ways as the episteme, the interstice, the level of "unspoken order," which is the gap between a culture's self-reflective laws and its fundamental codes and practices, that is, "the body of anonymous, historical rules, always determined in the time and space that have defined a given period, and for a given social, economic, geographical, or linguistic area the conditions of operation of the enunciative function." See Foucault, *Archaeology*, pp. 117. In other words, by examining texts, Foucault reveals the system regulating textual production, the "grid" that determines which texts are acceptable in a given community and which are not. This grid applies rules of inclusion and exclusion and what Foucault calls "enunciative modalities," determining who speaks, what is said (and not said), and how it is said. The grid exercises an organizing power, which produces knowledge. See Michel Foucault, *The Order of Things: An Archaeology of the Human Sciences* (New York: Vintage-Random, 1973).

[42] Deleuze, p. 75.

[43] Both Thomas Kuhn and Jean-Francois Lyotard have pointed out that though the science community is often assumed to be the most stable of all communities, it is actually beset by paradoxes and inconsistencies. In fact, as Lyotard says, "consensus is a horizon never reached" (*The Postmodern Condition* 61). The system is by its nature unstable, and perhaps more than a little whimsical in its procedure. Chance and eccentricity play a part in the system, and perhaps make it interesting, and to that extent tolerable. Discoveries are, to Lyotard, "unpredictable." That is, it is the element of chance and paradox existing in any system, no matter how formalized the system, that leads to insight and discovery. See Kuhn; and Lyotard, *The PostModern Condition: A Report on Knowledge*, trans. Geoff Bennington and Brian Massumi (Minneapolis, MN: U of Minnesota P, 1984).

[44] Foucault, *Archaeology*, pp. 54–55.

[45] Foucault, *Archaeology*, pp. 59–60.

[46] Foucault, *Archaeology*, p. 41.

[47] Foucault, *Archaeology*, p. 42.

[48] John Kifner, "4 Kent State Students Killed by Troops," *New York Times* 5 May 1970: 1

[49] See Foucault, *Archaeology*, pp. 97–98.

[50] Chiefly, archaeological analysis involves analysis of the "texts" (in the broadest sense) of a culture. These texts certainly include written products. For instance, in *The Birth of the Clinic*, Foucault examines a wide range of medical articles, case studies, and government and hospital-bureaucracy reports in order to understand how funding and supervising agencies organized hospitals and clinics in France around 1800. But such an analysis also considers the support system for those written products—the social and institutional structures, the semiotic field, even the architecture (e.g., the construction of the prison and the hospital). It must not privilege one type of text over another; the least bureaucratic memo might be most revealing. The archaeologist examines the texts to uncover the system by which they can be classified, to see what it is they say and what they do not say, that is, to uncover their presuppositions and repressed agenda. See Michel Foucault, *The Birth of the Clinic: An Archaeology of Medical Perception*, trans. A. M. Sheridan Smith (New York: Vintage-Random, 1973).

[51] Foucault looks especially for discontinuities or ruptures within and between systems. Archaeology addresses "itself to the general space of knowledge, to its configurations, and to the mode of being of the things that appear in it, defines systems of simultaneity, as well as the series of mutations necessary and sufficient to circumscribe the threshold of a new positivity." See Michel Foucault, "Nietzsche, Genealogy, History," in *The Foucault Reader*, ed. Paul Rabinow (New York: Pantheon-Random, 1984), especially pp. 81–82; see also Foucault, *Order*, p. xxiii. In *Madness and Civilization*, for example, Foucault investigates why in the seventeenth century leper houses were suddenly and inexplicably turned into houses of confinement for the poor. See Michel Foucault, *Madness and Civilization*, trans. Richard Howard (New York: Pantheon-Random, 1965).

[52] The archaeologist discovers this "grid of intelligibility" by exploring (as Foucault has done) what a discursive formation says about itself; what institutions it develops or defines and allows to flourish (e.g., the hospital, the prison); how it organizes and classifies these institutions, and, in turn, how these institutions organize and classify the objects or "bodies" that they claim as their own; what kinds of hierarchies the discursive formation sets up; what it chooses to call things; how its vocabulary constrains discourse, either by providing elaborate technical distinctions (as in some cases) or by the act of *not* naming, by remaining silent.

[53] This point is suggested in James Berlin's "Contemporary Composition: The Major Pedagogical Theories," *College English* 44 (1982): 765–777.

[54] Jim W. Corder, "Hunting for *Ethos* Where They Say It Can't Be Found," *Rhetoric Review* 7 (1989), pp. 303–304.

[55] Kurt Spellmeyer, "A Common Ground: The Essay in the Academy," *College English* 51 (1989): 262–276.

56 Joseph Harris, "The Idea of Community in the Study of Writing," *College Composition and Communication* 40 (1989): 11–22.

57 Foucault, "Nietzsche, Genealogy, History," p. 82.

58 Harris, p. 20.

59 See Patricia Bizzell, "Foundationalism and Anti-Foundationalism in Composition Studies," *PRE/TEXT* 7 (1986): 37–56.

60 Foucault himself starts his analytic with traditional entry points, accepting traditional institutional boundaries (such as the prison and the hospital). After all, one always begins someplace. The key difference is that his analysis eventually ruptures the boundaries. The boundaries are not maintained as the unexamined arena for an internal critique. Rather, the boundaries themselves are inspected. Obviously, when this happens some new and usually implicit boundaries are generated.

Chapter 7

🐛 *Composing the Discourse Community*

> Social constructionist work in composition is based on the assumption that writing is primarily a social act. A writer's language originates with the community to which he or she belongs. We use language primarily to join communities we do not yet belong to and to cement our membership in communities we already belong to.[1]
>
> *Kenneth Bruffee*

There are important differences between what we might call the sociological (in the sense of "realistic") and poststructural views of community. A poststructural analysis of a community does not accept the foundational terminology of the community as a given for the inquiry but begins by investigating where the foundational terminology came from, in what ways it was developed and used rhetorically to establish itself as foundational. A poststructural analysis does not accept the community's announced borders but rather investigates the dynamic nature of communities, the fluctuating borders, the intermixing of communities. A poststructural approach to community examines the political ramifications of the community's own regulating principles, examining those rhetorical acts that define (and at times, marginalize) bodies, to determine how subject positions and power relations are formed within the community under investigation.

A poststructural approach is primarily a critique—a critique that has as its aim the exposure and perhaps ultimately the rejection of the system under analysis. It is at this precise point that I believe rhetoric and composition must abandon, or at least redirect, the poststructural agenda. But to say this suggests a certain view of rhetoric: it suggests a view of rhetoric as committed, finally, to identification (not disidentification), to negotiation and reconciliation (not rejection). This is not to say that rhetoric does not admit conflict or disidentification. Conflict, disagreement, disidentification—all are vital to rhetoric. But they are not the ends of rhetoric. A poststructural rhetoric has to turn, ultimately, and become *reconstructive*. (I consider this argument again in Chapter 8, where I discuss the ethical implications of a social approach to audience.)

In this chapter (and also in Appendix II), I consider how the social view of audience outlined theoretically in Chapter 6 can be placed into practice by the rhetor—whose authority I have challenged in this study but whose viewpoint I have not abandoned.

A Contingent Understanding of "Discourse Community"

We are now ready to dare a definition of "discourse community." A discourse community is a local and temporary constraining system, defined by a body of texts (or more generally, practices) that are unified by a common focus. A discourse community is a textual system with stated and unstated conventions, a vital history, mechanisms for wielding power, institutional hierarchies, vested interests, and so on. Thus, a *discourse* community cuts across sociological or institutional boundaries. For example, the group "Magnavox employees" is a corporately (or sociologically) circumscribed group that has its own announced identity: it is defined as those on the Magnavox payroll. However that group's discursive identity is more complex, since it is intersected by multiple discourse communities. On one level, we can see a division between "workers" and "management": workers may operate according to the principles of one discourse community, with a set of assumptions and operating procedures quite different from management. At the same time, Magnavox is saturated with the conventions of different disciplinary orientations and organizational affiliations: engineers negotiate with business people, people from local headquarters struggle with people from the main office, divisions and departments develop their own discursive habits, lawyers meet with executives to determine corporate policy—and all of this within the corporate boundaries. At the same time, Magnavox develops discursive interrelationships with other companies, with the geographical communities where its plants are located, with various governmental agencies (e.g., the FTC, the Department of Defense), with society at large. In other words, Magnavox is involved with an entire complex network of discursive interrelationships. When I as writer produce a text at Magnavox I create a discourse that arises out of and becomes part of this network.

The discourse community here is this network, in all its complexities. Now this "community" is quite different from Kuhn's sense of "paradigm,"[2] because there is more than one paradigm operating here. Writing within this community is much more complicated than merely determining a simple set of paradigmatic conventions. This discourse community has more open borders than Fish's "interpretive community" and is much broader than either Kinneavy's sense of "situational context" or Bitzer's sense of "rhetorical situation"—both of which vary from discourse to discourse.[3] This discourse community is not a nice, neat compartment built by the accumulation of knowledge from within (Kuhn's description of "normal science"). Rather, this discourse community is "an unstable assemblage of faults, fissures, and heterogeneous layers,"[4] a network of intersecting systems, institutions, values, and practices. This discourse community is *not*, however, the same as culture; this discourse community is unstable, changing, dynamic—it is a turbulent, chaotic system that nevertheless operates with some kind of regularity. The discourse community here is a "strange attractor"—a force field providing a unity for an entire set of dispersed practices.[5]

But how do we abide such complexity? Complicating our scene to such an extent can lead us to the kind of rhetorical despair where we conclude that we cannot hope to deal with the infinite variations of particular audiences. It is at this point that the notion of "forum" may help us.

A forum is a concrete, local manifestation of the operation of the discourse community. It is a physical location for discursive activity—such as a journal, a conference, a corporation, or a department within a corporation. Forums provide well-defined speaking and writing roles for its members, who are, in turn, defined by those roles. A forum shares assumptions about what objects are appropriate for examination and discussion, what operating functions are performed on those objects, what constitutes "evidence" and "validity," and what formal conventions are followed. A forum may have a well-established *ethos*, or it may have competing factions and indefinite boundaries. It may be in what Kuhn refers to as a "preparadigm" state, that is, having an ill-defined regulating system and no clear leadership. Some forums are firmly established, however, such as journals (like *Research in the Teaching of English*) that have articulated and explicit standards and conventions. In such forums, as Vincent Leitch says, a speaker must be "qualified" to talk; he has to belong to a community of scholarship; and he is required to possess a prescribed body of knowledge (doctrine). . . . [This system] operates to constrain discourse; it establishes limits and regularities. . . . who may speak, what may be spoken, and how it is to be said; in addition [rules] prescribe what is true and what false, what is reasonable and what foolish, and what is meant and what not. Finally, they work to deny the material existence of discourse itself.[6]

The forum is a *trace* of a discourse community, a defined place of assembly or means of publication for discourse communities. Each forum has a distinct history and rules governing appropriateness to which members are obliged to adhere. These rules may be more or less apparent, more or less institutionalized, more or less specific to each community. Examples of forums include professional publications like *Rhetoric Review*, *English Journal*, and *Computerworld*; public media like *Newsweek* and *Runner's World*; professional conferences (the annual meeting of fluid power engineers, the 4Cs); company board meetings; family dinner tables; and the monthly meeting of the Indiana chapter of the Izaak Walton League. Douglas Park has described forums as the central meeting place or defining scene for discourse:

> An audience can exist when there is (1) an established social institution or social relationship, a judicial system, a legislative process, an institutional hierarchy, a charitable foundation, a social compact of any sort, a club, a nation, even a friendship between two people; (2) and an evolved and understood function that discourse performs within and for that social relationship. Speech-act theory—and sociolinguistics in general—has taught us to see all discourse as representing action performed within and conditioned by a social situation. . . . all discourse, especially of the more public or formalized kind, functions in and can be described as part of a social transaction that has defined roles for both writers and readers. . . . (3) Finally, for an audience to "assemble," there must be a physical setting. For written discourse, the exact analog to the place of assembly is the means of publication or distribution.[7]

A text is "acceptable" within a forum when it upholds the community episteme. On a simple level, this means that a manuscript submitted for publication to the *Journal of Applied Psychology* should probably follow certain formatting conventions: it must have the expected sections conforming to the general expectations of the social science community (i.e., review of literature, methods, results, discussion), and it must use the journal's version of APA documentation. However, these are only the superficial features of the forum.

On a more essential level, the manuscript must have an *ethos* conforming to the standards of the forum. The discourse must demonstrate that it contributes knowledge to the field, it must demonstrate familiarity with the work of previous researchers, it must conform to the accepted standards for research design, and it must show sufficient data to support its conclusions. The manuscript is a discursive practice within the forum, but it also contributes to an entire discourse community, of which the forum is a sign. The manuscript becomes part of an epistemological grid supporting the formation and the power relations that support the grid. The expectations, conventions, and attitudes of this discourse community as well as the forum (the readers, writers, reviewers, and publishers of *Journal of Applied Psychology*) will influence aspiring psychology researchers, shaping not only how they write but also their character within the discourse community.

An important facet of both forum and discourse community, and perhaps the key to understanding them, is their intertextual nature (see Chapter 5 for a discussion of intertextuality). The texts produced within the forum refer to other texts within it and to some outside it; rely on sources (acknowledged and unacknowledged) for their meaning; and anticipate still other texts to come. One way to do audience analysis, as Douglas Park suggests, is to analyze the texts defining a particular forum. One determines the assumptions of the forum by reading its discourse, by observing its behavior, determining its classifying principles, rules of formation and (especially important) exclusion—what is not said. The writer comes to know the audience by immersing himself in the discourse of the community, by becoming an insider, and yet, paradoxically, by retaining the critical eye of the outsider. The goal of the writer is *socialization* into the discourse community, which requires an understanding of the community's assumptions as well as its explicit conventions and intertextual nature. The rhetor must come to understand the distinct intertextual nature of the discourse community she wishes to "identify" with.

Discourse Communities and the Development of the Writer[8]

The notions of forum and discourse community challenge the traditional romantic notion of the writer. And for this reason the notions trouble some because they appear to question the contribution of the individual, leaving little room for individuality.[9] The discourse community seems to do away with the freedom and autonomy of the writer. Discourse communities are sometimes seen in dire terms: "discursive formations," even to Foucault, control bodies, exert power, limit knowledge, constrain—and perhaps obliterate—the individual. This view seems deterministic, devaluing the contribution of individual writers and making them appear merely tools of the discourse community. If these regulating systems are so constraining, how can an individual emerge? What happens to the idea of the lone inspired writer and the sacred autonomous text?

Both notions take a pretty hard knock. Genuine originality is difficult within the confines of a well-regulated system. Genius is possible, but it may be constrained. Foucault cites the example of Gregor Mendel, whose work in the nineteenth century was excluded from the prevailing community of biologists because he "spoke of objects, employed methods and placed himself within a theoretical perspective totally alien to the biology of his time. . . . Mendel spoke the truth, but he was not *dans le vrai* (within the true)."[10] Frank Lentricchia cites a similar example from the literary community: Robert Frost "achieved magazine publication only five times between 1895 and 1912, a period during which he wrote a number of poems later acclaimed . . . [because] in order to write within the dominant sense of the poetic in the United States in the last decade of the nineteenth century and the first decade of the twentieth, one had to employ a diction, syntax, and prosody heavily favoring Shelley and Tennyson. One also had to assume a certain stance, a certain world-weary idealism which took care not to refer too concretely to the world of which one was weary."[11]

Both examples point to the exclusionary power of discourse communities and raise serious questions about the freedom of the writer: chiefly, does the writer have any?

A partial answer to this problem may be found in Thomas Kuhn's discussion of the paradigm. He points out that the members of a paradigm may be regulated and constrained by it, but at the same time, the paradigm's vitality requires change and growth. It encourages development even as it regulates. Mere repetition is rarely acceptable. The individual is encouraged to be a creative "puzzle solver," to work out problems and come to conclusions in a manner that the paradigm will accept. Members of a paradigm may also transport methods and concepts from one community to another, and in that way facilitate the growth of the paradigm. Discourse communities constrain individuals, but they also allow individuals a place for self-definition, for identification in Burke's sense. A forum is a place of development. Individuals do not develop in isolation; the individual requires the "other" to achieve self-definition.

Remember, too, that the discourse community is a dispersion of interrelated practices. There is a regularity but it is a dispersed regularity. I will not contribute very much to the discourse community if my discourse simply *conforms* to it. Rather, my discourse must *interrelate* with the discourse community by connecting and intersecting with other discursive practices. My discourse will not connect, however, unless I work to develop a sense of those other discursive practices and the position of my own discourse within their network—in other words, unless I have a sense of audience—that is, audience as a network of discursive practices.

A poststructural or social constructionist program such as outlined here is by no means antithetical to cognitivist approaches to composition—in fact, the two approaches are mutually supportive. The development of the individual writer (at least as an *ethos*) can be, indeed has been, linked to the social perspective. We can talk about the writer's growth within the social framework.

Cognitive development plays a part in defining the individual's relationship to the discourse community. Joseph Williams, for one, has developed a model (based on Kohlberg's theory of moral development) for describing the different types of relationships individuals may have to their discourse communities.[12] He identifies three stages of development: presocialized, socialized, and postsocialized.

The "presocialized writer" does not yet understand the conventions or assumptions of the discourse community (Williams cites as an extreme example the student whose paper for the English teacher begins "Shakespeare is a famous Elizabethan dramatist." The student demonstrates in this articulation that he has learned an important fact accepted by the discourse community he writes for; he has not yet learned that such a fact is presupposed knowledge.) This writer is not sufficiently immersed in the discourse community to produce competent discourse by its members' standards. This writer does not know what the community members know (does not know what can be presupposed), is not acquainted with its distinctive intertextuality, may be only superficially acquainted with explicit conventions, if at all.

The "socialized writer" is a full-fledged member, and believer in, the discourse community—perhaps corresponding to Perry's "dualistic thinker" in terms of her commitment to the community conventions. The socialized writer is aware of her position within the community and knows the conventions (at least tacitly, though perhaps not *as* conventions). This writer is fully conditioned to the community but is not yet conscious of the community's regulating system as a system. This writer will probably not challenge conventions (indeed would not dream of doing so) and is not likely to question the assumptions of the community.

The "postsocialized writer" has reached such a degree of confidence, authority, or achievement that she is able to challenge conventions and question assumptions without fear of exclusion. This writer understands the system *as* system and is probably capable of moving from one community to several others. This writer is often in a leadership role in the discourse community and thus takes part in directing community change. This writer has worked through the conventions of the discourse community, understands them and manages them to the point where she directs the development of the community. She maintains her beliefs in the community; at the same time she is capable of exercising a healthy skepticism that the community needs to survive.

A Social Form of Audience Analysis

Social constructionist and poststructural theories suggest a revision of the conventional conception of audience analysis. It would seem, first, that the most useful object for analysis would be discourses produced within forums.[13] The writer discovers the episteme of the community by reading the community's discourse, by observing its behaviors, and through them determining the classifying principles, rules of formation and exclusion, and so on.

Audience analysis is not, from this viewpoint, strictly a scientific, detached process. The writer is not a lab technician standing apart from the object of study, peering at it through a microscope. (We should not, perhaps, be calling it audience *analysis*.) The first goal of the writer is "socialization" into the community, which requires an understanding of the community's unstated assumptions as well as its explicit conventions and intertextuality. The writer has to become a full-fledged member in order to achieve identification within a community. Audience analysis is not merely collecting facts about the audience—these facts will not, as Douglas Park points out, help the writer produce effective discourse. Rather the writer's job is to understand the community and adopt an appropriate ethos within it. To a great extent, this requires a "creative imitation" of community conventions.

The heuristic I have proposed for this process is called "forum analysis" (see Appendix II).[14] A forum analysis is a set of questions, extending in part from archaeological analysis and Leitch's description of it,[15] that encourages writers to explore the forums they are trying to enter. It is a kind of audience analysis—but not focused on real readers. Rather, it assumes that audience is defined by the texts (oral and written) it produces and that the writer needs to systematically explore this textual field in order to produce acceptable discourse within it. The advantage of this approach to audience analysis is that what it produces is an image of the audience's discourse—an image the writer can imitate in preparing her own discourses.

It is dangerous, though, for the writer to stay locked within the forum. The writer must develop a sense of the discursive network that inter-relates with the forum—with the discourse community, in other words. The forum is only a local and concrete manifestation of an entire network of discursive practices. It is also necessary for the writer to understand the forum in terms of its relationships with various disciplines, organizations, attitudes, and beliefs.

The notion of audience as discourse community provides a mediating middle ground between the notion that there are universal stylistic or logical principles (the assumption of traditional rhetoric) and the ad hoc-ism of the realist approach that sees all readers as "real" and hence "new." According to John W. Murphy, audience must be addressed on this middle ground:

> If the rhetorician . . . is not to do violence to a community, an audience must be addressed in terms of its own logic if real discourse is to be engendered. Every audience must therefore not be treated as a hypothetical "universal

audience," but a community that is congealed by the "collective praxis" of its members. A community is not a genus but *praxis*, and it is this human action that unites a community and, accordingly, must be consulted if the rhetorician is to properly address an audience. Using Gadamer's example, the horizon of existence of the rhetorician must "fuse" with that advanced by a particular community if social competence is to be exhibited by the rhetorician.[16]

The aim of forum analysis is to uncover this particular "trace" of the discourse community, that is, the praxis that is its defining character. A forum analysis is a kind of archaeological study—a set of questions encouraging the rhetor to focus on the intertext, the presupposed knowledge of the community, and thereby to discover the motivations behind community action.

Forum analysis should reveal the "gaps" in the discourse community, that is, the knowledge bounded by the discourse community but not yet articulated by it. For a writer, then, "finding a topic" is not the simple task that current-traditional rhetoric assumes it is—namely, selecting a preestablished subject area like "abortion" or "nuclear arms." Knowledge in a discipline is, of course, never articulated in terms of simple noun phrases. Knowledge is constituted in value statements that capture the assent of an entire community (e.g., "All men are created equal") or provide a point of controversy between communities (e.g., "Abortion is immoral"). The rhetor who wishes to contribute within a community must learn and understand the preestablished knowledge within a subject area, must learn which statements are "debatable" (in some sense) within a discourse community, and must discover where the gaps lie.

The gaps in the community's knowledge provide writing roles ("topics," in current-traditional vocabulary), which provide the means for writers to contribute to the community—that is, remain within community constraints yet provide a new perspective for the community and thereby achieve writer self-identification.

This idea is best illustrated with an example from the traditional "review of literature" section in a typical social science research article. The "review of literature" is a well-established convention allowing writers to demonstrate acquaintance with a given field and in so doing acquire community credibility. Conventionally, too, the review of literature is the writer's means of discovering the gaps in the community's knowledge—those knowledge areas bounded by the community but as yet unarticulated by it.

An excerpt from an article published in the journal *Exceptional Children* provides an example. In this article, "Integrating Normal and Handicapped Preschoolers: Effects on Child Development and Social Interaction," the authors report the results of research on integrating normal and handicapped preschoolers in the same classroom. They have this to say about previous research:

Most research in this area has studied the effects of integration on social interaction during play periods (e.g., see Guralnick, 1980; Peterson & Haralick, 1977). It has not examined the effects of integration on more general measures of developmental change over an extended period of time (e.g., a full school year). Several prior investigations have touched on the developmental effects of integrated special education preschools regarding growth in cognitive skills . . . [Discussion of three studies] Although these studies support an integrated preschool model, they are quasiexperimental, lacking both a control group and the random assignment of students to classrooms. These threats to internal validity make it impossible to separate the effects of integration from those associated with either the general provision of preschool special education or from normal maturation alone. . . . No reported investigations of integrating handicapped children in education settings exist that qualify as true experiments (Guralnick, 1981a).[17]

In this literature review section, the authors establish their acquaintance with their particular subfield within special education, including the status of their own prior research. They establish what is known about this particular problem in the subfield (i.e., "the effects of integration on social interaction during play periods"), and they point to the gaps in current knowledge. One gap has been in the time span of previous studies: no previous study has studied the effects of integrating normal and handicapped preschoolers "over an extended period of time." Another gap in the knowledge involves the rigorousness and validity of research design: prior research has been quasiexperimental; there have not been any reports that "qualify as true experiments." These gaps provide the writers with a locus, a place to contribute to the discourse community, and an *ethos*, a definable character within that community.

Finally, I am arguing for a sophistic notion of audience. To see the audience as a dumb presence, a passive receptor of an already determined meaning is to imagine a system in which the construction of truth is the responsibility of an already established authority—the philosopher-king or, perhaps, in our own terminology the so-called expert—someone who already possesses truth (knowledge) and passes it on to those less informed. The methodology that produces or generates the truth is, in this system, anterior to rhetoric, not integral to it. In this conception of communication, the rhetor analyzes audience, but only to determine the most efficient means of constructing the message, which exists as a simple medium for meaning already formed. Rhetoric is still heavily committed to this managerial communication model, which is incipient in Aristotle's *Rhetoric* and which emerges into an articulated system in George Campbell's major work.

A poststructuralist view has in common with social constructionism the position of seeing audience as collaborative writer, as a force that shapes and influences the writer and hence the inscribed text. This audience already exists before writer puts pen to paper—not as a dumb, shapeless mass or as a group of people but as a vital force of beliefs, attitudes, knowledge, existing in writing, in pre-texts that the willing writer can consult. Kenneth Burke was conscious of this need for rhetoric to work first of all on the rhetor. In fact, the rhetor's act of producing discourse first demands that she be persuaded by the social sources with which she will identify:

> Such considerations make us alert to the ingredient of rhetoric in all *socialization*, considered as a *moralizing* process. The individual person, striving to form himself in accordance with the communicative norms that match the cooperative ways of his society, is by the same token concerned with the rhetoric of identification. To act upon himself persuasively, he must variously resort to images and ideas that are formative. Education ("indoctrination") exerts such pressure upon him from without; he completes the process from within. If he does not somehow act to tell himself (as his own audience) what the various brands of rhetorician have told him, his persuasion is not complete.[18]

That is, the act of rhetoric begins not with the rhetor persuading the audience but with the rhetor *being persuaded by*—in Burke's term, *identifying with*—social norms, customs, in another sense, the audience.

Let us consider how this approach might work in practice. Say that I am convinced of the necessity of having a university writing center to provide students with supplemental writing instruction and that I wish to persuade the university administration to allot funds for such a project. In the classical conception, the rhetor in this situation would attempt to produce a discourse (i.e., a grant proposal) that would, through its exercise of logical, emotional, and ethical appeal, attempt to sway the audience (administrators) in one inspired discourse burst.

That this rarely works in the real world is only too clear to those who have entered the grant-writing arena with these assumptions. Rather, we speak of "networking"—that is, working *with* the audience to forge a mutual position. (I hope to avoid here any of the cynical and manipulative connotations that may associate with "networking"; I mean it in the positive sense of constructive dialectic.) If I am to persuade administrators of the importance of such a writing center, I have to be willing as rhetor to understand their position—and I do not mean "understand" as a kind of distant, remote inventional exercise, as a kind of manipulation (the way textbooks sometimes tell students to "consider your audience"). Rather, I must identify with them as administrators: I must actually *become* an administrator—in effect, breaking down the artificial division that separates our roles—and *become* my audience.

A writer does not "analyze" an audience so much as become one with the audience; a writer must not simply "analyze" the emotions but must share the emotions, be of one mind and heart with the audience.[19] To do this, of course, threatens my original position. I may decide after all that the university writing center would not justify its costs, would not serve as many students as well as some other program. In short, as rhetor I might be changed by, rather than change, my audience. The intent to persuade, in this model, is a risk. I must be willing to enter this world, bringing my values, my assumptions about language and rhetoric, to this space we refer to as "university administration" simply because I bring pre-texts from another realm, a set of assumptions, beliefs, and the like, that are only partially, if at all, functional in this discourse community. I bring my pre-texts to this new community with the intent to add to its grid. I may be successful in reshaping or redirecting the community to see the value of the writing center, but I might be changed by that identification. To change my audience, I have to be willing to change, too. I must accept them as writer and see myself as, in part, audience: thus, the roles of audience and writer, these once-separate roles, become blurred, co-alesce in the notion of discourse community—Burke's parlor metaphor.

This conception of audience is certainly a sophistic one—or perhaps a neosophistic one. It supposes that truth and knowledge do not lie absolutely with the rhetor, who discovers truth through some prior and unrelated activity. Rather, truth is probable, local, and temporary. It is "rhetorically negotiated,"[20] or "discovered" through active dialectic, in *praxis*, and it changes as circumstances change. My task as rhetor is to bring what I can to the dialectic but to enter the dialectic as a participant, not as an absolute speaker of the truth or as a passive receptor of someone else's truth.

The social view of audience has not been favored or even much acknowledged in rhetoric and composition until recently. Views identifying the writer as the instigator of the composing act have tended to predominate. It may be that treating the audience in social terms threatens long-held assumptions about the nature of the writing process. Treating audience in such terms may threaten a cherished assumption—the belief in the autonomous status of the writer as privileged ground of discourse, as independent *cogito*.

Perhaps this subordination of the social view has occurred out of maliciousness or whimsy or political design. However, it is more likely that certain assumptions about the nature of the composing process lead, inevitably, to certain views of audience, views that diminish its role in composing. For example, expressivist rhetoric, which has invested itself in a romantic view of the writer as potential genius and which sees invention as a mysterious process defying description, assigns little value to audience. The cognitive-process view, while declaring audience an important concern, cannot satisfactorily account for its presence in terms of the writer's cognitive operations (or at least has not yet done so) and thus subordinates it by consigning it to the realm of "task environment."

The social view of audience has been generally neglected in composition studies. Poststructuralist criticism recalls our attention to this view—but at the same time cautions us about simplifying the view: audience may be "community," but that community means far more than "real people." The audience-as-community perspective offers us a view that both mediates between and encompasses the other, more prevalent treatments. This approach will certainly not undermine or supplant the traditional treatments of audience, but it will complement them by providing the missing social angle that recognizes more fully the contribution of the audience to the creation of discourse.

NOTES
Chapter 7

[1] Kenneth A. Bruffee, "Social Construction, Language, and the Authority of Knowledge: A Bibliographical Essay," *College English* 48 (1986), p. 784.

[2] Thomas Kuhn, *The Structure of Scientific Revolutions*, 2nd ed. (Chicago: U of Chicago P, 1971).

[3] See Stanley Fish, *Is There a Text in This Class? The Authority of Interpretive Communities* (Cambridge: Harvard UP, 1980); James L. Kinneavy, "The Relation of the Whole to the Part in Interpretation Theory and in the Composing Process," in *Linguistics, Stylistics, and the Teaching of Composition*, ed. Donald A. McQuade (Akron, OH: U of Akron English Department, 1979), 1–23; and Lloyd F. Bitzer, "The Rhetorical Situation," *Philosophy and Rhetoric* 1 (1968): 1–14.

[4] Michel Foucault, "Nietzsche, Genealogy, History," in *The Foucault Reader*, ed. Paul Rabinow (New York: Pantheon-Random, 1984), p. 82.

[5] See James Gleick, *Chaos: Making a New Science* (New York: Penguin, 1987).

[6] Vincent B. Leitch, *Deconstructive Criticism: An Advanced Introduction* (New York: Columbia UP, 1983), p. 145.

[7] Douglas Park, "Analyzing Audiences," *College Composition and Communication* 37 (1986), pp. 482–483.

[8] The discussion in this section is a revised version of material that appears in James E. Porter, "Reading Presences in Texts: Audience as Discourse Community," in *Oldspeak/Newspeak: Rhetorical Transformations*, ed. Charles Kneupper (Arlington, TX: Rhetoric Society of America, 1985), 241–256.

[9] For critiques of the concept of discourse community, see Joseph Harris, "The Idea of Community in the Study of Writing," *College Composition and Commu-*

nication 40 (1989): 11–22; Jim W. Corder, "Hunting for *Ethos* Where They Say it Can't be Found," *Rhetoric Review* 7 (1989): 299–316; and Kurt Spellmeyer, "A Common Ground: The Essay in the Academy," *College English* 51 (1989): 262–276. This criticism of the social view of rhetoric is discussed in more detail in Chapter 6.

[10] Michel Foucault, "The Discourse on Language," in *The Archaeology of Knowledge and the Discourse on Language*, trans. A. M. Sheridan Smith (New York: Pantheon-Random, 1972), p. 224.

[11] Frank Lentricchia, *After the New Criticism* (Chicago: The U of Chicago P, 1980), pp. 197, 199.

[12] Joseph M. Williams, "Cognitive Development, Critical Thinking, and the Teaching of Writing," paper presented at the Conference on Writing, Meaning, and Higher Order Reasoning, University of Chicago, Chicago, IL, May 15, 1984.

[13] Art Walzer advises that "since an interpretive community is defined by the specialized *topoi* that characterize its discourse . . . our heuristic for the analysis of audience should have students analyze specialized journals in terms of such general *topoi* as the roles played by scholars working in a discipline, etc." See Arthur E. Walzer, "Articles from the 'California Divorce Project': A Case Study of the Concept of Audience," *College Composition and Communication* 36 (1985), p. 156.

[14] For an example of an extended forum analysis, see Carol Berkenkotter, "Evolution of a Scholarly Forum: *Reader*, 1977–1988," in *A Sense of Audience in Written Communication*, ed. Gesa Kirsch and Duane H. Roen (Newbury Park, CA: Sage, 1990), 191–215. See also the student samples collected in Appendix II.

[15] See Leitch, pp. 151–152.

[16] John W. Murphy, "Jacques Derrida: A Rhetoric That Deconstructs Common Sense," *Diogenes* 128 (1984), p. 140.

[17] Joseph R. Jenkins, Matthew L. Speltz, and Samuel L. Odom, "Integrating Normal and Handicapped Preschoolers: Effects on Child Development and Social Interaction," *Exceptional Children* 52 (1985), p. 8.

[18] Kenneth Burke, *A Rhetoric of Motives* (Berkeley, CA: U of California P, 1969), p. 39. See also, pp. 56–57.

[19] Several rhetoricians have identified the importance of the rhetor "becoming one with" the audience. Kenneth Burke refers to this as "identification." Daniel Fogarty calls it "consubstantiality." And Richard Young, Alton Becker, and Kenneth Pike discuss it under the principle of "assumption of similarity." See Kenneth Burke, *A Grammar of Motives* (Berkeley, CA: U of California P, 1969), pp. 19–23; Daniel J. Fogarty, S. J., *Roots for a New Rhetoric* (New York: Russell and Russell, 1959), pp. 75–76; and Richard E. Young, Alton L. Becker, and Kenneth L. Pike, *Rhetoric: Discovery and Change* (New York: Harcourt, 1970), p. 275.

[20] See Louise Wetherbee Phelps, "Audience and Authorship: The Disappearing Boundary," in *A Sense of Audience in Written Communication*, ed. Gesa Kirsch and Duane H. Roen (Newbury Park, CA: Sage, 1990), 153–174.

Chapter 8

ᘒ Conclusion: The Ethical Implications of a Social Vision of Audience

> Every political deliberation and decision, either explicitly or implicitly, involves a reference to and, as much as possible, an answer to the issue of what "we" ought to be or become in the present circumstances. The "we" at stake here thus designates a community whose existence belongs to the determination of what we ought to be or become and indeed to the determination of how to do it. . . . Whatever the question, an obligation is implied.[1]
>
> *Jean-Francois Lyotard*

Pedagogies that emphasize the social view of writing do not necessarily diminish the role of the writer, as their critics charge. To write is to enter into a cooperative relationship with another: it always requires securing the cooperation of the audience, who is only a passive receptor if we choose to regard him or her as such. Rather than diminishing me, or threatening my personality, the social view is elevating, enabling and also

119

ethical. The kind of accommodation it encourages aims for a "good" that is greater than the individual elements of me the writer or you the audience.

We have not yet in composition really begun to think seriously about the question, Why should writers write? We have tended to answer the question of purpose in terms of the personal desires or intents of the writer: I write to express myself, I write to inform others, I write to persuade them—all these articulations assuming the "I" as the center of discovery, as the authority over the audience. We may have a warm feeling that we are writing ultimately for the good of the audience—but this view is a paternalistic one: the rhetor deciding what is good for the audience. We need to question some of these managerial assumptions about composing—and to begin thinking of *purpose* in terms of the "good" of something. But what? The *polis*? That concept isn't functional for us, but I am thinking of something akin to that: "discourse community" strikes me as suitable for the time being—its flexibility (or ambiguity, if you prefer) being its most attractive feature.[2]

Rhetoric must have an aim, and not simply an internal or tautological aim either. It is not enough to say that I am writing to persuade my readers. *Why* am I trying to persuade them? *Why* should they accept my position? Because it is *good* for them. To exercise rhetoric, the rhetor needs a notion of "the good"—at least a selfish notion of what is good for the self, if not a sense of what is good for "all." And of course "the good" in any ethical system would mean the good of the audience as well as the rhetor. Since determining what is "good" and "right" is not always so easy, rhetoric needs ethics—which we should understand as the study of ways of determining what is good.

There is an entire literature bordering on rhetoric that deals with ethics. In Aristotle's *Rhetoric*, the common ground between rhetor and audience was the *topoi*, common patterns of thinking that provide a basis for cooperation between rhetor and audience. The purpose of the enterprise was the good of the *polis*. Thus, the act of composing a speech was situated within an ethical and political framework. Aristotle's *Nicomachean Ethics* is integrally tied to the *Rhetoric* (as is his *Politics*). The *Rhetoric* leans heavily on the description of "the good" in *Nicomachean Ethics;* since the rhetor must have "the good of the state" as his ultimate aim, determining what is good is part of the rhetorical enterprise. Much of Book 2 of *Rhetoric* is devoted to describing "the good life," which was integrally tied to the good of the *polis* and to the strategies that motivate people and that the rhetor can use to motivate audiences. Augustine was also conscious of the ethical foundations of rhetoric; in *De Doctrina Christiana* he points out that moral rhetoric must by necessity regard the truth value of statements and the ethical stance of the speaker and have as its proper aim the good of the individual (which was ultimately, for Augustine, the salvation of the soul). The works of the *ars praedicandi* assume as ultimate aim the salvation of the Christian. In contemporary rhetoric, the good (when it is discussed at all) is considered in terms of social and political interests. But ethics also has a role to play in business and technical writing, where the rhetor mediates (either consciously or unconsciously) between the good of the corporation, the good of the state, and perhaps an alternative moral good (borrowed from another system).

Ethics is another topic that, like audience, has been lost to rhetoric—divided from it by the slow development of airtight disciplines, a trend encouraged particularly by Peter Ramus, the greatest of curricular dividers. Through the history of rhetoric, ethics was appropriated by philosophy and theology and disconnected from rhetoric. Twentieth-century rhetoricians like Richard Weaver and Karl Wallace have attempted to reconnect ethics and rhetoric, but their efforts have not been successful, perhaps because their sense of ethics is ahistorical and idealistic rather than local or contextual.[3]

A full consideration of the connections between ethics and rhetoric would require another volume—yet it is an important matter to consider in conjunction with audience. The interaction between rhetor and audience must be governed ultimately by something outside rhetoric. That something may well be audience *belief* (which, though it may be "outside" rhetoric, may still be accessible *through* it).[4] Aristotle places incredible faith in rhetoric in viewing it as the means by which truth can be achieved. "Rhetoric is useful," says Aristotle, "because things that are true and things that are just have a natural tendency to prevail" (*Rhetoric*, Book 1.1). The truth is likely to prevail because, in Chaim Perelman's terms, audience will function as a verifying ground, serving as judge of ideas: "In Aristotle's view, every audience is a judge which in the end must decide the superiority of one disputed thesis over the other when neither is obviously compelling."[5] Perelman urges us to place more trust in the principles of our discipline—to recognize that we need audience and that we need to have a faith in and respect for (not simply tolerance of) audience and in belief (the basis for audience change):

> Instead of searching for a necessary and self-evident first truth from which all our knowledge would be suspended, let us recast our philosophy in terms of a vision in which people and human societies are in interaction and are solely responsible for their cultures, their institutions, and their future—a vision in which people try hard to elaborate reasonable systems, imperfect but perfectible.[6]

This view of rhetoric is sophistic, its view of the role of audience echoing Protagoras' perception of "man as the measure of all things." It does not solve our problems, however. I would not offer Perelman's position as an answer to the struggles within critical theory and rhetoric and composition. His trust in the "universal audience" is problematic for those who see multiple audiences or discourse communities struggling over disciplinary issues. Where is this universal audience? How do we know which audience is the *universal* one? Perelman does not provide us with a satisfactory answer—but I think he points out where we should be looking: toward audience and toward some notion of belief.

We can also look to postmodern theory for a treatment of ethics. We should understand ethics here in several senses. First, ethics is the determination of the "should" for the "we": What should we (in various communities) do, believe, think? And how do we justify those actions, those beliefs, those thoughts? Second, and extending from this, ethics is a study of the definition and constitution of the self. Assuming that the self is at least in part (and perhaps entirely) constituted within discursive practices, what roles are available to the self? How does the self achieve identity? Self in the postmodern sense is not to be understood as transcendental, a priori, or un-self-determined. Rather, self is postures evident in discourses, positions taken or adopted. Ethics, then, comes closer to the classical notion of *ethos*—character. How does one make value assertions? How does one justify them? By what authority?

The notion of the good is tied to a "we," and every action (including every discursive action) invokes the "we" in some sense. According to Jean-Francois Lyotard,

> every political deliberation and decision, either explicitly or implicitly involves a reference to and, as much as possible, an answer to the issue of what "we" ought to be or become in the present circumstances. The "we" at stake here thus designates a community whose existence belongs to the determination of what we ought to be or become and indeed to the determination of how to do it. . . . Whatever the question, an obligation is implied.[7]

In *Peregrinations*, Lyotard examines various critical postures that he himself held at various times, including indifference (discussed in his first chapter, "Clouds") and irony (considered in his second essay, "Touches"). Rejecting both indifference and irony as viable critical postures, he arrives at duty, at obligation: not a duty or obligation to a particular position, but rather a duty "to be obliged" (that is, to something), an attachment, a commitment, a belief. Lyotard goes on to describe the "pure obligation," the "duty of being obliged,"[8] which must, for him, drive political action. This duty extends beyond, I believe, to all community action, however variously "communities" may be defined.

This duty, this drive to action derives from community, but not community in the sense of universal common ground—not, in other words, the Kantian *sensus communis* (which supports "pure" judgments), or the universal audience of Perelman, or the horizon of expectations of Jauss. Rather, this duty derives from a "local we"—a "we" that is bound and localized in several ways—perhaps by culture, by disciplinary affiliations, by formal conventions, by religious convictions, by theological predispositions, and certainly by some combination of these (and other) influences.

This "local we" is not a static entity. It moves, changes, adapts, as it "touches" other communities, blends into them, moves away from them.

Let me back out of this abstruse discussion to generalize somewhat. Certainly, it is a good thing to "analyze" audience—if by this we mean "come to understand" our audience. But this is not enough. We must move beyond the managerial communication model presumed by such an articulation to understand the audience as a community, as a "local we," which serves as a ground (local ground, remember) for beliefs, values, attitudes, actions—elements integrally tied to the question of ethics (What should we do?), as well as to questions of identity (What should we be?), argument (How do we justify ourselves?), invention (How should we think?), and other rhetorical concerns as well.

The implications of this position are, I hope, clear. We must reinstantiate audience, and the accompanying concern for ethics, into the discipline, reviving a consideration for the implications of audience in rhetoric. Such an invigoration means much more than simply adding mandatory new chapters on audience and ethics to all our freshman composition texts. It means in part changing the *ethos* of those textbooks—redirecting them politically, recharging them with a new vocabulary, changing their entire slant and posture.

Obviously this project is a vast one. Let me offer one brief and reductive example to make my point. Most freshman composition texts begin with some kind of statement about the purpose of writing, and very often that purpose statement is couched in terms something like these: "Writing is an important means of expressing yourself" or "Writing is an important way you communicate with others." This kind of statement is so common, so seemingly innocuous, that we may not even recognize its problematic ideology.

A textbook based on a community perspective valuing audience and ethics would begin much differently. Maybe like this: "You have a duty and an obligation to write, not because you have 'the truth' and must share it with others, but because *we* need to discover truths and we need all the help we can get, yours included. You write because you have an obligation to do so."

The posture of this fictional opening is somewhat different. This articulation is a call to action. It is an invitation to the writer to participate in a discussion already in progress. It does not advise the writer to "go out and find" an audience—because the audience is already *here*, as the voice of the textbook, and it got "here" before the writer did. Join us, the audience tells the writer, we need your help. The audience is not outside the textbook. The audience, indeed numerous audiences are already within the book, voices calling the writer to participate with a "local we."

To adopt this approach, we do not have to throw out all the traditional practices and principles of rhetoric and composition. In fact, we can keep most of them. But we will need to rearrange these principles and practices in a different framework, one founded on a different ethical relationship between audience and writer.

We may be uncomfortable dealing with the ethics of writing. But whether we like it or not, we *are* teaching an ethics of writing—now, implicitly, in our pedagogies. The practice of ignoring audiences, or of treating all audiences with generic strategies, or indeed any approach to audience, has ethical implications. We need to begin to examine that ethics—and to begin to question the conventional understanding of the relationship between writer and audience.

In *The Order of Things*, Foucault notes that within disciplinary matrices certain terms are "outside knowledge" and, for that reason, are "conditions of knowledge." They provide a ground for classifying objects, or, as Foucault says, they "totalize phenomena and express the *a priori* coherence of empirical multiplicities."[9] "Madness," for example, is *not* a pure and prior state of being but is a defined condition created by a knowledge system. "Labor," "life," and "language" are other such terms. "Audience" is yet another.

"Audience" is a kind of god term (or "ultimate term," in Richard Weaver's terminology). As such, it is very often not defined but is accepted as a precondition of knowledge (like "writer") within rhetoric and composition. At the same time, the meaning of the term slides, and the term takes on different values within different rhetoric epistemologies.[10]

My analysis of audience has proceeded from the start based on the assumption that the models we employ to describe the "reality" of the writing process or the writing situation rely on a classifying grid that empowers certain characteristics and disenfranchises others. In fact, when we talk about the writing process, we are engaging in metaphor. Often, we are activating the "conduit metaphor"[11] and likening the process to a telephone wire (or sewer pipeline), other times to a chemical or industrial sequence, or to a computer model. When we liken the composing process to a set of stages in the manufacture of a product, we are isolating for observation "the process" but are abstracting the writer from that process, in a sense privileging the writer by placing him outside the process. When we employ the dramatic metaphor of "situation," we call to mind a *scene* or dramatic moment that privileges the interaction of characters but that thereby subordinates process. The situation metaphor calls attention to the static dialectic and contextual properties of writing but deemphasizes the developmental and diachronic aspects.

I have attempted to demonstrate (in Chapter 2) that the role of audience was established fairly early on—hypostatized in Aristotle's classification schema—and that subsequent treatments, though they suffer slight shifts and modifications, have by and large accepted the grid provided in

Aristotle. A comparable argument might be championed that Aristotle developed the classificatory system that split rhetoric from logic, in fact creating two distinct types of discourse around which developed two competing and unequal systems of thought. Perhaps Aristotle intended a more cooperative sense of the audience-rhetor relationship, as some have argued. However, his penchant for classifying led to hypostatization: this grid became *the* grid. Subsequent rhetoricians developed the split, adopted and eventually assimilated the conduit metaphor, and deposited the audience at the receiving end of the pipe: audience thus becomes, to extend the Lakoff and Johnson metaphor, the town dump—or perhaps the sewage treatment plant. Contemporary composition suggests that the writer look down the pipe to see who's getting the garbage and how they feel about it—but that is the extent to which the rhetor has been obligated to deal with audience. The pipe line is one-way.

The social view that sees audience as discourse community offers a useful, indeed a necessary, alternative to the pipeline metaphor. The metaphor of "community" is, for many, a powerful and attractive one. Some may associate it positively with the "communal movements" of the 1960s. For others, the term may have religious and spiritual connotations. For some, the terms "social" and "communal" suggest positive political action. But by adopting this metaphor we can examine a number of issues and concepts in rhetoric and composition. This different perspective will enable us to understand old rhetorical concepts (e.g., writer, text, style) in new ways. Obviously, this will be an exhaustive enterprise, providing a research program for rhetoric and composition for some time to come.

NOTES
Chapter 8

[1] Jean-Francois Lyotard, *Peregrinations: Law, Form, Event* (New York: Columbia UP, 1988), p. 35.

[2] See Carolyn Miller, "The Discourse Community as *Polis*," paper presented at the Modern Language Association Conference, New Orleans, LA, 1988.

[3] Louise Wetherbee Phelps discusses the relationship between composition and ethics in *Composition as a Human Science: Contributions to the Self-Understanding of a Discipline* (New York: Oxford UP, 1988). See especially Chapter 9, "Toward a Human Science Disciplined by Practical Wisdom."

⁴ Where do we find the authority necessary to make value statements? The rhetorician has to begin somewhere, with something. Perhaps the starting point is belief, as Richard Weaver thinks (174–175). Perhaps we have only faith, as Burke's final words in *A Rhetoric of Motives* suggest: "But since, for better or worse, the mystery of the hierarchic is forever with us, let us, as students of rhetoric, scrutinize its range of entrancements, both with dismay and in delight. And finally let us observe, all about us, forever goading us, though it be in fragments, the motive that attains its ultimate identification in the thought, not of the universal holocaust, but of the universal order— as with the rhetorical and dialectic symmetry of the Aristotelian metaphysics, whereby all classes of beings are hierarchally arranged in a chain or ladder or pyramid of mounting worth, each kind striving towards the *perfection* of its kind, and so towards the kind next above it, while the strivings of the entire series head in God as the beloved cynosure and sinecure, the end of all desire" (333). See Kenneth Burke, *A Rhetoric of Motives* (Berkeley, CA: U of California P, 1969). Burke seems to be suggesting that rhetoric should reencounter ethics, or beyond that, theology. He is acknowledging that rhetoric must have an aim—it must be directed toward something.

⁵ Chaim Perelman, *The Realm of Rhetoric*, trans. William Kluback (Notre Dame, IN: U of Notre Dame P, 1982), p. 155.

⁶ Perelman, *Realm*, p. 160.

⁷ Lyotard, *Peregrinations*, p. 35.

⁸ Lyotard, *Peregrinations*, p. 35.

⁹ Michel Foucault, *The Order of Things: An Archaeology of the Human Sciences* (New York: Vintage-Random, 1973), p. 244.

¹⁰ Weaver refers to the tendency of ultimate terms to change their references over time as "semantic shift." See Richard M. Weaver, "Relativism and the Use of Language," in *Language Is Sermonic*, p. 130.

¹¹ George Lakoff and Mark Johnson, *Metaphors We Live By* (Chicago: The U of Chicago P, 1980).

Appendix I

ॐ *Audience in Professional Writing*[1]

Audience has been an important concern in professional writing research and textbooks for some time—and there is certainly a substantial amount of research on the role of audience in professional writing.[2] While audience analysis is sometimes a feature of freshman composition texts, such strategies have been widely used in professional writing textbooks.[3] In fact, professional writing readily accepts the need to consider issues of audience: There has not been anything like a call to ignore the audience—though some approaches (such as certain readability assessments) do assume that audience needs are best met by attention to style—and there has not been much impetus toward expressivism.[4]

Discussions of audience in professional writing have, naturally enough, paralleled discussions in rhetoric and composition generally. There is, in fact, a regular practice of researchers borrowing from rhetoric theory to develop new approaches. (For example, some researchers have applied reader-response criticism to develop a theory of the implied reader for professional writing.[5]) However, advances in professional writing have not been exclusively derivative from rhetoric and composition. The borrowing has not been all one way. In some interestingly distinct ways, rhetoric and composition have been influenced by professional writing. For instance, research in readability, usability, and organizational commu-

127

nication has influenced, and promises to continue to enlighten, our ideas about audience.

Readability Formulas and the Shannon-Weaver Model

Though audience analysis is a generally accepted and recommended strategy in professional writing, such analysis is often couched in a strongly managerial composing ideology. The traditional model guiding work in professional communications has been the Shannon-Weaver model, which employs a telecommunications metaphor in describing the writing process.[6] In this model, communication is perceived in physical terms as a broadcast. The aim of communication is to reduce the level of "noise" in the "transmission." Communicating effectively requires that the speaker or writer develop the clearest transmission possible, creating a direct path between his idea and the reader's reception of it. The model strongly influenced treatment of composing, and general approaches to technical and business communications, at least in part because it was a model "irresistibly easy to grasp."[7]

The readability formulas developed in the 1940s and 1950s rest on Shannon-Weaver assumptions—viewing the text as a physical medium, like a telephone wire, conveying the writer's ideas to the reader. The term "readability" refers to the accessibility of a given text to a given reader or readers. Readability refers broadly to anything from changing the typeface or format of a report, to reconstructing sentences, to applying readability formulas, to reorganizing. The most widely used method of assessing readability is the application of readability formulas (such as the Flesch Reading Ease Scale, the Gunning Fog Index, and the Dale-Chall formula), which are generally based on document variables such as number of syllables, vocabulary difficulty, and word and sentence length. These formulas have proven attractive because they are easy to apply and generate an exact and fairly reliable score, which can be useful for comparative purposes. These measures are limited though, and have been criticized for not considering important variables of rhetorical context—such as cultural factors, content and readers' prior knowledge of it, text structure and format, syntax—and for not providing writers with guidance in revision.[8]

Readability formulas are inadequate measures of a text's accessibility because they rely on a limited set of variables. Readability formulas consider the text "in itself," and do not consider how a text might be read by different readers. An example will serve to illustrate the problem. The word "waive" has only one syllable and is thus likely to improve the readability score of a document. Yet its meanings on income tax forms can be varied and complicated; it is not necessarily a simple word for the inexpert income tax preparer. Conversely, although "elevator" is a four-syllable word—and would thus increase difficulty level on most scales—it is a relatively accessible concept. Word and sentence length are not always significant factors in determining the "difficulty" of a text.

In their reductiveness, readability formulas are not adequate measures of overall text accessibility. Despite such limitations, however, readability formulas are achieving greater stature, as more and more states are passing "plain English laws" mandating the use of these formulas to determine the readability of legal documents such as warranties and contracts.[9]

Other approaches to readability focus on the formal features of texts without quantifying them within a formula. Daniel Felker et al.'s *Guidelines for Document Designers*, for instance, provides basic instructions for making documents "easier to read and understand,"[10] assuming that readability can be treated almost exclusively as a function of formal features of text. The authors offer such current-traditional advice as "use the active voice" and "use short sentences." Such advice assumes that reader needs are best met through attention to formal features (e.g., sentence length, syntactic construction, graphic devices) and that these principles are general to all readers.

The epistemology supporting these readability approaches is a current-traditional one: "meaning" exists prior to text and is embodied in the text, however perfectly or imperfectly. The act of writing is the task of creating a "transparent" text, or of "adapting" the text to make it as nearly transparent as possible, a text that will pose the fewest obstacles between the reader and "the meaning"—or, in Shannon-Weaver terms, keep "noise" to a minimum. Though such approaches aim to make texts more readable, ironically enough they obscure the presence of the reader by using oversimplified measures and by failing to consider how readers *contribute* to meaning.

Cognitive/Linguistic Approaches to Readability

Generally, readability research has developed well beyond the use of formulas (though much public policy is still being decided on the basis of formulas). Supported in part by the Document Design Center in Washington, DC, readability researchers have developed a more mature sense of what "readability" means, calling on insights from, primarily, cognitive psychology and linguistics and testing these theories empirically (often with usability studies). Readability researchers working from the assumptions of cognitive psychology and text (or functional) linguistics attempt to assess readability by connecting the formal features of discourse (particularly syntactic and graphic elements) to cognition and, consequently, to audience receptibility. Thus, such assessments attempt to account for reader variation. These cognitive/linguistic assessments do not count words and syllables but instead examine the relationships between syntactic structures and reader psychology/knowledge.[11]

These cognitive/linguistic assessments are based on "schema theory," which Thomas Huckin describes as follows:

> [Schema theory postulates] that the human mind routinely constructs, on the basis of patterns of experience, abstract generic concepts or "schemata." These schemata are stored in long-term memory and thereafter guide the way we perceive and remember things. . . . The power of schemata in the communication process resides largely in their ability to induce inference from the reader (listener, viewer, etc.). This process of schema-based inferring works as follows. When the writer and reader share a schema, that is, when their respective schemata for a particular concept are essentially similar, the writer does not have to refer explicitly to all the details of that schema for those details to be conveyed to the reader: the reader will simply supply any missing details by inference.[12]

Such assessments focus on the arrangement of information in a document, stressing syntactic coherence as well as conceptual and grammatical parallelism and, especially in their application to technical communication, promoting the use of lists, of forecasting statements and of metadiscourse (i.e., reading cues). From such a perspective, for instance, sentence *length* per se is not as important a factor in determining readability as sentence *syntax*, that is, the arrangement of clauses within and between sentences.

One principle extending from this theory advises the writer to begin sentences with noun phrases (or general concepts) referring to information familiar to the reader. Newer (or less familiar) information and complicated concepts should come at the end of sentences and paragraphs. Another principle advises that writers can best help inexpert readers by using guiding metadiscourse, because inexpert readers need the cues such metadiscourse provides to determine what is important (and what is not) in a given passage. As Thomas Huckin points out, expert readers do not require as much metadiscourse, because they can call on prior knowledge and experiences external to the text to evaluate and classify what they are reading.[13]

These cognitive/linguistic assessments account more satisfactorily than readability formulas for reader diversity. They develop a notion of textual coherence, for instance, that allows for the contribution that the reader brings to the text (represented as "schematic framework"). Nevertheless, these assessments still focus on textual features, relying on an often generic cognitive theory that posits preconceived notions of "expert" and "inexpert" reader and assumes a vision of reader as "information processor." Such a conception does not account satisfactorily for distinct, unusual, or interactive rhetorical contexts. These assessments also do not offer strategies for determining readers' schemas. They suffer from the same limitation as the real-reader heuristic: How do we determine the reader's schema? How do we collect evidence about it and, assuming we could collect such information, how would we use it to create a piece of writing? Such assessments seem to offer more potential as guides to editing an already existing document, to "adapting a discourse to its end," rather than as aids to invention.[14]

Readability assessments assume the managerial communication model, focusing on the ways that an already established discourse can be made more user friendly or writer based—in other words, "adapted" to fit the needs of real readers. In their focus on adaptation, readability assessments do not help us very much in considering how audience can or should influence invention. Like most approaches assuming a managerial communication model, readability assessments obscure the social elements and the contributions of the audience. Both the readability formulas and the cognitive/linguistic assessments imagine the reader as a property of text, though the latter examines how textual structures are tied to cognitive considerations. Information attained through these assessments can be helpful to the writer in developing an overall sense of audience. However, the writer using these methods must be aware of their limitations—of what aspects of the audience and readability they do not account for. "Readability" as a term is no more or less slippery than "audience."

Usability Research

One of the more promising audience-related developments in professional writing is usability research. "Usability" refers to a range of methods for determining the "usefulness" of, usually, a piece of functional or instructional writing (such as computer documentation). In a usability study of a piece of computer documentation, for instance, the researcher

> gathers empirical information about actual users [i.e., real readers] engaged in using a computer system, at some point in time during the development of a product, for the specific purposes of diagnosis, feedback, validation, or critique, and for the general purposes of improving computer systems or learning more about how users interact with systems.[15]

A usability study—often referred to as a "user test"—provides an opportunity for direct interaction between writer and reader. Audience analysis in a usability study is more than imaginative speculation. In a user test, the researcher directly observes someone using (or trying to use) a set of instructions. User testing is sometimes a face-to-face, personal meeting—or at least some type of direct observation of a reader *doing* something. User testing works best of course with functional documents—that is, with writing that asks the reader to *do* something that can be observed.

Janice Redish and Jack Selzer argue that user testing is the best method of assessing the readability of a given document.[16] In a user test, the writer presents the actual, real readers—or representatives of that group—with the document in question and then observes and evaluates their use of the document, in some cases using reading comprehension tests or protocols to describe and evaluate reader response.[17] User testing can expose the weaknesses and strengths of a document with its actual readers; thus, it is probably the most valid of the common assessments. Usability testing as a method seems particularly useful for evaluation of functional documents—that is, training and procedural documents written for users who are "reading to do" (as opposed to reading to learn). With this type of reader, usability studies can provide important information about reading behaviors, which can help in the design and editing of functional documents. It is less useful as an assessment of nonfunctional documents—that is, those documents where the reader's response may be less obvious or only indirectly observable.

A weakness of usability testing is its focus on a limited set of behaviors—usually, a few moments of a few readers—and its use of those moments as a basis for an overall judgment about the document being tested. These observations of a few moments can be useful heuristically, but we must remember that a number of important variables may not be accounted for. When real readers use computer manuals, for instance, they bring to their reading certain experiences, attitudes, expectations, and beliefs. They are coming out of a variety of discourse communities about which the usability researcher may have very little knowledge. That user brings to the usability test a range of reading experiences, a range of preconceptions about reading, about manuals, about computers, about tasks, about following directions. The person comes to the manual with an ideology, a perspective that includes attitudes toward authority. The manual reading or consulting moment, then, places the user in a political context—and the effect of that context, as well as the prior dispositions of the user, may be difficult to determine within the conventional usability parameters.

Like most methods, though, the effectiveness of usability research depends on how it is conducted. When used in the latter stages of document development, user testing serves the purpose of audience adaptation: that is, we test an already existing document to see what changes (usually editorial) we need to make. When used earlier in the development of a document, a usability study can serve a more heuristic purpose—guiding the writer's design (or invention). The usability test is a useful way for the writer to encounter the "real reader"—and to learn more about audience from her specific observations of that single real reader. The misuse of such a test would be for the writer to see the single user as representing the audience. The writer must avoid exaggerating the value of a single reader's or a few readers' responses. The more helpful and valid use of the test is to see the single reader as providing an *example* of a real reader—an example that can serve heuristically to help the writer develop a more mature understanding of audience.[18]

The Social and Organizational Perspective

Professional writing recognizes, perhaps more than other areas of writing research, the complexity of the organizational communication situation—and has long recognized that the professional writer faces a multitude of audiences.[19] There is also an increasing recognition that the commonly used models—certainly the strictly linear managerial Shannon-Weaver communication model but even the new rhetorical sense of "rhetorical situation"—are inadequate for explaining the intricacies of corporate composing.[20] We need a more *social* model to talk about composing in the workplace.[21]

Linda Driskill notes that a composing model for professional writing has to do more than simply consider purpose, audience, and role. She argues that

> a full rhetorical context should go beyond these three factors to include the relation between the organizational situation and the rhetorical situation, and the culture, values, history, and ways of thinking that determine the criteria for judging communication practice in a real organization. . . . Definitions of situation reflect the values of corporate culture, the requirements of organizational structure, the influences of the firm's external environment, and ways of thinking and arguing that derive from the individual's training, education, and professional role.[22]

Communication practices within a corporation are guided by more than simply the dictates of a single rhetorical situation. They are written in a discursive network that is influenced by "the corporate culture," as well as by documents outside the walls of the corporation. These discursive practices include activities as well as documents. As Driskill points out, this situation

> involves nonrhetorical elements: actions such as delivering goods to a particular location, manufacturing, operating machinery, or making calculations.[23]

Driskill urges researchers (and practitioners) of professional writing to develop a new sense of situation and a model providing ways to describe the network of discursive practices that influences composing.

Driskill maps a direction toward which professional writing might be moving: toward the social/organizational perspective, and toward seeing "audience" as a field of discursive practices located in social/organizational networks. Such a perspective moves professional writing research well ahead, I believe, of developments in rhetoric and composition. Professional writing research may well advance our understanding of the ways in which audience operates as a discourse community.

NOTES
Appendix I

1. As used here, the term "professional writing" refers to a broad range of workplace writing—and includes what would in a more conventional classification be considered perhaps as "technical writing," "business writing," or "advertising." The designation refers to documents such as letters, memos, internal and external reports, promotional and informational brochures, news releases, computer documentation and other types of instructions and manuals, product packaging, advertising, policy statements, and other writing produced regularly by employees at all organizational levels, whether written for customers and other companies (or for "the public" generally) or whether written internally within the organization.

2. See Michael Keene and Marilyn Barnes-Ostrander, "Audience Analysis and Adaptation," in *Research in Technical Communication: A Bibliographic Sourcebook*, ed. Michael G. Moran and Debra Journet (Westport, CT: Greenwood, 1985), 163–191; and Carl G. Wagner, "The Technical Writing Audience: A Recent Bibliography," *The Technical Writing Teacher* 14 (1987): 243–263.

3. Textbooks that stress audience factors include Leslie Olsen and Thomas N. Huckin's *Principles of Communication for Science and Technology* (New York: McGraw-Hill, 1983); Rebecca Burnett Carosso's *Technical Communication* (Belmont, CA: Wadsworth, 1986); and Paul V. Anderson's *Technical Writing: A Reader-Centered Approach* (San Diego, CA: Harcourt, 1987).

    Generally, approaches to audience in professional writing textbooks have focused on identification and analysis of—usually through a series of questions—the real reader. However, professional writing has tended to be fairly eclectic in its approaches to audience. There is also an established convention of seeing audience in terms of organizational characterizations, a treatment of audience comparable to the audience types catalogued in Book 2 of Aristotle's *Rhetoric*. Thomas Pearsall's audience characterizations have been widely used. Pearsall identifies five types of audience—layman, executive, expert, technician, and operator—and makes generalizations about the needs and perspectives of each type. See Thomas Pearsall, *Audience Analysis for Technical Writing* (Beverly Hills, CA: Glencoe, 1969).

4. The practical needs of the workplace, the constraints of organizational writing, and the heavy emphasis on functional documents would seem to discourage expressivist approaches.

5. The importance of the implied reader has been recognized by professional

writing researchers. Mary Coney has argued for the importance of the "mock reader" in "The Use of the Reader in Technical Writing," *Journal of Technical Writing and Communication* 8 (1978): 97–106. David Carson has called for more research in the area of reader psychology in an effort to narrow the gap between real and implied reader. He believes that the resemblance between fictive and actual reader should be closer—if possible, exact—in technical writing. See David L. Carson, "Audience in Technical Writing: The Need for Greater Realism in Identifying the Fictive Reader," *The Technical Writing Teacher* 7 (1979): 8–11.

Some researchers have recognized the limitations of the managerial notion of audience and of conventional audience analysis and have looked for help to the notion of the implied reader. See, for example, Charlotte Thralls et al., "Real Readers, Implied Readers, and Professional Writers: Suggested Research," *Journal of Business Communication* 25 (1988): 47–65; and James Suchan and Ron Dulek, "Toward a Better Understanding of Reader Analysis," *Journal of Business Communication* 25 (1988): 29–45.

[6] See Claude Shannon and Warren Weaver, *The Mathematical Theory of Communication* (Urbana, IL: U of Illinois P, 1949).

[7] Linda Driskill, "Understanding the Writing Context in Organizations," in *Writing in the Business Professions*, ed. Myra Kogen (Urbana, IL: NCTE & ABC, 1989), p. 128.

[8] For criticisms of readability formulas, see Avon Crismore, "Readability and the Black Box," *Indiana Reading Quarterly* 14 (1982): 14–16, 23–25; Janice C. Redish, "Understanding the Limitations of Readability Formulas," *IEEE Transactions on Professional Communication* 24.1 (1981): 46–48; Janice C. Redish and Jack Selzer, "The Place of Readability Formulas in Technical Communication," *Technical Communication* (1985): 46–52; and Jack Selzer, "What Constitutes a 'Readable' Technical Style?" in *New Essays in Technical and Scientific Communication: Research, Theory, Practice*, ed. Paul V. Anderson et al. (Farmingdale, NY: Baywood Press, 1983), 71–89.

[9] For further details, see Rebecca Pressman, *Legislative and Regulatory Progress on the Readability of Insurance Policies* (Washington, DC: Document Design Center-American Institutes for Research, 1979).

[10] See Daniel B. Felker et al., *Guidelines for Document Designers* (Washington, DC: American Institutes for Research, 1981).

[11] For cognitive/linguistic treatments of readability as applied to general composition as well as professional writing, see Joseph M. Williams, *Style: Ten Lessons in Clarity and Grace*, 3rd ed. (Glenview, IL: Scott, Foresman, 1988); William Vande Kopple, *Clear and Coherent Prose: A Functional Approach* (Glenview, IL: Scott, Foresman, 1989); Thomas N. Huckin, "A Cognitive Approach to Readability," in *New Essays in Technical Communication: Research, Theory, Practice*, ed. Paul V. Anderson et al. (Farmingdale, NY: Baywood Press, 1983), 90–108; and Olsen and Huckin, "Making Your Writing Readable," in *Principles of Communication for Science and Technology*.

[12] Huckin, "Cognitive Approach," pp. 92–93.

[13] See Huckin, "Cognitive Approach," p. 101 for a list of other guidelines for producing readable prose.

[14] Much has been written in professional writing about "audience adaptation." While audience analysis is something the writer applies to the real reader, audience adaptation is something the writer does to the text—that is, adapt it for and make it more readable to the real reader. See Paul V. Anderson, *Teaching Technical Writing: Teaching Audience Analysis and Adaptation* (Bloomington, MN: Association of Teachers of Technical Writing, 1980).

[15] Patricia A. Sullivan, *Examining the Usability of Documentation*, unpublished manuscript, 1990.

[16] See Redish and Selzer, "The Place of Readability Formulas."

[17] See, for example, Janice C. Redish, Daniel B. Felker, and A. Rose, "Evaluating the Effects of Document Design Principles," *Information Design Journal* 2 (1981): 236–243.

[18] See Patricia A. Sullivan and James E. Porter, "User Testing: The Heuristic Advantages at the Draft Stage," *Technical Communication* 37 (1990): 78–80.

[19] J. C. Mathes and Dwight Stevenson provide an extensive discussion of the many audience levels involved in a technical communication, of the routes a technical document may travel, and of the different purposes it may serve. Their treatment is a relatively early recognition of the presence of multiple audiences, but in a sense it also presents an early vision of audience as community (in this case the organization). See J. C. Mathes and Dwight W. Stevenson, *Designing Technical Reports: Writing for Audiences in Organizations* (Indianapolis, IN: Bobbs-Merrill, 1976). See also L. Lee Forsberg, "Who's Out There Anyway? Bringing Awareness of Multiple Audiences Into the Business-Writing Class," *Iowa State Journal of Business and Technical Communication* 1 (1987): 45–69; Rachel Spilka, "Interacting with Multiple Readers: A Significant Component of Document Design in Corporate Environments," *Technical Communication* 36 (1989): 368–372; Rachel Spilka, "Orality and Literacy in the Workplace: Process- and Text-Based Strategies for Multiple-Audience Adaptation," *Journal of Business and Technical Communication* 4 (1990): 44–67; and Rachel Spilka, "Studying Writer-Reader Interactions in the Workplace," *The Technical Writing Teacher* 15 (1988): 208–221.

[20] See Driskill.

[21] See Lester Faigley, "Nonacademic Writing: The Social Perspective," in *Writing in Nonacademic Settings*, ed. Lee Odell and Dixie Goswami (New York: Guilford, 1985).

[22] Driskill, pp. 142, 138.

[23] Driskill, p. 138.

Teaching a Community View of Audience

Discourse community may be a somewhat nebulous concept, but we can partially locate discourse communities in what I am calling "forums." One pedagogical strategy for learning more about the discourse community is "forum analysis"—which is a type of audience analysis, but different from the conventional real-reader heuristics. Forum analysis is a kind of textual analysis that aims to uncover the characterizing *ethos* of a particular discourse community.

Conventional audience heuristics generally focus on analyzing the audience "in itself." (See Figure 1 for a sample audience analysis heuristic.) Our representative heuristic, taken from *Four Worlds of Writing*, is actually a much-better-than-typical sample.[1] In fact, this audience heuristic is perhaps the most developed strategy for considering audience to be found in any composition textbook. (We have to remember that most composition texts and handbooks, though they advise the writer to "consider" audience, do no more than that. Very few provide any kind of audience heuristic, much less one as developed as our sample.)

This sample represents an advance from the typical treatments of audience, first in providing a heuristic at all, and second in prompting the writer to consider relational roles (in items 5 and 6). At the same time, the heuristic focuses on the audience as a set of real readers existing apart from and prior to the discourse (see, for example, items 2 and 3). Where is the writer to find this audience or to verify responses to these prompts? The guide encourages the writer to collect her thoughts to build an imaginative construct of the audience—but the construct is likely to be faulty or incomplete if the writer has limited prior experience with the audience. (See Chapter 1 on the problem of locating audiences.)

Forum analysis, by contrast, focuses the writer's attention on discursive practices rather than imagined "real readers." (See Figure 2 for a sample forum analysis heuristic.[2]) Forum analysis is an inquiry procedure that relies on more than merely imaginative speculation. To respond to the prompts in a forum analysis the writer must examine discourse (both oral and written) produced by the forum under consideration. In other words, the writer must collect samples and do some research to plan how her discourse will interrelate with those discursive practices of the community. Forum analysis maps a strategy for the writer to become a contributing voice within the community—and so perhaps is a strategy for a long-term commitment rather than a momentary one.

There is certainly some overlap between audience analysis and forum analysis. Forum analysis, however, has several distinct features. First, forum analysis has a different emphasis; it calls attention to audiences as themselves primarily speakers and writers of discourse (not just silent, passive receptors of the writer's message). Forum analysis begins by casting the audience in the role of participant in a social dialogue. Forum analysis encourages the writer to begin analysis by *listening* to what the audience has to say, to determine why they say it, how they say it, and to whom they say it. Thus, forum analysis establishes an altogether different relational role between writer and reader. The writer learns *from*, not just *about*, the audience.

The prompts under "Background" encourage the writer to explore the historical and political background of the forum under investigation. Borrowing from Douglas Park's terminology, it asks the writer to consider what situation brings this audience together in the first place.[3] How did this forum come to be? Why does it exist? How does it define itself? Also, situation here is defined differently from the conventional rhetorical situation. The situation here is not the occasion provided by the writer's single text (forum analysis does not privilege the lone text) but rather the entire field of discursive practice with which the writer's lone text will establish some kind of interrelationship.

Several examples will serve to demonstrate how forum analysis works in practice. (All three samples were written by seniors at Purdue University enrolled in a professional writing class taught during the Fall 1988 semester. I should add that I regard all three samples as *excellent*, in that all three writers demonstrate a fairly advanced understanding of the forums they are investigating.)

Sample 1 was written by Kent, who was editor of his residence hall newsletter, *The Clarion*. Kent did a forum analysis for his publication in an effort to understand better the organizational context in which his publication functioned. Notice how his discussion starts out to be an analysis of a forum but turns into a consideration of organizational character. His stated purpose is to do a "forum analysis of *The Clarion*," yet his analysis begins with a discussion of the history and organization of the residence hall itself, Cary Quadrangle. A forum may function within a larger organization—and both contribute to and develop out of the character of that organization. The forum is *not* the same as the discourse community, of course, but it does show a trace of the community's activities.

In effect, Kent does an archaeological analysis of his forum in an attempt to understand something about the "grid" (in Foucault's terms, *dispositif*) which supports that community. He attempts to understand "Cary Quadrangle." What is Cary Quadrangle? Most obviously, it is a building—a residence hall, to be exact. More importantly in terms of rhetorical understanding, it represents an *ethos*, a collected set of beliefs, a campus identity. (Just as "Washington" within the American episteme represents more than just a geographical place; it represents an entire set of associations, attitudes, values.) Where does this identity come from? From discourse. The attitudes, beliefs, positions are developed over a period of time through discourse within and about the Quadrangle—perhaps largely through informal oral discourse ("table talk") that becomes formalized and monumentalized through repetition (e.g.,in newsletters).

The newsletter also has the potential to influence, as well as reflect, the *ethos*, as Kent's discussion of the history of the newsletter suggests. At one point, he says, the newsletter served a "rah-rah" function; it served patriotically to stimulate support and pride in the organization. As Kent comments, in the late 1950s and 1960s pride in Cary was developed out of an abstract sense of "duty": one was loyal to Cary and took pride in it because it was one's residence hall; one had an obligation to be loyal to it. Now, says Kent, we cannot appeal to an abstracted sense of duty. Rather, efforts to build unity must be predicated on a sense of pride that is tied not to an abstract sense of obligation and duty but to a more practical appeal to concrete benefits: we should be loyal to Cary because it offers us more than other residence halls or fraternities. In this portion of his analysis, Kent achieves a kind of historical insight, not only about the forum but about the discourse community as well. In part, Kent articulates how arguments are now made within this forum (compared to how they used to be developed). This difference in "argumentative technique" bespeaks a basic epistemological shift. It may be the same newsletter—but the discursive field has certainly changed.

The unspoken "opposition" in Kent's analysis is other halls and fraternities: Cary is for those males who do not like what they see as the trivial "clubbiness" and the "stupid regulations" of fraternities. Thus, the newsletter also serves to create a separate identity for Cary: it is a residence hall whose character offers something better than the fraternities. Forums are always expressions of value. The aim of a forum analysis is, partly, to uncover the characterizing *ethos* as well as the values that give the community its identity.

Doug's project is to write a brochure describing the Purdue University honors program (see Sample 2). An "honors program" is a concept specific to any university but not to any particular discipline within the university. Such a forum certainly cuts across disciplinary lines. What is it that characterizes "the honors program"? We might see its chief feature as that of elitism—and you can attach both negative and positive connotations to that term. Honors programs exist to create a separate identity, for both faculty and students, an identity of separateness that is founded on a real or imagined academic and intellectual superiority. This *ethos* can be characterized in terms of a certain language, a certain appeal to central beliefs: the appeal to high culture, for example, or to the notion of a rigorous academic curriculum that is "higher than" what normally goes on.

To write an honors brochure, a writer must be in tune with this *ethos*, which means, in part, being aware of the conventions of the honors brochure (which the writer can partly glean by studying honors brochures from various universities). The writer must be aware of the audience presuppositions, beliefs, attitudes, and values. But more important than knowing who the real audience is, the writer must have a sense of the tradition of the honors concept. Conventional audience analysis will be of very little help to the writer here. No matter who the real readers may be, the document needs to be written with a sense of the honors ethos. The writer must be reasonably consistent with an ethos that the readers will adopt, in a sense being "true" to a traditional role more than directing the discussion at real readers. (Here is a context where an *ethos* of disdain may be the preferred strategy.) There is no effective method for user testing a document like an honors brochure—or a short story. Forum analysis is particularly well suited to such contexts because forum analysis takes a historical perspective, looking to uncover the characterizing episteme of a community.

Cassie's project was to produce a set of programs for the Purdue University swim team (see Sample 3). The background section of her forum analysis indicates that she has a very good grasp of the role her document will play in providing an identity for the team and in developing and maintaining a relationship between the swim team and the home boosters, such as Purdue students and faculty, alumni, and parents and friends. As Cassie points out, the members of this forum are diverse, they have many roles. But her document need only address them in one particular role. There is a unifying factor for this community, as she says, "An interest in swimming competition." Thus a diverse group of readers assembles within this forum for a particular purpose and with particular needs and interests.

Cassie recognizes several purposes for her document within this forum. First, she knows sports programs exist to inform the public, but she is also attempting to promote the program more than was done in the past, to instill a greater sense of identity (and perhaps loyalty as well). She plans to expand the format of the programs. Thus, though Cassie is writing *within* the constraints of the discourse community, she is also contributing to its growth and well being. In other sections of her analysis, she recognizes the various interest groups the program represents (such as coaches, players, media advisors). There are a variety of interests and concerns— and all these groups will, in a sense, collaborate on the writing of the document. Even though Cassie is, technically speaking, the writer, she writes under advice and with the consent of a network of concerns. She ghostwrites for a community.

Her analysis considers conventional and formal features of the final document. She feels that there should be some continuity between her programs and past team programs, so she plans to keep some familiar material and formatting. At the same time, she will attempt to improve the design somewhat (e.g., by using laser technology) and to apply her talents as a graphics artist to improve the "look" of the programs.

All three of these writers show an awareness of how their planned discourses will fit into a network of discursive practices. All three writers begin by looking at an immediate document—a residence hall newsletter, an honors progrom program brochure, a swimming meet program—but the forum analysis encourages them to imagine that document, and to plan for composing it, within a larger framework of concerns. To think of audience only as the receivers of these documents is not ultimately going to be very helpful to any of these writers. Rather, seeing their documents as existing in a field of already established practices helps them develop some concrete strategies for producing the documents.

Notice that Doug and Cassie in particular end by focusing on the design of their documents. Once they understand something about their respective discourse communities, they can make design decisions based on principles other than generic ones. The documents they are planning will be partly reliant on, but also partly independent of, their predecessors. Cassie, for instance, establishes as a rhetorical value that she will maintain some continuity with previous programs: she applies ideas from her graphic arts background—but applies them with a consciousness of community constraints. All three writers notice the constraints. At the same time, they exercise a creativity within those constraints—bringing perspectives from other communities, for instance. These writers map out a territory in the existing discourse network—and indeed all successful writers do—planning their writing with an awareness of the discursive field they are entering.

The value of forum analysis is not so much in the particular questions asked. (In fact, I can imagine alternate strategies for conducting forum analysis.) Rather, its value is in the perspective it takes toward audience. I believe we need to develop audience heuristics that begin by placing the writer and audience on a different relational footing altogether: that begin by guiding the writer toward interaction with (not control over) audience.

NOTES
Apppendix II

[1] Janice M. Lauer, Gene Montague, Andrea Lunsford, and Janet Emig, *Four Worlds of Writing*, 2nd ed. (New York: Harper & Row, 1985). The third edition of *Four Worlds* includes material that asks student writers to consider the writing communities they participate in.

[2] This forum analysis heuristic appears as an Appendix in James E. Porter, "Intertextuality and the Discourse Community," *Rhetoric Review* 5 (1986), pp. 46–47.

[3] See Douglas B. Park, "Analyzing Audiences," *College Composition and Communication* 37 (1986): 478–488.

FIGURE 1. Audience Analysis Heuristic

Audience Guide

1. State your audience and the reasons for choosing it.
2. Analyze the audience in itself.
   a. Identify the levels and types of experiences that your audience has had (cultural, recreational, educational, and so on).
      • What is the median level of education in your audience?
      • Are most of your audience males or females?
      • What is the median age of your audience?
      • Is there anything special about your audience that will affect their image of you and themselves (racial, cultural, recreational, occupational, etc.)?
   b. Identify the hierarchy of values that your audience holds (money, power, friendship, security, intellectual growth).
3. Analyze the audience in relation to the subject.
   a. Identify the knowledge and opinion your audience holds on the subject.
   b. Determine how strongly your audience holds those views.
   c. Assess how willing your audience is to act on its opinion—if acting is appropriate.
4. In light of the information you gained above, determine the specific role your audience will play.
5. Repeat steps 2 and 3, but this time analyze only the *specific* role you want the audience to play.
   a. Determine what levels and types of experience fit the role your audience will play.
   b. Identify the values that fit that role.
   c. Determine what opinion you want your audience to hold in that role, how strongly you want the audience to hold it, and whether you want the audience to act on it.
6. Determine your voice and the *relational* role you want your audience to play. State why you have chosen that relationship.

Quoted with permission from Janice M. Lauer et al., *Four Worlds of Writing*, 2nd ed. New York: Harper and Row, 1985, pp. 47–48.

FIGURE 2.   Forum Analysis Heuristic*

Forum Analysis

———— *Background* ————

— Identify the forum by name and organizational affiliation.
— Is there an expressed belief, editorial policy, philosophy? What purpose does the forum serve? Why does it exist?
— What is the disciplinary orientation?
— How large is the forum? Who are its members? Its leaders? Its readership?
— In what manner does the forum assemble (e.g., newsletter, journal, conference, weekly meeting)? How frequently?
— What is the origin of the forum? Why did it come into existence? What is its history? Its political background? Its traditions?
— What reputation does the forum have among its own members? How is it regarded by others?

———— *Discourse Conventions* ————

Who Speaks/Writes?
— Who is granted status as speaker/writer? Who decides who speaks/writes in the forum? By what criteria are speakers/writers selected?
— What kind of people speak/write in this forum? Credentials? Disciplinary orientation? Academic or professional background?
— Who are the important figures in this forum? Whose work or experience is most frequently cited?
— What are the important sources cited in the forum? What key works, events, experiences is it assumed members of the forum know?

To Whom Do They Speak/Write?
— Who is addressed in the forum? What are the characteristics of the assumed audience?
— What are the audience's needs assumed to be? To what use(s) is the audience expected to put the information?
— What is the audience's background assumed to be? Level of proficiency, experience, and knowledge of subject matter? Credentials?
— What are the beliefs, attitudes, values, prejudices of the addressed audience?

What Do They Speak/Write About?
— What topics or issues does the forum consider? What are allowable subjects? What topics are valued?
— What methodology or methodologies are accepted? Which theoretical approaches are preferred: deduction (theoretical argumentation) or induction (evidence)?
— What constitutes "validity," "evidence," and "proof" in the forum (e.g., personal experience/observation, testing and measurement, theoretical or statistical analysis)?

How Do They Say/Write It?

    Form
- What types of discourse does the forum admit (e.g., articles, reviews, speeches, poems)? How long are the discourses?
- What are the dominant modes of organization?
- What formatting conventions are present: headings, tables and graphs, illustrations, abstracts?

    Style
- What documentation form(s) is used?
- Syntactic characteristics?
- Technical or specialized jargon? Abbreviations?
- Tone? What stance do writers/speakers take relative to audience?
- Manuscript mechanics?

Other Considerations?

*Quoted with permission from James E. Porter, "Intertextuality and the Discourse Community," *Rhetoric Review* 5 (1986), pp. 46–47.

SAMPLE 1.   Forum Analysis of *The Clarion*

TO: Professor James Porter, English 515 Instructor
FROM: Kent, English 515 Student
DATE: November 10, 1988
SUBJECT: Forum Analysis of *The Clarion*: Background and Discourse Conventions

----

——— *Background* ———

History. Cary Quadrangle is the largest residence hall at Purdue, and is the largest all-male residence hall in the country. The 1500 men of Cary represent a broad crosssection of Purdue—in both major and semester classification. *The Clarion*, the official newspaper of and for the residents of Cary Quadrangle, was founded in 1938. This newspaper has chronicled the happenings of the 1500 men who have lived in Cary for each of its 50 years, and for most of its history has been an important unifying voice for Cary residents.

The newspaper expresses the "editorial policy," if you will, of the residence hall. It is really more of a philosophy: open communication to create an awareness of what Cary can offer to its residents, as well as what it means to be a resident in Cary—the traditions, the fraternity, and the opportunities.

Organization. The formal organization for the forum has four parts. The first is the Cary student government. The government is subdivided into the executive and unit councils. The executive council is somewhat analogous to a cabinet and is composed of the top officers (president, vice-president, secretary, treasurer), unit presidents (eight total), and sub-club presidents (*The Clarion*, WCCR [radio station], go-kart club, etc.). This body makes broad policy decisions and provides the top-level student leadership. The unit council is the main legislative body of Cary, and is composed of the unit presidents, representatives, and the freshman council members. Both of the councils hold weekly meetings.

The second part of the forum organization is the counseling staff. These older students live on each floor, maintaining discipline and helping the residents with academic and social issues. These counselors are opinion leaders for the floors, and are paid employees of Purdue University. The counselors receive almost daily communication from the management, and have occasional meetings.

The third part of the forum organization is the management of Cary. This includes the manager, assistant managers, the food service, and maintenance. These people are the backbone of Cary, and have considerable power to ensure things flow smoothly every day—whether it be disciplinary action or scheduling various events. The management has weekly meetings with the residence hall administration.

The fourth and largest part of the forum organization is the student population of Cary. This majority of this group are freshmen, new to Cary and Purdue. Their voices are heard mainly indirectly through the unit and executive councils, along with counselor reports and feedback. Floors hold occasional, informal meetings, usually arranged by the counselors.

Reputation/Image. Cary has a lot of pride in itself, especially this year, as it is celebrating its 60th anniversary. Cary has long been recognized as the residence hall with the most activities and services for students. It has gained, in the past ten years or so, the reputation as a freshman dorm, and therefore perhaps a little more wild than the norm. The current management and government has been working to overcome that image and has been fairly successful. *The Clarion* is playing a major role in projecting an image of a mature, fun place to live, and has helped to further the goal of unity among the residents.

Discourse Conventions

Who Speaks/Writes? Because Cary is a college residence hall, some of the normal forum analysis criteria for technical or scientific organizations need to be modified. If the forum is thought of as the four-part organization described above, then it can be fairly easily seen that many people can speak or write in it. No one really needs "permission" to communicate. For example, students can post notices with items for sale on each unit's bulletin boards freely. In other words, lots of speaking and writing occurs every day, most of it informal. Members of each of the parts communicate with each other continuously.

Most of the few formal communications originate from the management in the front office—whether it be the day's dining room table notices, instructions for the counseling staff, or a letter from the manager to another unit of the university. The manager holds the most authority when speaking or writing, perhaps—yet it is a two-edged sword. If he over-emphasizes his importance/authority, his word will be largely ignored by the residents. In other words, he has to communicate tactfully at all times and project a willingness to work with people, not simply tell them what to do.

The Clarion has a unique role. It is, simultaneously, the voice of the students and the management. Any student is welcome to write articles and be heard through *The Clarion,* and the management often suggests articles and occasionally writes its own. The people writing for the paper don't have as much authority as the office personnel, but they do have a voice that makes a difference.

The management as a whole references past procedures and especially university policy when making formal announcements or decisions. It is assumed that people understand the parts of Cary (the various buildings and units) in all internal communications, and that the source for the communication need only briefly be identified (memo format) or even not at all (in the case of the table notices). The same is true in the paper—we assume that people reading it, for the most part, understand the environment about which it speaks. Recent campus and Cary events are categories of assumed knowledge, as well as well-known cultural events or icons.

To Whom Do They Speak/Write? The largest part of the discourse from the forum is directed at the residents of the hall. This audience, as mentioned previously, is an all-male, college student population, although of various levels of knowledge about Purdue. The residents all have different interests, as any collection of people roughly the same age would, but the majority of them do share some common broad interests: automobiles, music, sports, and news about the place they live.

This group has a need, as recognized by management and *The Clarion* staff, to know about the happenings in Cary Quad. With 1500 residents divided up into five buildings, it's pretty easy to lose touch (or never learn about) particular events and people. Because Cary has over one-half new freshmen each fall, the audience's proficiency with the discourse environment begins low and rises as the year moves on.

The upperclassmen who stay on at Cary are about the only people who have definable attitudes about issues. The freshmen really spend most of their first year forming and then trying out conceptual frameworks for understanding Purdue (i.e. College Life). The upperclassmen generally are prejudiced against fraternity life—if they liked it, they would be living in such an environment. Also, the upperclassmen are generally busy people, and bothered by things that get in their way ("stupid" regulations and inconsiderate neighbors, for example).

What Do They Speak/Write About? The various elements of the forum generate a wide variety of discourse. Nothing is really a prohibited topic, although each of the various "discourse vehicles" has its own certain topical limits. The management usually focuses on administrative issues, policy announcements, and disciplinary actions. The student government focuses on legislative and activity issues, the counselors on awareness and disciplinary issues, and the students on general communication.

The Clarion, by sitting in the middle of all of these elements, can accept all of these forms as valid, and does. Each of these categories maps into a part of the paper, whether it be a particular theme, column, strategy, or picture. Each of the kinds of discourse, in other words, is valuable in its own way, as long as it is "newsworthy" and relatively timely.

This forum departs from the careful scientific standards of deduction vs. induction and doesn't have formal definitions for validity, evidence, or proof. Rather, the community is continuously changing from year to year, and accepts something as valid or insightful from a source that might once would have been considered unrealible. For example, the various student governments have had different amounts of success in communicating with the residents over the years. Some years the government seems to really be in tune with the students, yet other years it seems to make rules and host events that the residents think are inappropriate (i.e., not fun) and therefore largely ignored.

How Do They Write/Say It?—Form. The Cary forum admits many types of discourse, although most of the important communication is written. The entire forum is assembled only once a year, so clear written communication is a necessity. The main types of written discourse are:

- Memos from the office to students, counselors, and people outside the forum
- Table notices
- *The Clarion*

The Clarion is definitely the most formal, traditional type of discourse. It is also the longest, at 6–8 pages per issue, while the other two types are generally limited to one page. For the newspaper, the dominant organization is traditional newspaper style, with the major stories on the front page, the editorials on page two, the "newsy" stories on page three, etc.

The Clarion is really a cross between a newspaper and a newsletter. As such, people are emphasized as well as stories, and interesting tables and charts are welcome to add a creative, community feeling to the publication. Otherwise, the paper follows traditional newspaper heading, spacing, and presentation standards.

How Do They Write/Say It?—Style. As Cary follows a modified newspaper form, many of the things associated with this particular style are also present. The writing style is very "newsy" on the general news stories, but there is a very relaxed style for the features. This style projects the familiarity between the writer and the reader, to break down any barriers and get the reader involved (not necessarily agreeing, just actively reading and thinking). Technical jargon really isn't present in *The Clarion*, as it is a general-focus publication, although some jargon is used in the album and automobile columns to give them flavor and credibility with the readers. Abbreviations are kept to a minimum, although ones for Purdue/Cary organizations are used often since they are usually in common usage.

The tone of the paper is friendly and even conspiratorial at times (the Quad against the world, etc.). The staff understands that the paper is for, about, and by the residents, so it must be on their level. The writer is often a partner with the reader, and very seldom a cold, removed entity, except for the major news stories, which remain objective. Even the unit news has a light tone to keep it from being just a boring statement of facts and activities.

The conventions for the paper have changed down through the years. In the 1950's and 60's, the paper was much more formal (although inconsistently so), and seems to have been more of a propaganda tool for the management and university (Rah-rah Cary, Go Purdue, etc). The staff feels that style is very inappropriate considering the average reader today seems to be much more aware of subtle propaganda. This style would end up being very insulting—and the paper would be an unread failure.

——— *Conclusions* ———

I have worked this year with the Cary management and government to develop an exciting, informative publication that represents the Cary forum. The staff's goal is to provide news that is interesting and relevant to Cary residents. We try to cover news that other area newspapers don't, or emphasize certain topics that the others won't. Cary, many people feel, is a much closer organization this year. I would hope that *The Clarion* had a lot to do with this close, almost family, atmosphere by making people aware of their fellow "Quad Dogs," activities, and opportunities. Every large forum needs a publication to hold it together, and the newspaper tries to fulfill this role.

SAMPLE 2.   Forum Analysis of Purdue Honors Program

TO: Professor James Porter
FROM: Doug
DATE: November 8, 1988
SUBJECT: *Forum Analysis for Honors Program Brochure*

On October 3, 1988 I began designing an informational/promotional brochure for the Purdue Honors Program. Assigned by the Director of Honors, Dr. Clayton D. Lein, to create the brochure, I have focused on departmental needs and audience interests while writing and editing the brochure's text. I will have completed three variations of the brochure by December 12, 1988, the date on which I will provide Dr. Lein with a final brochure design. This forum analysis will detail the context of the project, my audience analysis, the organizational constraints under which I worked, and the design of the actual brochure.

——— *Honors Program Needs* ———

Because the Purdue University HSSE Honors Program has grown by almost 200% in the past few years, the new director, Dr. Lein believed that the Program needed at least one document on which to publicize the Honors Program and to inform interested audiences about what the Program means. Since I had approached him about designing some publications, Dr. Lein asked me to create a general, all-purpose brochure similar to, but more imaginative than, brochures from the Honors Programs of other Big Ten schools. Currently no single form of Honors documentation exists—only semester newsletters and personal letters from the Honors Office. Dr. Lein decided that for the Program to continue its maturation, he would need to offer a campus-wide brochure.

Although this main brochure, including all three variations, will be used primarily for bargaining purposes, I am supposed to treat it as a final, print-ready document. Since Dr. Lein will not be able to secure funding from the HSSE Directors until the summer of 1989, the brochure will not be published before the fall semester next year. At that time, copies would be sent to incoming freshmen (and their parents) who meet the HSSE requirements for academically gifted students. Most of these students would be Dean's Freshman Scholars. Not all accepted freshmen would receive a copy of the brochure unless they requested one. Some brochures would also be distributed throughout the normal distribution sites across the Purdue campus.

——— *Audience Analysis* ———

Because the brochure must serve a variety of purposes, it must be general enough to address a number of audiences, yet still be imaginative enough to draw interest from a wide array of readers. Because the most affected audience is the incoming freshmen, I have worked on designing the text to answer questions a student might have concerning the Honors Program and what it stands for. Because these students are obviously intelligent, the brochure had to be written for an educated audience. Although the text reads easily, I rarely made it simple, fearing a too-friendly tone would alienate the academic audience Dr. Lein suggested I appeal to. On the other hand, I could not alienate the parents of the students since they often encourage their sons and daughters to pursue the stronger academic path.

Another audience I had to consider was the on-campus students who had not received information about the Honors Program but wanted to join. According to Dr. Lein, he has almost fifty requests for information every semester. With the general brochure, he could satisfy these students quickly and easily. Honors students themselves could benefit from an informative brochure since they also need to learn about the requirements and benefits the Honors Program offers.

Organizational Constraints

One of the major organizational constraints governing my brochure design was that I had to produce a clean, sharp academic image which relied solely on text design and appropriate wording. Although I focused on three variations based on sophistication of graphics, I knew that the best two copies would probably be used only as bargaining tools to obtain funding for the least expensive design. I have not had to consider cost restraints in my work, but I have attempted to limit my design to the point that it would have no trouble passing through the standards of the HSSE office and the university.

Time constraints have played a role as well since I have had to work around the schedules of the Honors Director, numerous Honors students and instructors, and university photographers. Because these people have aided me by providing their input to my project, I do not want to pressure them to work hurriedly. I will, nonetheless, have a set of three camera-ready brochures by December 12.

Perhaps the most difficult constraint to follow was Dr. Lein's request that I be as creative and imaginative as I wanted. Although this prompted me to work with virtually no constraint, it did pressure me to explore many types of text design and page layout. Since the brochure has to represent an Honors Program full of academic prestige, I could not design a wildly creative brochure without alienating the audiences. The major decisions on these issues affected primarily the tone of my brochure and the sections of text included within it.

Actual Brochure Design

The manner in which I approached the design of my brochure enabled me to study the situation in depth immediately before I had to begin working. My initial planning was to interview Dr. Lein about the Honors Program needs and about what he needed from me as a writing specialist. Knowing the direction in which he wanted to steer the publication, I researched brochures from over fifty colleges, including many from Purdue. I then researched the Purdue Honors Program as thoroughly as I could in order to view any existing publications. Because there was only one page of published material other than newsletters, I realized that I needed to draw the useful material from the newsletters or find it through primary research.

After I had researched the situation thoroughly, I decided that the best way to present the Honors Program was through a relatively short (approximately ten to 12 pages) brochure in a 7 1/2 inches by 3 1/2 inches format. Most college texts are of this general size, and Purdue University often employs a similar style in its publications. In order for the text to appear neat and clear, I needed to limit the columns to one per page in a ten-point Times font, unjustified to improve readability. The headings (which are basically questions the audience might ask the Honors Office) are 14-point italicized Times. The brochure's cover would be a thick linen type with an embossed seal of Purdue and the wording, "The Honors Program At Purdue University" in an italicized 18-point Palatino font.

The reason I decided to prepare the brochure in such a way is that I needed a familiar mode of providing information. It is designed to meet the audience needs by answering its own questions, section by section. To insure the Director's voice throughout, I have submitted my work for him to edit, and I have asked him to write a short introductory "letter" which will appear at the beginning of the brochure. By including Dr. Lein's voice, I can effectively address some of the issues that concern him.

To try to personalize the brochure and work on the theme of the total Honors Experience, I have included photographs and statements from three students and three instructors active in the Honors Program. Because of their input, I believe the brochure will take on a more personal approach while still providing the information that the Honors Program is a diverse, flexible program. The Director, student, and instructor comments are the only pieces of text I have not written, except for one section concerning Honors Program requirements which I selected from the earliest publication.

The actual sections include some statistics/findings from the Honors Office, but overall, the voice and tone are consistent throughout the entire publication. The tone itself is friendly, yet hardly cute or colloquial, relying instead on an educated audience reading for information rather than out of curiousity. This will follow with other Honors announcements and writings—formal yet reader-oriented.

Conclusion

Because the scope of the audience is virtually unknown at this time, the brochure might be too limited, yet it must be until the Honors Office can evaluate its needs more effectively. Whatever the case, the brochure is conservative enough to pass university standards and to represent the Honors Program without remaining a basic, boring publication.

SAMPLE 3.   Forum Analysis of Purdue Swimming Program

Cassie
11/7/88
English 515

Forum Analysis: Purdue Swimming Programs

─────── *Background* ───────

Athletic programs are traditionally made available to the public, free of charge, at all competitions held at Purdue University. Programs usually list the home team's rosters and competitive schedules and sometimes include the visiting team's roster as well. Programs are informative and are designed to present spectators of athletic competitions with information—about the competitor's athletic events and awards, their class in school, and their hometown. Information about the team's schedule and upcoming competitions is also presented.

The forum includes all spectators of Purdue swim meets held either at Purdue or another *home* facility, i.e. the IUPUI Natatorium in Indianapolis. Readers include swimmers either affiliated with Purdue or any other competitive group (including recruits visiting the university), coaches of the same, parents and relatives of the competitors, alumni, members of the Purdue athletic department or office of sports information and any other fans attending a competition. The forum is diverse in all aspects except the one unifying factor—an interest in swimming competition.

Spectators assemble for Purdue swimming competitions at Lambert Field-house in West Lafayette, IN, and other locations around the Midwest for away meets. There are approximately 15 competitions annually. Between 5–8 of these are usually at Purdue where programs are made available.

In the past, programs were created to inform the public about the team members, coaching staff and competitive schedule of the Purdue swimming teams. Recently, there has been an increased concern with promoting the team's achievements and goals and publicizing the accomplishments of its members. The coaches voiced an interest in expanding both the purpose and design of the programs, from straightforward information giving and listings, to a format which would also entertain and publicize. It was recommended that the new programs take advantage of some of the strengths of the team's media guides, including writing and a more extensive use of graphics.

Media guides are another form of publication created by Purdue's office of sports information to promote the athletic teams. These guides are substantially longer and contain complete team histories, background information about Purdue University, team schedules, and photographs and personal information about each swimmer and the coaches. Expanding the programs to include more extensive use of writing and graphics similar to the media guides was one idea for improving the new swimming programs.

———— *Discourse Conventions* ————

Who Speaks/Writes?
   Purdue's office of sports information is responsible for creating and distributing the programs and media guides for all athletic teams at Purdue. In the past, student interns of this office have been responsible for the work, but upon the coaches request and permission by Al Schenoe of the sports information office, special permission was granted for a Purdue student to create this year's programs.

To Whom Do They Speak/Write?
   Spectators of Purdue's swim meets are addressed in the forum. This includes people of all ages, interests and professions. Their unifying characteristics are an interest in swimming in general, and in the Purdue athletes and coaches in specific. The readers of the programs want to know about the athletes they are watching and the coaches who train them. They are interested in the personalities, interests and habits of the competitors, and the philosophies and practices of the coaches behind the scenes.
   The spectators gather to watch athletes they are familiar with compete against athletes from other teams. They are fans, either of Purdue swimmers, or a visiting team, and have at least a general understanding of the sport of swimming. The programs serve as a source of information to the fans and make them more familiar with the athletes they are watching. Fans tend to watch those athletes they know or recognize. Programs help generate interest in the athletes and excitement about the team's goals and achievements by introducing them to the public.

What Do They Speak/Write About?
   This year's programs include a variety of information in addition to the rosters and team schedule that traditionally make up the bulk of an athletic program. Article topics are generated by the writer and reviewed by the coaching staff. Those that promote the goals of the team are researched and written to be included in the programs. The articles are based on interviews of athletic department staff, coaches, athletes and anyone who might otherwise become associated with the activities of the swimming team. They are given credibility with the use of direct quotes.
   Topics that might be included in the programs included information about upcoming competitions—swimmers to watch, good races to look for, and directions to away facilities. Special activities of the team, such as summer training, clinics for diving and stretching, and the three-week Christmas training trip. Other articles spotlight coaches and/or athletes that are outstanding for a particular reason, i.e. Purdue's new diving coach, the team captains, senior members of the team, etc. All the articles are written to promote the coaches' philosophies and the goals of the team.

How Do They Say/Write It?
   Articles, graphics and listed information make up the content of the swimming programs. The space allotted to these elements varies according to their importance and the overall visual impact of the publication. In the past, the programs were simply information listed into blocks, but attempts are being made to vary the format and content of the programs so they will be more interesting and visually effective. Headlines, photographs, illustrations and

rules are now being used to format the programs more effectively although previously few or no graphics were included in the program's main body.

Stories in the first programs this year were written as feature articles in basic journalistic style and attributed quotes were used to document them. The language used in the programs doesn't include much technical jargon and is easily understood by the audience. For the most part, the readers are familiar with the sport of swimming and somewhat familiar with at least a few of the competitors and coaches. Light in tone, the articles were written by a friend and equal of reader/spectator, to inform him about what goes on behind the scenes, at practices and school, not just at the meets. The programs were intended to generate interest in the personalities and philosophies of the athletes and coaches, and to publicize and promote the team in as entertaining a way as possible.

Other Considerations

The form of the athletic programs is being experimented with because the traditional purpose, subject matter and format of the publication is being expanded to meet new needs. For this reason, the range of material included, the ideas expressed and the way they are presented are not yet permanently established. Eager to explore the potential uses of this publication, the coaching staff is investigating the possible effects it may have in generating interest and enthusiasm for their program. They welcome experimentation with content, form and style in order to determine the format which is most effective at creating positive publicity and participation by their fans.

Bibliographies of Audience

Ede, Lisa. "Audience: An Introduction to Research." *College Composition and Communication* 35 (1984): 140–154.

Hillocks, George, Jr., with Larry Johannessen, "Audience." *Research on Written Composition: New Directions for Teaching*. Urbana, IL: NCRE and ERIC/RCS, 1986. 84–91.

Keene, Michael, and Marilyn Barnes-Ostrander. "Audience Analysis and Adaptation." *Research in Technical Communication: A Bibliographic Sourcebook*. Ed. Michael G. Moran and Debra Journet. Westport, CT: Greenwood, 1985. 163–191.

Wagner, Carl G. "The Technical Writing Audience: A Recent Bibliography." *The Technical Writing Teacher* 14 (1987): 243–263.

Young, Richard. "Recent Developments in Rhetorical Invention." *Teaching Composition: Twelve Bibliographical Essays*. Ed. Gary Tate. Fort Worth, TX: Texas Christian UP, 1987. 1–38. (Audience discussed on pp. 15–18.)

Bibliography

Abrams, M. H. *The Mirror and the Lamp: Romantic Theory and the Critical Tradition*. London: Oxford UP, 1953.

Anderson, Paul V., ed. *Teaching Technical Writing: Teaching Audience Analysis and Adaptation*. Bloomington, MN: Association of Teachers of Technical Writing, 1980.

Anderson, Paul V. *Technical Writing: A Reader-Centered Approach*. San Diego, CA: Harcourt, 1987.

Anson, Chris. "Writing in Place:Studies of Writers' Transitions Into New Discourse Communities." Applied Linguistics Section, Midwest MLA Conference. Columbus, OH, November 12, 1987.

Aristotle. *The Ethics of Aristotle: The Nicomachean Ethics*. Trans. J. A. K. Thomson. London: Penguin, 1976.

—. *Posterior Analytics—Topica*. Ed. Hugh Tredennick and E.S. Forster. Cambridge, MA: Loeb-Harvard UP, 1960.

—. *The Rhetoric and Poetics of Aristotle*. Intro. Edward P. J. Corbett. New York: Modern Library-Random, 1984.

Atkins, G. Douglas, and Michael L. Johnson, eds. *Writing and Reading Differently: Deconstruction and the Teaching of Composition and Literature*. Lawrence, KS: UP of Kansas, 1985.

Augustine. *On Christian Doctrine*. Trans. D. W. Robertson, Jr. Indianapolis, IN: Bobbs-Merrill, 1958.

Bain, Alexander. *English Composition and Rhetoric*. Enlarged Edition. New York: Appleton, 1887.

Baker, Sheridan. *The Complete Stylist and Handbook.* 3rd ed. New York: Harper & Row, 1984.

—. *The Practical Stylist.* 4th ed. New York: Crowell, 1977.

Barthes, Roland. "The Death of the Author." *Image—Music—Text.* Trans. Stephen Heath. New York: Hill and Wang, 1977. 142–148.

—. "Writers, Intellectuals, Teachers." *Image—Music—Text.* Trans. Stephen Heath. New York: Hill and Wang, 1977. 190–215.

Bator, Paul. "Aristotelian and Rogerian Rhetoric." *College Composition and Communication* 31 (1980): 427–432.

Bazerman, Charles. "Physicists Reading Physics: Schema-Laden Purposes and Purpose-Laden Schema." *Written Communication* 2 (1985): 3–23.

—. "Scientific Writing as a Social Act: A Review of the Literature of the Sociology of Science." *New Essays in Technical and Scientific Communication: Research, Theory, Practice.* Ed. Paul V. Anderson et al. Farmingdale, NY: Baywood, 1983. 156–184.

—. "What Written Knowledge Does: Three Examples of Academic Discourse." *Philosophy of the Social Sciences* 11 (1981): 361–387.

—. "The Writing of Scientific Non-Fiction: Contexts, Choices, Constraints." *PRE/TEXT* 5 (1984): 39–74.

Beach, Richard, and Joanne Liebman-Kleine. "The Writing/Reading Relationship: Implications of Recent Research in Cognition for Reading and Writing." *Reader* 11 (1984): 23–37.

Becker, Carl. *The Declaration of Independence.* 2nd ed. New York: Vintage-Random, 1942.

Berger, Peter L., and Thomas Luckmann. *The Social Construction of Reality.* Garden City, NY: Doubleday, 1966.

Berkenkotter, Carol. "Evolution of a Scholarly Forum: *Reader*, 1977–1988." *A Sense of Audience in Written Communication.* Ed. Gesa Kirsch and Duane H. Roen. Newbury Park, CA: Sage, 1990. 191–215.

—. "Understanding a Writer's Awareness of Audience." *College Composition and Communication* 32 (1981): 388–399.

Berlin, James A. "Contemporary Composition: The Major Pedagogical Theories." *College English* 44 (1982): 765–777.

—. "Revisionary History: The Dialectical Method." *PRE/TEXT* 8 (1987): 47–61.

—. *Rhetoric and Reality: Writing Instruction in American Colleges, 1900–1985.* Carbondale, IL: Southern Illinois UP, 1987.

—. *Writing Instruction in Nineteenth-Century American Colleges.* Carbondale, IL: Southern Illinois UP, 1984.

Berlin, James A., and Robert P. Inkster. "Current-Traditional Rhetoric: Paradigm and Practice." *Freshman English News* 8 (1980): 1–4, 13–14.

Bernstein, Basil. *Class, Codes, and Control.* New York: Schocken, 1975.

Bevilacqua, Vincent M. "Philosophical Origins of George Campbell's *Philosophy of Rhetoric.*" *Speech Monographs* 32 (1965): 1–12.

Bitzer, Lloyd. "Aristotle's Enthymeme Revisited." *Quarterly Journal of Speech* 45 (1959): 399–408.

—. "Hume's Philosophy in George Campbell's *Philosophy of Rhetoric.*" *Philosophy and Rhetoric* 2 (1969): 139–166.

—. Introduction. *The Philosophy of Rhetoric,* by George Campbell. Carbondale, IL: Southern Illinois UP, 1963. ix–xxxvii.

—. "The Rhetorical Situation." *Philosophy and Rhetoric* 1 (1968): 1–14.

—. "Rhetoric and Public Knowledge." *Rhetoric, Philosophy, and Literature.* Ed. Don Burks. West Lafayette, IN: Purdue UP, 1978. 67–93.

Bizzell, Patricia. "Cognition, Convention, and Certainty: What We Need to Know about Writing." *PRE/TEXT* 3 (1982): 213–243.

—. "College Composition: Initiation into the Academic Discourse Community." *Curriculum Inquiry* 12 (1982): 191–207.

—. "Foundationalism and Anti-Foundationalism in Composition Studies." *PRE/TEXT* 7 (1986): 37–56.

—. "Thomas Kuhn, Scientism, and English Studies." *College English* 40 (1979): 764–771.

Black, Edwin. "The Second Persona." *Quarterly Journal of Speech* 56 (1970): 109–119.

Blair, Hugh. *Lectures on Rhetoric and Belle Lettres.* 2 vols. Ed. Harold F. Harding. Carbondale, IL: Southern Illinois UP, 1965.

Bleich, David. *Readings and Feelings: An Introduction to Subjective Criticism.* Urbana, IL: NCTE, 1975.

Booth, Wayne C. "The Rhetorical Stance." *College Composition and Communication* 14 (1963): 139–145.

—. *The Rhetoric of Fiction.* Chicago: The U of Chicago P, 1961.

Bradford, Annette N., and Merrill D. Whitburn. "Analysis of the Same Subject in Diverse Periodicals: One Method for Teaching Audience Adaptation." *The Technical Writing Teacher* 9 (1982): 58–64.

Bramer, George. *Writing for Readers.* Columbus, OH: Merrill, 1981.

Branham, Robert J., and W. Barnett Pearce. "Between Text and Context: Toward a Rhetoric of Contextual Reconstruction." *Quarterly Journal of Speech* 71 (1985): 19–36.

Britton, James, et al. *The Development of Writing Abilities (11–18).* London: Macmillan, 1975.

Brooke, Robert, and John Hendricks. *Audience Expectations and Teacher Demands.* Carbondale, IL: Southern Illinois UP, 1989.

Brooks, Cleanth, and Robert Penn Warren. *Modern Rhetoric*. 2nd ed. New York: Harcourt, 1958.

Brown, Gillian, and George Yule. *Discourse Analysis*. Cambridge: Cambridge UP, 1983.

Brown, Maurice. "Creating a Critical Audience." *College Composition and Communication* 14 (1963): 263–264.

Brown, Stuart, Duane Roen, and Zita Ingham. "The Reader as Entity." *Journal of Business Communication* 23 (1986): 13–21.

Brown, Stuart C., and Thomas Willard. "George Campbell's Audience: Historical and Theoretical Considerations." *A Sense of Audience in Written Communication*. Ed. Gesa Kirsch and Duane H. Roen. Newbury Park, CA: Sage, 1990. 58–72.

Bruffee, Kenneth A. "Social Construction, Language, and the Authority of Knowledge: A Bibliographical Essay." *College English* 48 (1986): 773–790.

Bruner, Jerome S. "The Social Context of Language Acquisition." *Language and Communication* 1 (1981): 155–178.

Buck, Gertrude. "Recent Tendencies in the Teaching of English Composition." *Education Review* 22 (1901): 371–383.

Burke, Kenneth. *A Grammar of Motives*. Berkeley, CA: U of California P, 1969.

—. *The Philosophy of Literary Form*. 3rd ed. Berkeley, CA: U of California P, 1973.

—. *A Rhetoric of Motives*. Berkeley, CA: U of California P, 1969.

Campbell, George. *The Philosophy of Rhetoric*. Ed. Lloyd F. Bitzer. Carbondale, IL: Southern Illinois UP, 1963.

Carey, Robert F. "Theory and Research in Reading: Insights from Socio-Psycholinguistics." *Reader* 10 (1983): 1–13.

Carson, David L. "Audience in Technical Writing: The Need for Greater Realism in Identifying the Fictive Reader." *The Technical Writing Teacher* 7 (1979): 8–11.

Carosso, Rebecca Burnett. *Technical Communication*. Belmont, CA: Wadsworth, 1986.

Ceccio, Joseph F., and Michael J. Rossi. "Inventory of Students' Sex Role Biases: Implications for Audience Analysis." *The Technical Writing Teacher* 8 (1981): 78–82.

[Cicero.] *Ad C. Herennium—De Ratione Dicendi (Rhetorica ad Herennium)*. Trans. Harry Caplan. Cambridge, MA: Loeb-Harvard UP, 1954.

Cicero. *De Inventione—De Optimo Genere Oratorum—Topica*. Trans. H. M. Hubbell. Cambridge, MA: Loeb-Harvard UP, 1949.

—. *De Oratore*. 2 vols. Trans. E. W. Sutton and H. Rackham. Cambridge, MA: Loeb-Harvard UP, 1942.

Clark, Gregory. *Dialogue, Dialectic, and Conversation: A Social Perspective on the Function of Writing*. Carbondale, IL: Southern Illinois UP, 1990.

Clarke, Jennifer, and Peter Elbow. "Desert Island Discourse: On the Benefits of Ignoring Audience." *The Journal Book.* Ed. Toby Fulwiler. Montclair, NJ: Boynton, 1987.

Clevenger, Theodore, Jr. *Audience Analysis.* Indianapolis, IN: Bobbs-Merrill, 1966.

Coe, Richard M. *Form and Substance: An Advanced Rhetoric.* New York: Wiley, 1981.

Collins, James L., and Michael M. Williamson. "Assigned Rhetorical Context and Semantic Abbreviation in Writing." *New Directions in Composition Research.* Ed. Richard Beach and Lillian S. Bridwell. New York: Guilford, 1984. 285–296.

Coney, Mary B. "The Use of the Reader in Technical Writing." *Journal of Technical Writing and Communication* 8 (1978): 97–106.

Connors, Robert J. "Textbooks and the Evolution of the Discipline." *College Composition and Communication* 37 (1986): 178–194.

Connors, Robert J., Lisa S. Ede and Andrea A. Lunsford. "The Revival of Rhetoric in America." *Essays on Classical Rhetoric and Modern Discourse.* Ed. Robert J. Connors, Lisa S. Ede, and Andrea A. Lunsford. Carbondale, IL: Southern Illinois UP, 1984. 1–15.

Consigny, Scott. "Rhetoric and Its Situations." *Philosophy and Rhetoric* 7 (1974): 175–186.

Cooper, Martha. "Reconceptualizing Ideology According to the Relationship Between Rhetoric and Knowledge/Power." *Rhetoric and Ideology: Compositions and Criticisms of Power.* Ed. Charles W. Kneupper. Arlington, TX: Rhetoric Society of America, 1989. 30–41.

Corbett, Edward P. J. *Classical Rhetoric for the Modern Student.* 2nd ed. New York: Oxford UP, 1971.

—. *The Little Rhetoric and Handbook.* 2nd ed. Glenview, IL: Scott, Foresman, 1982.

Corder, Jim W. "Hunting for *Ethos* Where They Say It Can't Be Found." *Rhetoric Review* 7 (1989): 299–316.

Crismore, Avon. "Readability and the Black Box." *Indiana Reading Quarterly* 14 (1982): 14–16, 23–25.

Crosswhite, James. "Universality in Rhetoric: Perelman's Universal Audience." *Philosophy and Rhetoric* 22 (1989): 157–173.

Crowhurst, Marion, and Gene L. Piché. "Audience and Mode of Discourse Effects on Syntactic Complexity in Writing at Two Grade Levels." *Research in the Teaching of English* 13 (1979): 101–109.

Crowley, Sharon. "The Current-Traditional Theory of Style: An Informal History." *Rhetoric Society Quarterly* 16 (1986): 233–250.

—. "The Evolution of Invention in Current-Traditional Rhetoric: 1850–1970." *Rhetoric Review* 3 (1985): 146–162.

—. "On Post-Structuralism and Compositionists." *PRE/TEXT* 5 (1984): 185–195.

Culler, Jonathan. *On Deconstruction: Theory and Criticism after Structuralism.* Ithaca, NY: Cornell UP, 1982.

—. *The Pursuit of Signs: Semiotics, Literature, Deconstruction*. Ithaca, NY: Cornell UP, 1981.

Daiute, Colette A. "The Computer as Stylus and Audience." *College Composition and Communication* 34 (1983): 134–145.

D'Angelo, Frank J. *Process and Thought in Composition*. 3rd ed. Boston: Little, Brown, 1985.

Däumer, Elisabeth. "Gender Bias in the Concept of Audience." *Reader* 13 (1985): 32–44.

Davidson, Arnold I. "Archaeology, Genealogy, Ethics." *Foucault: A Critical Reader*. Ed. David Couzens Hoy. Oxford: Basil Blackwell, 1986. 221–233.

Davis, Ken. "The Circle Game: A Heuristic for Discovering Rhetorical Situations." *College Composition and Communication* 29 (1978): 285–287.

Dearin, Ray D. "The Philosophical Basis of Chaim Perelman's Theory of Rhetoric." *Quarterly Journal of Speech* 55 (1969): 213–224.

Deleuze, Gilles. *Foucault*. Trans. and ed. Séan Hand. Minneapolis, MN: U of Minnesota P, 1988.

Derrida, Jacques. *Dissemination*. Trans. Barbara Johnson. Chicago: The U of Chicago P, 1981.

—. "Signature Event Context." *Glyph* 1 (1977): 172–197.

Diggs, B. J. "Persuasion and Ethics." *Quarterly Journal of Speech* 50 (1964): 369–373.

Dillon, George L. *Constructing Texts: Elements of a Theory of Composition and Style*. Bloomington, IN: Indiana UP, 1981.

—. *Rhetoric as Social Imagination*. Bloomington IN: Indiana UP, 1986.

Dilworth, Collett B., Jr., and Robert W. Reising. "Writing as a Moral Act: Developing a Sense of Audience." *English Journal* 67 (November 1978): 76–78.

Dobrin, David N. *Writing and Technique*. Urbana, IL: NCTE, 1989.

Doheny-Farina, Stephen. "Writing in an Emerging Organization: An Ethnographic Study." *Written Communication* 3 (1986): 158–185.

Dreyfus, Hubert C., and Paul Rabinow. *Michel Foucault: Beyond Structuralism and Hermeneutics*. 2nd ed. Chicago: The U of Chicago P, 1983.

Driskill, Linda. "Understanding the Writing Context in Organizations." *Writing in the Business Professions*. Ed. Myra Kogen. Urbana, IL: NCTE & ABC, 1989. 125–145.

Dumbauld, Edward. *The Declaration of Independence*. 2nd ed. Norman, OK: U of Oklahoma P, 1968.

Eagleton, Terry. *Literary Theory: An Introduction*. Bloomington, MN: U of Minnesota P, 1983.

Ede, Lisa. "Audience: An Introduction to Research." *College Composition and Communication* 35 (1984): 140–154.

—. "Is Rogerian Rhetoric Really Rogerian?" *Rhetoric Review* 3 (1984): 40–48.

—. "On Audience and Composition." *College Composition and Communication* 30 (1979): 291–295.

—. "Rhetoric vs. Philosophy: The Role of the Universal Audience in Chaim Perelman's *The New Rhetoric.*" *Central States Speech Journal* 32 (1981): 118–125.

Ede, Lisa, and Andrea Lunsford. "Audience Addressed/Audience Invoked: The Role of Audience in Composition Theory and Pedagogy." *College Composition and Communication* 35 (1984): 155–171.

Elbow, Peter. "Closing My Eyes as I Speak: An Argument for Ignoring Audience." *College English* 49 (1987): 50–69.

—. "Preface 4: The Doubting Game and the Believing Game." *PRE/TEXT* 3 (1982): 339–351.

—. *Writing Without Teachers.* New York: Oxford UP, 1973.

—. *Writing With Power.* New York: Oxford UP, 1981.

Emig, Janet. *The Composing Processes of Twelfth Graders.* Urbana, IL: NCTE, 1971.

Enos, Richard Leo, and Jeanne L. McClaran. "Audience and Image in Ciceronian Rome: Creation and Constraints of the *Vir Bonus* Personality." *Central States Speech Journal* 29 (1978): 98–106.

Ewald, Helen Rothschild. "The Implied Reader in Persuasive Discourse." *Journal of Advanced Composition* 8 (1988): 167–178.

Ewald, Helen Rothschild, and Donna Stine. "Speech Act Theory and Business Communication Conventions." *Journal of Business Communication* 20 (1983): 13–25.

Faigley, Lester. "Competing Theories of Process: A Critique and a Proposal." *College English* 48 (1986): 527–542.

—. "Nonacademic Writing: The Social Perspective." *Writing in Nonacademic Settings.* Ed. Lee Odell and Dixie Goswami. New York: Guilford, 1985. 231–248.

Felker, Daniel B., ed. *Document Design: A Review of the Relevant Research.* Washington, DC: American Institutes for Research, 1980.

Felker, Daniel B., et al. *Guidelines for Document Designers.* Washington, DC: American Institutes for Research, 1981.

Fetterley, Judith. *The Resisting Reader: A Feminist Approach to American Fiction.* Bloomington, In: Indiana UP, 1978.

Feyerabend, Paul. "Creativity—A Dangerous Myth." *Critical Inquiry* 13 (1987): 700–711.

—. "How to Be a Good Empiricist—A Plea for Tolerance in Matters Epistemological." *Challenges to Empiricism.* Ed. Harold Morick. Belmont, CA: Wadsworth, 1972.

Fish, Stanley. *Is There A Text in This Class? The Authority of Interpretive Communities.* Cambridge, MA: Harvard UP, 1980.

Floreak, Michael J. "Designing for the Real World: Using Research to Turn a 'Target Audience' into Real People." *Technical Communication* 36 (1989): 373–381.

Flower, Linda. "Cognition, Context, and Theory Building." *College Composition and Communication* 40 (1989): 282–311.

—. *Problem-Solving Strategies for Writing.* 2nd ed. New York: Harcourt, 1985.

—. "Writer-Based Prose: A Cognitive Basis for Problems in Writing." *College English* 41 (1979): 19–38.

Flower, Linda, and John R. Hayes. "The Cognition of Discovery: Defining a Rhetorical Problem." *College Composition and Communication* 31 (1980): 21–32.

—. "A Cognitive Process Theory of Writing." *College Composition and Communication* 32 (1981): 365–387.

—. "The Dynamics of Composing: Making Plans and Juggling Constraints." *Cognitive Processes in Writing.* Ed. Lee W. Gregg and Erwin R. Steinberg. Hillsdale, NJ: Erlbaum, 1980. 31–50.

Flower, Linda, et al. "Detection, Diagnosis, and the Strategies of Revision." *College Composition and Communication* 37 (1986): 16–55.

Flynn, Elizabeth, and Patrocinio P. Schweickart, eds. *Gender and Reading: Essays on Readers, Texts, and Contexts.* Baltimore: The Johns Hopkins UP, 1986.

Fogarty, Daniel, S. J. *Roots for a New Rhetoric.* New York: Russell and Russell, 1959.

Fontaine, Sheryl I. "The Unfinished Story of the Interpretive Community." *Rhetoric Review* 7 (1988): 86–96.

Forman, Janis. "The Discourse Communities and Group Writing Practices of Management Students." *Worlds of Writing: Teaching and Learning in Discourse Communities of Work.* Ed. Carolyn B. Matalene. New York: Random House, 1989: 247–254.

Forsberg, L. Lee. "Who's Out There Anyway? Bringing Awareness of Multiple Audiences into the Business-Writing Class." *Iowa State Journal of Business and Technical Communication* 1 (1987): 45–69.

Foss, Sonja K., Karen A. Foss, and Robert Trapp. *Contemporary Perspectives on Rhetoric.* Prospect Heights, IL: Waveland Press, 1985.

Foucault, Michel. *The Archaeology of Knowledge and the Discourse on Language.* Trans. A. M. Sheridan Smith. New York: Pantheon-Random, 1972.

—. *The Birth of the Clinic: An Archaeology of Medical Perception.* Trans. A. M. Sheridan Smith. New York: Vintage-Random, 1973.

—. *Discipline and Punish: The Birth of the Prison.* Trans. Alan Sheridan. New York: Vintage-Random, 1979.

—. "History, Discourse and Discontinuity." Trans. Anthony M. Nazzaro. *Salmagundi* 20 (1972): 229–233.

—. *The History of Sexuality: Volume I: An Introduction.* Trans. Robert Hurley. New York: Vintage-Random, 1980.

—. *Madness and Civilization*. Trans. Richard Howard. New York: Pantheon-Random, 1965.

—. "Nietzsche, Genealogy, History." *The Foucault Reader*. Ed. Paul Rabinow. New York: Pantheon-Random, 1984. 76–100.

—. *The Order of Things: An Archaeology of the Human Sciences*. New York: Vintage-Random, 1973.

—. *Power/Knowledge: Selected Interviews and Other Writings, 1972–1977*. Ed. Colin Gordon. New York: Pantheon-Random, 1980.

—. "The Subject and Power." *Critical Inquiry* 8 (1982): 777–795.

—. *This Is Not A Pipe*. Trans. James Harkness. Berkeley, CA: U of California P, 1983.

—. "What Is an Author?" *The Foucault Reader*. Ed. Paul Rabinow. New York: Pantheon-Random, 1984. 101–120.

Freed, Richard C., and Glenn J Broadhead. "Discourse Communities, Sacred Texts, and Institutional Norms." *College Composition and Communication* 38 (1987): 154–165.

Fulkerson, Richard. "Four Philosophies of Composition." *College Composition and Communication* 30 (1979): 343–348.

Funkhouser, G. Ray, and Nathan Maccoby. "Communicating Specialized Information to a Lay Audience." *Journal of Communication* 21 (1971): 58–71.

Gage, John T. "An Adequate Epistemology for Composition: Classical and Modern Perspectives." *Essays on Classical Rhetoric and Modern Discourse*. Ed. Robert J. Connors, Lisa S. Ede, and Andrea A. Lunsford. Carbondale, IL: Southern Illinois UP, 1984. 152–169.

Gallagher, Brian. "A Critique of the Rhetorical and Organizational World of Business Communication Texts." *Writing in the Business Professions*. Ed. Myra Kogen. Urbana, IL: NCTE & ABC, 1989. 222–245.

Geertz, Clifford. *Local Knowledge: Further Essays in Interpretive Anthropology*. New York: Basic, 1983.

Genung, John Franklin. *The Practical Elements of Rhetoric*. Boston: Ginn, 1892.

—. *The Working Principles of Rhetoric*. Boston: Ginn, 1900.

George, Diana, and Diane Shoos. "The Culture of the Bath: Cigarette Advertising and the Representation of Leisure." *Reader* 23 (1990): 50–66.

Gere, Ann Ruggles. *Writing Groups: History, Theory, and Implications*. Carbondale, IL: Southern Illinois UP, 1987.

Gergen, Kenneth J. "The Social Constructionist Movement in Modern Psychology." *American Psychologist* 40 (1985): 266–275.

Gleick, James. *Chaos: Making a New Science*. New York: Penguin, 1987.

Golden, James L. "Plato Revisited: A Theory of Discourse for All Seasons." *Essays on Classical Rhetoric and Modern Discourse*. Ed. Robert J. Connors, Lisa S. Ede, and Andrea A. Lunsford. Carbondale, IL: Southern Illinois UP, 1984. 16–36.

Golden, James L., Goodwin F. Berquist, and William E. Coleman. *The Rhetoric of Western Thought*. Dubuque, IA: Kendall/Hunt, 1976.

Gragson, Gay, and Jack Selzer. "Fictionalizing the Readers of Scholarly Articles in Biology." *Written Communication* 7 (1990): 25–58.

Grice, H. P. "Logic and Conversation." *The Logic of Grammar*. Ed. Donald Davidson and Gilbert Herman. Encino, CA: Dickenson, 1975. 64–75.

Grimaldi, William M. A., S. J. *Aristotle, Rhetoric I: A Commentary*. New York: Fordham UP, 1980.

Gumperz, John J. "Linguistics: The Speech Community." *International Encyclopedia of the Social Sciences*. Ed. David L. Sills. New York: Macmillan, 1968. 9:381–386.

Hacking, Ian. "The Archaeology of Foucault." *Foucault: A Critical Reader*. Ed. David Couzens Hoy. Oxford: Basil Blackwell, 1986. 27–40.

Hagaman, John. "George Campbell and the Creative Management of Audience." *Rhetoric Society Quarterly* 13 (1983): 21–24.

Hairston, Maxine C. "Carl Rogers' Alternative to Traditional Rhetoric." *College Composition and Communication* 27 (1976): 373–377.

—. *Successful Writing: A Rhetoric for Advanced Composition*. New York: Norton, 1981.

—. "Using Carl Rogers' Communication Theories in the Composition Classroom." *Rhetoric Review* 1 (1982): 50–55.

—. "The Winds of Change: Thomas Kuhn and the Revolution in the Teaching of Writing." *College Composition and Communication* 33 (1982): 76–88.

Halloran, Michael. "Aristotle's Concept of Ethos, or if not His, Somebody Else's." *Rhetoric Review* 1 (1982): 58–63.

Halpern, Jeanne W. "What Should We Be Teaching Students in Business Writing?" *Journal of Business Communication* 18 (1981): 39–53.

Hamermesh, Madeline. "Sharpening the Old Saws: Speech-Act Theory and Business Communication." *Journal of Business Communication* 18 (1981): 15–22.

Harned, Jon. "Stanley Fish's Theory of the Interpretive Community: A Rhetoric for Our Time?" *Freshman English News* 14 (1985): 9–13.

Harris, Joseph. "The Idea of Community in the Study of Writing." *College Composition and Communication* 40 (1989): 11–22.

Hartley, James. *Designing Instructional Text*. 2nd ed. London: Kogan Page, 1987.

Havelock, Eric. *The Muse Learns to Write*. New Haven, CN: Yale UP, 1986.

Hawkes, Terence. *Structuralism and Semiotics*. Berkeley, CA: U of California P, 1977.

Heath, Shirley Brice. *Ways with Words*. New York: Cambridge UP, 1983.

Hemingway, Ernest. *A Farewell to Arms*. New York: Scribner's, 1929.

Herrstrom, David Sten. "A Matrix of Audience Responses for the Internal Proposal." *The Technical Writing Teacher* 10 (1983): 101–107.

Hill, Adams Sherman. *The Principles of Rhetoric.* New York: Harper and Brothers, 1895.

Hill, Forbes I. "The Rhetoric of Aristotle." *A Synoptic History of Classical Rhetoric.* Ed. James J. Murphy. Davis, CA: Hermagoras, 1983. 19–76.

Hillocks, George, Jr. *Research on Written Composition: New Directions for Teaching.* Urbana, IL: NCRE and ERIC/RCS, 1986.

Hirsch, E. D., Jr. *Cultural Literacy: What Every American Needs to Know.* New York: Vintage-Random, 1988.

Holland, Norman. *Five Readers Reading.* New Haven, CN: Yale UP, 1975.

Holtzman, Paul D. *The Psychology of Speakers' Audiences.* Glenview, IL: Scott, Foresman, 1970.

Holub, Robert C. *Reception Theory: A Critical Introduction.* London: Methuen, 1984.

Horner, Winifred Bryan. "Speech-Act Theory and Writing." *fforum: Essays on Theory and Practice in the Teaching of Writing.* Ed. Patricia L. Stock. Upper Montclair, NJ: Boynton/Cook, 1983. 96–98.

Huckin, Thomas N. "A Cognitive Approach to Readability." *New Essays in Technical Communication: Research, Theory, Practice.* Ed. Paul V. Anderson et al. Farmingdale, NY: Baywood Press, 1983. 90–108.

Hughes, Richard E., and P. Albert Duhamel. *Rhetoric: Principles and Usage.* 2nd ed. Englewood Cliffs, NJ: Prentice-Hall, 1967.

Irmscher, William F. *The Holt Guide to English.* 2nd ed. New York: Holt, Rinehart, 1976.

Iser, Wolfgang. *The Implied Reader.* Baltimore, MD: Johns Hopkins UP, 1974.

Jarratt, Susan C. "The First Sophists and the Uses of History." *Rhetoric Review* 6 (1987): 67–78.

Jauss, Hans Robert. *Toward an Aesthetic of Reception.* Trans. Timothy Bahti. Minneapolis, MN: U of Minnesota P, 1982.

Jenkins, Joseph R., Matthew L. Speltz, and Samuel L. Odom. "Integrating Normal and Handicapped Preschoolers: Effects on Child Development and Social Interaction." *Exceptional Children* 52 (1985): 7–17.

Johnson, Nan. "Reader-Response and the *Pathos* Principle." *Rhetoric Review* 6 (1988): 152–166.

Johnstone, Henry W., Jr. "The Idea of a Universal Audience." *Validity and Rhetoric in Philosophical Argument.* University Park, PA: Dialogue, 1978. 101–106.

Juhl, P. D. "Stanley Fish's Interpretive Communities and the Status of Critical Interpretation." *Comparative Criticism* 5 (1983): 47–58.

Jurkiewicz, Kenneth. "How to Begin to Win Friends and Influence People: The Role of the Audience in the Prewriting Process." *College Composition and Communication* 26 (1975): 173–176.

Karlinsky, Stewart S., and Bruce S. Koch. "Readability Is in the Mind of the Reader." *Journal of Business Communication* 20 (1983): 57–69.

Keene, Michael, and Marilyn Barnes-Ostrander. "Audience Analysis and Adaptation." *Research in Technical Communication: A Bibliographic Sourcebook.* Ed. Michael G. Moran and Debra Journet. Westport, CN: Greenwood, 1985. 163–191.

Kennedy, George. *The Art of Persuasion in Greece.* Princeton, NJ: Princeton UP, 1963.

—. *The Art of Rhetoric in the Roman World.* Princeton, NJ: Princeton UP, 1972.

Kerferd, G. B. *The Sophistic Movement.* Cambridge: Cambridge UP, 1981.

Kifner, John. "4 Kent State Students Killed by Troops."*New York Times* 5 May 1970: 1.

Kinneavy, James L. "The Relation of the Whole to the Part in Interpretation Theory and in the Composing Process." *Linguistics, Stylistics, and the Teaching of Composition.* Ed. Donald A. McQuade. Akron, OH: U of Akron English Department, 1979. 1–23.

—. *A Theory of Discourse: The Aims of Discourse.* Englewood Cliffs, NJ: Prentice-Hall, 1971.

—. "Writing Across the Curriculum." *Teaching Composition: Twelve Bibliographical Essays.* Ed. Gary Tate. Fort Worth, TX: Texas Christian UP, 1987. (See especially pp. 368–371.)

Kinneavy, James L., John Q. Cope, and J. W. Campbell. *Aims and Audiences in Writing.* Dubuque, IA: Kendall/Hunt, 1976.

Kirsch, Gesa, and Duane H. Roen, eds. *A Sense of Audience in Written Communication.* Newbury Park, CA: Sage, 1990.

Kneupper, Charles. "Argument: A Social Constructivist Perspective." *Journal of the American Forensic Association* 17 (1981): 183–189.

Knoblauch, C. H. "Intentionality in the Writing Process: A Case Study." *College Composition and Communication* 31 (1980): 153–159.

Kogen, Myra. "The Role of Audience in Business and Technical Writing." *The Bulletin* of the Association for Business Communication 46 (December 1983): 2–4.

Kroll, Barry M. "Audience Adaptation in Children's Persuasive Letters." *Written Communication* 1 (1984): 407–427.

—. "Cognitive Egocentrism and the Problem of Audience Awareness in Written Discourse." *Research in the Teaching of English* 12 (1978): 269–281.

—. "Developing a Sense of Audience." *Language Arts* 55 (1978): 828–831.

—. "Rewriting a Complex Story for a Young Reader: The Development of Audience-Adapted Writing Skills." *Research in the Teaching of English* 19 (1985): 120–139.

—. "Writing for Readers: Three Perspectives on Audience." *College Composition and Communication* 35 (1984): 172–185.

Kuhn, Thomas S. *The Structure of Scientific Revolutions.* 2nd ed. Chicago: The U of Chicago P, 1970.

Laclau, Ernesto, and Chantal Mouffe. *Hegemony and Socialist Strategy: Towards a Radical Democratic Politics.* Trans. Winston Moore and Paul Cammack. Thetford, England: The Thetford Press, 1985.

Lakoff, George, and Mark Johnson. *Metaphors We Live By.* Chicago: The U of Chicago P, 1980.

Lamb, Catherine E. "Less Distance, More Space: A Feminist Theory of Power and Writer/Audience Relationships." *Rhetoric and Ideology: Compositions and Criticisms of Power.* Ed. Charles W. Kneupper. Arlington, TX: Rhetoric Society of America, 1989. 99–104.

Lanham, Richard A. *A Handlist of Rhetorical Terms.* Berkeley, CA: U of California P, 1969.

Lauer, Janice, Gene Montague, Andrea Lunsford, and Janet Emig. *Four Worlds of Writing.* New York: Harper & Row, 1981; 2nd ed. 1985.

LeFevre, Karen Burke. *Invention as a Social Act.* Carbondale, IL: Southern Illinois UP, 1987.

Leggett, Glenn, et al, eds. *Prentice-Hall Handbook for Writers.* 9th ed. Englewood Cliffs, NJ: Prentice-Hall, 1985.

Leitch, Vincent B. *Deconstructive Criticism: An Advanced Introduction.* New York: Columbia UP, 1983.

Lemert, Charles C., and Garth Gillan. *Michel Foucault: Social Theory as Transgression.* New York: Columbia UP, 1982.

Lentricchia, Frank. *After the New Criticism.* Chicago: The U of Chicago P, 1980.

Locker, Kitty. "Theoretical Justifications for Using Reader Benefits." *Journal of Business Communication* 19 (1982): 51–66.

Long, Russell C. "Writer-Audience Relationships: Analysis or Invention?" *College Composition and Communication* 31 (1980): 221–226.

Lovejoy, Kim Brian. "Discourse Communities in the Academy: A Cohesion Analysis of Texts in Three Disciplines." Applied Linguistics Section, Midwest MLA Conference. Columbus, OH, November 12, 1987.

Lundberg, Patricia Lorimer. "Dialogically Feminized Reading: A Critique of Reader-Response Criticism." *Reader* 22 (1989): 9–37.

Lunsford, Andrea. "Aristotelian vs. Rogerian Rhetoric: A Reassessment." *College Composition and Communication* 30 (1979): 146–151.

Lunsford, Andrea A., and Lisa S. Ede. "Classical Rhetoric, Modern Rhetoric, and Contemporary Discourse Studies." *Written Communication* 1 (1984): 78–100.

—. "On Distinctions Between Classical and Modern Rhetoric." *Essays on Classical Rhetoric and Modern Discourse.* Ed. Robert J. Connors, Lisa S. Ede, and Andrea A. Lunsford. Carbondale, IL: Southern Illinois UP, 1984. 37–49.

Lyotard, Jean-Francois. *Peregrinations: Law, Form, Event.* New York: Columbia UP, 1988.

—. *The Postmodern Condition: A Report on Knowledge.* Trans. Geoff Bennington and Brian Massumi. Minneapolis, MN: U of Minnesota P, 1984.

Macdonald, Kathleen. *When Writers Write*. Englewood Cliffs, NJ: Prentice-Hall, 1983.

MacDonald, Susan Peck. "Problem Definition in Academic Writing." *College English* 49 (1987): 315–331.

Macrorie, Ken. *Telling Writing*. 2nd ed. Rochelle Park, NJ: Hayden, 1976.

—. *Uptaught*. New York: Hayden, 1970.

Mailloux, Steven. *Interpretive Conventions: The Reader in the Study of American Fiction.* Ithaca, NY: Cornell UP, 1982.

—. "Learning to Read: Interpretation and Reader-Response Criticism." *Studies in the Literary Imagination* 12 (1979): 93–108.

—. "Reader-Response Criticism?" *Genre* 10 (1977): 413–431.

Maimon, Elaine P. "Knowledge, Acknowledgement, and Writing Across the Curriculum." *The Territory of Language: Linguistics, Stylistics, and the Teaching of Composition*. Ed. Donald A. McQuade. Carbondale, IL: Southern Illinois UP, 1986. 89–100.

Maimon, Elaine P., et al. *Readings in the Arts and Sciences*. Boston: Little, Brown, 1984.

Makay, John J. *Speaking with an Audience: Communicating Ideas and Attitudes*. Dubuque, IA: Kendall/Hunt, 1984.

Matalene, Carolyn B., ed. *Worlds of Writing: Teaching and Learning in Discourse Communities of Work*. New York: Random, 1989.

Mathes, J. C., and Dwight W. Stevenson. *Designing Technical Reports: Writing for Audiences in Organizations*. Indianapolis, IN: Bobbs-Merrill, 1976.

Mathews, William. *Oratory and Orators*. Chicago: Griggs, 1883.

McClearey, Keven E. "Audience Effects of Apologia." *Communication Quarterly* 31 (1983): 12–20.

McConnell-Ginet, Sally. "The Sexual (Re)Production of Meaning: A Discourse-Based Theory." *Language, Gender, and Professional Writing: Theoretical Approaches and Guidelines for Nonsexist Usage*. Ed. Francine Wattman Frank and Paula A. Treichler. New York: Modern Language Association. 35–50.

McCrimmon, James M. *Writing with a Purpose*. 3rd ed. Boston: Houghton Mifflin, 1963.

McDermott, Douglas. "George Campbell and the Classical Tradition." *Quarterly Journal of Speech* 49 (1963): 403–409.

McDonald, John C. "Taste and the Shaping of Audience in Hugh Blair." *Visions of Rhetoric*. Ed. Charles W. Kneupper. Arlington, TX: Rhetoric Society of America, 1987. 22–29.

Miller, Carolyn R. "The Discourse Community as *Polis*." Conference of the Modern Language Association, New Orleans, LA, 1988.

—. "Genre as Social Action." *Quarterly Journal of Speech* 70 (1984): 154–167.

—. "Public Knowledge in Science and Society." *PRE/TEXT* 3 (1982): 31–49.

Miller, James E., Jr. *Word, Self, Reality: The Rhetoric of Imagination.* New York: Harper & Row, 1972.

Miller, Keith D. "Martin Luther King, Jr. Borrows a Revolution: Argument, Audience, and Implications of a Secondhand Universe." *College English* 48 (1986): 249–265.

Mills, Carl. "Linguistic Models, Research Designs, and Discourse Communities." Applied Linguistics Section, Midwest MLA Conference. Columbus, OH, November 12, 1987.

Mills, C. B., and K. L. Dye. "Usability Testing: User Reviews." *Technical Communication* 32 (1985): 40–45.

Minot, Walter. "Response to Russell C. Long, 'Writer-Audience Relationships: Analysis or Invention?' " *College Composition and Communication* 32 (1981): 335–337.

Mitchell, Ruth, and Mary Taylor. "The Integrating Perspective: An Audience-Response Model for Writing." *College English* 41 (1979): 247–271.

Moffett, James. *Teaching the Universe of Discourse.* Boston: Houghton Mifflin, 1968.

Monahan, Brian D. "Revision Strategies of Basic and Competent Writers as They Write for Different Audiences." *Research in the Teaching of English* 18 (1984): 288–304.

Moxley, Joseph M. "Commentary: The Myth of the Technical Audience." *Journal of Technical Writing and Communication* 18 (1988): 107–109.

Murphy, James J. *Rhetoric in the Middle Ages: A History of Rhetorical Theory from Saint Augustine to the Renaissance.* Berkeley, CA: U of California P, 1974.

Murphy, John W. "Jacques Derrida: A Rhetoric That Deconstructs Common Sense." *Diogenes* 128 (1984): 125–140.

Murray, Donald M. "Teaching the Other Self: The Writer's First Reader." *College Composition and Communication* 33 (1982): 140–147.

—. *A Writer Teaches Writing.* 2nd ed. Boston: Houghton Mifflin, 1985.

Myers, Greg. "The Social Construction of Two Biologists' Proposals." *Written Communication* 2 (1985): 219–245.

—. "Text as Knowledge Claims: The Social Construction of Two Biologists' Articles." *Social Studies of Science* 15 (1985): 593–630.

—. "Writing Research and the Sociology of Scientific Knowledge: A Review of Three New Books." *College English* 48 (1986): 595–610.

Neel, Jasper. *Plato, Derrida, and Writing.* Carbondale, IL: Southern Illinois UP, 1988.

Norris, Christopher. *Deconstruction: Theory and Practice.* London: Methuen, 1982.

Noujain, Elie Georges. "History as Genealogy: An Exploration of Foucault's Approach to History." *Contemporary French Philosophy.* Ed. A. Phillips Griffiths. Cambridge: Cambridge UP, 1987. 157–174.

Nystrand, Martin. "Rhetoric's 'Audience' and Linguistics' 'Speech Community': Implications for Understanding Writing, Reading, and Text." *What Writers Know.* Ed. Martin Nystrand. New York: Academic Press, 1982. 1–28.

Odell, Lee, and Dixie Goswami, eds. *Writing in Nonacademic Settings.* New York: Guilford, 1985.

Olsen, Leslie, and Thomas N. Huckin. "Making Your Writing Readable." *Principles of Communication for Science and Technology.* New York: McGraw-Hill, 1983. 289–301.

Ong, Walter, S. J. *Orality and Literacy: The Technologizing of the Word.* London: Methuen, 1982.

—. "The Writer's Audience Is Always a Fiction." *PMLA* 90 (1975): 9–21.

Overington, Michael A. "The Scientific Community as Audience: Toward a Rhetorical Analysis of Science." *Philosophy and Rhetoric* 10 (1977): 143–164.

Park, Douglas. "Analyzing Audiences." *College Composition and Communication* 37 (1986): 478–488.

—. "The Meanings of 'Audience.' " *College English* 44 (1982): 247–257.

—. "Perelman's Universal Audience." Conference on College Composition and Communication. St. Louis, MO, March 18, 1988.

Pearsall, Thomas. *Audience Analysis for Technical Writing.* Beverly Hills, CA: Glencoe, 1969.

Perelman, Chaim. *The Realm of Rhetoric.* Trans. William Kluback. Notre Dame, IN: U of Notre Dame P, 1982.

Perelman, Chaim, and L. Olbrechts-Tyteca. *The New Rhetoric.* Trans. William Kluback. Notre Dame, IN: U of Notre Dame P, 1969.

Pfister, Fred R., and Joanne F. Petrick. "A Heuristic Model for Creating a Writer's Audience." *College Composition and Communication* 31 (1980): 213–220.

Phelps, Louise Wetherbee. "Audience and Authorship: The Disappearing Boundary." *A Sense of Audience in Written Communication.* Ed. Gesa Kirsch and Duane H. Roen. Newbury Park, CA: Sage, 1990. 153–174.

—. *Composition as a Human Science: Contributions to the Self-Understanding of a Discipline.* New York: Oxford UP, 1988.

Pirsig, Robert M. *Zen and the Art of Motorcycle Maintenance: An Inquiry into Values.* Toronto: Bantam, 1974.

Plato. *Euthyphro—Apology—Crito—Phaedo—Phaedrus.* Trans. Harold North Fowler. Cambridge, MA: Loeb-Harvard UP, 1914.

Porter, James E. "*Divisio* as Em-/De-Powering Topic: A Basis for Argument in Rhetoric and Composition." *Rhetoric Review* 8 (1990): 191–205.

—. "Intertextuality and the Discourse Community." *Rhetoric Review* 5 (1986): 34–47.

—. "The Problem of Defining Discourse Communities." Conference on College Composition and Communication. St. Louis, MO, March 19, 1988.

—. "Reading Presences in Texts: Audience as Discourse Community." *Oldspeak/ Newspeak: Rhetorical Transformations.* Ed. Charles Kneupper. Arlington, TX: Rhetoric Society of America, 1985. 241–256.

—. "Re-Situating the Audience in Composition Theory." Conference on College Composition and Communication. Seattle, WA, March 16, 1989.

—. "This Is Not A Review of Foucault's *This Is Not A Pipe.*" *Rhetoric Review* 4 (1986): 210–219.

—. "Truth in Technical Advertising: A Case Study." *IEEE Transactions on Professional Communication* 30 (1987): 182–189.

Porter, Jeffrey. "The Reasonable Reader: Knowledge and Inquiry in Freshman English." *College English* 49 (1987): 332–344.

Pratt, Mary Louise. *Toward a Speech Act Theory of Literary Discourse.* Bloomington, IN: Indiana UP, 1977.

Pressman, Rebecca. *Legislative and Regulatory Progress on the Readability of Insurance Policies.* Washington, DC: Document Design Center-American Institutes for Research, 1979.

Purves, Alan C. "Putting Readers in Their Places: Some Alternatives to Cloning Stanley Fish." *College English* 42 (1980): 228–236.

—. "That Sunny Dome: Those Caves of Ice: A Model for Research in Reader Response." *College English* 40 (1979): 802–812.

Quintilian. *The Institutio oratoria of Quintilian.* Trans. H. E. Butler. 4 vols. Cambridge, MA: Loeb-Harvard UP, 1974.

Rabinowitz, Peter J. "Assertion and Assumption: Fictional Patterns and the External World." *PMLA* 96 (1981): 408–419.

—. "Truth in Fiction: A Reexamination of Audiences." *Critical Inquiry* 4 (1977): 121–141.

Rafoth, Bennett A. "Audience Adaptation in the Essays of Proficient and Nonproficient Freshman Writers." *Research in the Teaching of English* 19 (1985): 237–253.

—. "The Concept of Discourse Community Descriptive and Explanatory Adequacy in the Concept of Discourse Community." *A Sense of Audience in Written Communication.* Ed. Gesa Kirsch and Duane H. Roen. Newbury Park, CA: Sage, 1990. 140–152.

Raymond, James C. "Enthymemes, Examples, and Rhetorical Method." *Essays on Classical Rhetoric and Modern Discourse.* Ed. Robert J. Connors, Lisa S. Ede, and Andrea A. Lunsford. Carbondale, IL: Southern Illinois UP, 1984. 140–151.

Redish, Janice C. *Beyond Readability: How to Write and Design Understandable Life Insurance Policies.* Washington, DC: American Council of Life Insurance.

—. "Understanding the Limitations of Readability Formulas." *IEEE Transactions on Professional Communication* 24.1 (1981): 46–48.

Redish, Janice C., Daniel B. Felker, and A. Rose. "Evaluating the Effects of Document Design Principles." *Information Design Journal* 2 (1981): 236–243.

Redish, Janice C., and Jack Selzer. "The Place of Readability Formulas in Technical Communication." *Technical Communication* (1985): 46–52.

Roberts, David D., and Patricia A. Sullivan. "Beyond the Static Audience Construct: Reading Protocols in the Technical Writing Class." *Journal of Technical Writing and Communication* 14 (1984): 143–153.

Rod, David K. "Kenneth Burke and Susanne K. Langer on Drama and Its Audience." *Quarterly Journal of Speech* 89 (1986): 306–317.

Romaine, Suzanne. "What Is a Speech Community?" *Sociolinguistic Variation in Speech Communities.* Ed. Suzanne Romaine. London: Edward Arnold, 1982. 13–24.

Ronald, Kate. "On the Outside Looking In: Students' Analyses of Professional Discourse Communities." *Rhetoric Review* 7 (1988): 130–149.

Rosenbaum, Stephanie, and R. Dennis Walters. "Audience Diversity: A Major Challenge in Computer Documentation." *IEEE Transactions on Professional Communication* 29 (1986): 48–55.

Rosenblatt, Louise. *The Reader, the Text, the Poem: The Transactional Theory of the Literary Work.* Carbondale, IL: Southern Illinois UP, 1978.

Rosner, Mary. "Style and Audience in Technical Writing: Advice from the Early Texts." *The Technical Writing Teacher* 11 (1983): 38–45.

Ross, William T. "Self and Audience in Composition." *Freshman English News* 13 (Spring 1984): 14–16.

Roth, Robert G. "The Evolving Audience: Alternatives to Audience Accommodation." *College Composition and Communication* 38 (1987): 47–55.

Roundy, Nancy. "Audience Analysis: A Guide to Revision in Technical Writing." *The Technical Writing Teacher* 10 (1983): 94–100.

Rubin, Donald L. "Social Cognition and Written Communication." *Written Communication* 1 (1984): 211–245.

Rubin, Donald L., and Gene L. Piché. "Development in Syntactic and Strategic Aspects of Audience Adaptation Skills in Written Persuasive Communication." *Research in the Teaching of English* 13 (1979): 293–316.

Schenck, Eleanor M. "Technical Writers, Readers, and Context Clues." *Journal of Technical Writing and Communication* 10 (1980): 189–194.

Schweickart, Patrocinio P. "Add Gender and Stir." *Reader* 13 (1985): 1–9.

Scott, Fred Newton, and Joseph Villiers Denney. *Elementary English Composition.* Boston: Allyn and Bacon, 1908.

Selden, Raman. "Reader-Oriented Theories." *A Reader's Guide to Contemporary Literary Theory.* Lexington, KY: The UP of Kentucky, 1985. 106–127.

Selzer, Jack. "What Constitutes a 'Readable' Technical Style?" *New Essays in Technical and Scientific Communication: Research, Theory, Practice.* Ed. Paul V. Anderson et al. Farmingdale, NY: Baywood Press, 1983. 71–89.

Shannon, Claude, and Warren Weaver. *The Mathematical Theory of Communication.* Urbana, IL: U of Illinois P, 1949.

Spellmeyer, Kurt. "A Common Ground: The Essay in the Academy." *College English* 51 (1989): 262–276.

—. "Foucault and the Freshman Writer: Considering the Self in Discourse." *College English* 51 (1989): 715–729.

Spilka, Rachel. "Interacting with Multiple Readers: A Significant Component of Document Design in Corporate Environments." *Technical Communication* 36 (1989): 368–372.

—. "Orality and Literacy in the Workplace: Process- and Text-Based Strategies for Multiple-Audience Adaptation." *Journal of Business and Technical Communication* 4 (1990): 44–67.

—. "Studying Writer-Reader Interactions in the Workplace." *The Technical Writing Teacher* 15 (1988): 208–221.

Stewart, Donald C. "Textbooks Revisited." *Research in Composition and Rhetoric: A Bibliographic Sourcebook.* Ed. Michael G. Moran and Ronald F. Lunsford. Westport, CN: Greenwood, 1984. 453–468.

Street, Richard L., Jr. "Lexical Diversity as an Indicator of Audience Adaptation in Ciceronian Orations." *Central States Speech Journal* 30 (1979): 286–288.

Strunk, William, Jr. and E. B. White. *The Elements of Style.* Revised Edition. New York: Macmillan, 1962.

Suchan, James, and Ron Dulek. "Toward a Better Understanding of Reader Analysis." *Journal of Business Communication* 25 (1988): 29–45.

Suleiman, Susan R. "Introduction: Varieties of Audience-Oriented Criticism." *The Reader in the Text: Essays on Audience and Interpretation.* Ed. Susan R. Suleiman and Inge Crosman. Princeton, NJ: Princeton UP, 1980. 3–45.

Sullivan, Patricia. *Examining the Usability of Documentation.* Unpublished manuscript, 1990.

Sullivan, Patricia, and Linda Flower. "How Do Users Read Computer Manuals? Some Protocol Contributions to Writers' Knowledge." *Convergences: Essays on Reading, Writing, and Literacy.* Ed. B. T. Peterson. Urbana, IL: NCTE, 1986. 163–178.

Sullivan, Patricia A., and James E. Porter. "User Testing: The Heuristic Advantages at the Draft Stage." *Technical Communication* 37 (1990): 78–80.

Swales, John, and Hazem Najjar. "The Writing of Research Article Introductions." *Written Communication* 4 (1987): 175–191.

Thomas, Gordon P. "Mutual Knowledge: A Theoretical Basis for Analyzing Audience." *College English* 48 (1986): 580–594.

Thralls, Charlotte, Nancy Roundy Blyler, and Helen Rothschild Ewald. "Real Readers, Implied Readers, and Professional Writers: Suggested Research." *Journal of Business Communication* 25 (1988): 47–65.

Tierney, Robert J. "Writer-Reader Transactions: Defining the Dimensions of Negotiation." *fforum: Essays on Theory and Practice in the Teaching of Writing.* Ed. Patricia L. Stock. Upper Montclair, NJ: Boynton/Cook, 1983. 147–151.

Tompkins, Jane P. Introduction. *Reader-Response Criticism: From Formalism to Post-Structuralism.* Ed. Jane P. Tompkins. Baltimore, MD: Johns Hopkins UP, 1980. ix–xxvi.

Toulmin, Stephen. *The Uses of Argument.* Cambridge: Cambridge UP, 1958.

Vande Kopple, William. *Clear and Coherent Prose: A Functional Approach.* Glenview, IL: Scott, Foresman, 1989.

Van Maanen, John. *Tales of the Field: On Writing Ethnography.* Chicago: The U of Chicago P, 1988.

Vatz, Richard E. "The Myth of the Rhetorical Situation."*Philosophy and Rhetoric* 6 (1973): 154–161.

Wagner, Carl G. "The Technical Writing Audience: A Recent Bibliography." *The Technical Writing Teacher* 14 (1987): 243–263.

Wallace, Karl. "The Substance of Rhetoric: Good Reasons." *Quarterly Journal of Speech* 49 (1963): 239–249.

Walzer, Arthur E. "Articles from the 'California Divorce Project': A Case Study of the Concept of Audience." *College Composition and Communication* 36 (1985): 150–159.

Washington, Gene. "The Nature of 'Audience' " (editor's note). *Rhetoric Review* 3 (1985): 218–219.

Weaver, Richard M. *Language Is Sermonic.* Ed. Richard L. Johannesen et al. Baton Rouge, LA: Louisiana State UP, 1970.

Welch, Kathleen Ethel. "Keywords from Classical Rhetoric: The Example of *Physis.*" *Rhetoric Society Quarterly* 17 (1987): 193–204.

Wendell, Barrett. *English Composition.* New York: Scribner's, 1912.

Wexler, Joyce. "Modernist Writers and Publishers." *Studies in the Novel* 17 (1985): 286–295.

Whitburn, Merrill D. "The First Day in Technical Communication: An Approach to Audience Adaptation." *The Technical Writing Teacher* 3 (1976): 115–118.

White, Edward M. "Post-Structural Literary Criticism and the Response to Student Writing." *College Composition and Communication* 35 (1984): 186–195.

White, Hayden. *Metahistory: The Historical Imagination in Nineteenth-Century Europe.* Baltimore, MD: Johns Hopkins UP, 1973.

Willard, Charles Arthur. *Argumentation and the Social Grounds of Knowledge.* University, AL: U of Alabama P, 1983.

Willard, Thomas, and Stuart C. Brown. "The One and the Many: A Brief History of the Distinction." *A Sense of Audience in Written Communication.* Ed. Gesa Kirsch and Duane H. Roen. Newbury Park, CA: Sage, 1990. 40–57.

Williams, Joseph M. "Cognitive Development, Critical Thinking, and the Teaching of Writing." Conference on Writing, Meaning, and Higher Order Reasoning. University of Chicago, Chicago, IL, May 15, 1984.

—. *Style: Ten Lessons in Clarity and Grace*. 3rd ed. Glenview, IL: Scott, Foresman, 1988.

Wilson, W. Daniel. "Readers in Texts." *PMLA* 96 (1981): 848–863.

Winterowd, W. Ross. *The Contemporary Writer*. New York: Harcourt, 1975.

— (with Dorothy Augustine). "Speech Acts and the Reader-Writer Transaction." *Composition/Rhetoric: A Synthesis*. Carbondale, IL: Southern Illinois UP, 1986. 175–193.

Wolford, Chester L. "Teaching Audience in Technical Writing, or the Technical Writing Teacher as Weekend Novelist." *The Technical Writing Teacher* 7 (1979): 12–14.

Woodson, Linda. *A Handbook of Modern Rhetorical Terms*. Urbana, IL: NCTE, 1979.

Youga, Jan. *The Elements of Audience Analysis*. New York: Macmillan, 1989.

Young, Richard E. "Concepts of Art and the Teaching of Writing." *The Rhetorical Tradition and Modern Writing*. Ed. James J. Murphy. New York: MLA, 1982. 130–141.

—. "Paradigms and Problems: Needed Research in Rhetorical Invention." *Research in Composing*. Ed. Charles Cooper and Lee Odell. Urbana, IL: NCTE, 1978. 29–47.

—. "Recent Developments in Rhetorical Invention." *Teaching Composition: Twelve Bibliographical Essays*. Ed. Gary Tate. Fort Worth, TX: Texas Christian UP, 1987. 1–38.

Young, Richard E., Alton L. Becker, and Kenneth L. Pike. *Rhetoric: Discovery and Change*. New York: Harcourt, 1970.

Zappen, James P. "The Discourse Community in Scientific and Technical Communication: Institutional and Social Views." *Journal of Technical Writing and Communication* 19 (1989): 1–11.

—. "Rhetorical and Technical Communication: An Argument for Historical and Political Pluralism." *Iowa State Journal of Business and Technical Communication* 1 (1987): 29–44.

Ziman, John Michael. *Public Knowledge: An Essay Concerning the Social Dimension of Science*. Cambridge: Cambridge UP, 1968.

Zolten, J. Jerome. *Speaking to an Audience: A Practical Method of Preparing and Performing*. Indianapolis, IN: Bobbs-Merrill, 1984.

❧   *Author Index*

A

Abrams, M. H., 39, 47, 48, 156
Anderson, Paul V., 134, 135, 136, 156, 166, 173
Anson, Chris, 156
Aristotle, 2, 3, 4, 9, 10, 11, 14, 15–21, 24, 25, 26, 27, 30, 31, 32, 34, 53, 55, 57, 59, 114, 120, 121, 124, 125, 156
Atkins, G. Douglas, 156
Augustine, 24, 28, 120, 156
Augustine, Dorothy, 176

B

Bain, Alexander, 35, 46, 156
Baker, Sheridan, 29, 45, 47, 156, 157
Barnes-Ostrander, Marilyn, 134, 156, 167
Barthes, Roland, 10, 14, 68, 157

Bator, Paul, 62, 157
Bazerman, Charles, 83, 98, 157
Beach, Richard, 157
Becker, Alton L., 2, 11, 55, 58, 59, 62, 72, 76, 77, 118, 176
Becker, Carl, 76, 157
Berger, Peter L., 86, 99, 157
Berkenkotter, Carol, 118, 157
Berlin, James, 6, 27, 30, 31, 36, 38, 39, 45, 46, 47, 48, 52, 55, 60, 61, 102, 157
Bernstein, Basil, 87, 99, 157
Berquist, Goodwin F., 26, 61, 165
Bevilacqua, Vincent M., 46, 158
Bitzer, Lloyd, 27, 45, 46, 53, 60, 107, 117, 158
Bizzell, Patricia, 83, 98, 99, 103, 158
Black, Edwin, 158
Blair, Hugh, 25, 30, 31–32, 45, 158
Bleich, David, 64, 75, 158
Blyler, Nancy, (See also Roundy) 173, 174

179

Booth, Wayne C., 39, 48, 53, 60, 158
Bradford, Annette N., 158
Bramer, George, 158
Branham, Robert J., 158
Britton, James, 158
Broadhead, Glenn J., 164
Brooke, Robert, 158
Brooks, Cleanth, 33, 45, 158
Brown, Gillian, 27, 159
Brown, Maurice, 159
Brown, Stuart C., 28, 45, 159, 175
Bruffee, Kenneth A., 83, 98, 105, 115, 117, 159
Bruner, Jerome S., 159
Buck, Gertrude, 39, 48, 159
Burke, Kenneth, 14, 16, 25, 28, 52, 59, 79, 80, 81, 97, 110, 116, 118, 126, 159

——— C ———

Campbell, George, 9, 10, 14, 25, 30, 31, 32–34, 35, 36, 41, 43, 45, 46, 48, 55, 114, 159
Campbell, J. W., 61, 167
Carey, Robert F., 159
Carosso, Rebecca Burnett, 134, 159
Carson, David L., 135, 159
Ceccio, Joseph F., 159
Cicero, 1, 11, 16, 19–21, 26, 159
Clark, Gregory, 159
Clarke, Jennifer, 159
Clevenger, Theodore, Jr., 11, 160
Coe, Richard M., 160
Coleman, William E., 16, 61, 165
Collins, James L., 160
Coney, Mary B., 135, 160
Connors, Robert J., 26, 27, 28, 48, 160, 164, 168, 172
Consigny, Scott, 60, 61, 160
Cooper, Charles, 45, 176
Cooper, Martha, 160
Cope, John Q., 61, 167
Corbett, Edward P. J., 11, 25, 55, 59, 61, 62, 160

Corder, Jim W., 94, 102, 118, 160
Crismore, Avon, 135, 160
Crosman, Inge, 75, 174
Crosswhite, James, 160
Crowhurst, Marion, 160
Crowley, Sharon, 46, 160
Culler, Jonathan, 64, 69, 76, 97, 160

——— D ———

Daiute, Colette A., 161
D'Angelo, Frank J., 2, 11, 55, 77, 161
Daumer, Elisabeth, 75, 161
Davidson, Arnold I., 14, 161
Davidson, Donald, 165
Davis, Ken, 161
Dearin, Ray D., 161
Deleuze, Gilles, 13, 14, 92, 100, 101, 161
Denney, Joseph Villiers, 39, 40, 48, 173
Derrida, Jacques, 27, 28, 68, 82, 161
Diggs, B. J., 161
Dillon, George L., 11, 13, 161
Dilworth, Collett B., Jr., 161
Dobrin, David N., 161
Doheny-Farina, Stephen, 161
Dreyfus, Hubert C., 14, 100, 101, 161
Driskill, Linda, 133, 135, 136, 161
Duhamel, P. Albert, 55, 61, 166
Dulek, Ron, 12, 135, 174
Dumbauld, Edward, 76, 161
Dye, K. L., 170

——— E ———

Eagleton, Terry, 161
Ede, Lisa S., 6, 7, 12, 18, 19, 26, 27, 28, 62, 63, 73, 74, 77, 156, 160, 161, 162, 164, 168, 172
Elbow, Peter, 31, 37, 47, 159, 162

Emig, Janet, 11, 61, 77, 142, 162, 168
Enos, Richard Leo, 27, 162
Ewald, Helen Rothschild, 162, 174

——— F ———

Faigley, Lester, 136, 162
Felker, Daniel B., 129, 135, 136, 162, 172
Fetterley, Judith, 64, 162
Feyerabend, Paul, 162
Fish, Stanley, 64, 74, 75, 88, 89, 99, 107, 117, 162
Floreak, Michael, 163
Flower, Linda, 41–43, 48, 49, 163, 174
Flynn, Elizabeth, 163
Fogarty, Daniel, S. J., 45, 52, 53, 59, 60, 118, 163
Fontaine, Sheryl I., 163
Forman, Janis, 163
Forsberg, L. Lee, 136, 163
Foss, Karen A., 163
Foss, Sonja K., 163
Foucault, Michel, 8, 10, 13, 14, 25, 28, 68, 88, 89–94, 95, 97, 100, 101, 102, 103, 109, 117, 118, 124, 126, 163, 164
Frank, Francine Wattman, 169
Freed, Richard C., 164
Fulkerson, Richard, 164
Fulwiler, Toby, 159
Funkhouser, G. Ray, 164

——— G ———

Gage, John T., 27, 164
Gallagher, Brian, 164
Geertz, Clifford, 99, 164
Genung, John Franklin, 29, 35, 38, 44, 46, 164
George, Diana, 75, 164
Gere, Ann Ruggles, 98, 164
Gergen, Kenneth J., 164

Gillan, Garth, 14, 168
Gleick, James, 100, 117, 164
Golden, James L., 26, 61, 164, 165
Gordon, Colin, 164
Goswami, Dixie, 136, 162, 171
Gragson, Gay, 76, 165
Gregg, Lee W., 49, 163
Grice, H. P., 165
Griffiths, A. Phillips, 170
Grimaldi, William M. A., S. J., 26, 165
Gumperz, John J., 99, 165

——— H ———

Hacking, Ian, 165
Hagaman, John, 45, 165
Hairston, Maxine C., 11, 60, 62, 165
Halloran, Michael, 165
Halpern, Jeanne W., 165
Hamermesh, Madeline, 165
Harding, Harold F., 45, 158
Harned, Jon, 165
Harris, Joseph, 94, 95, 103, 117, 165
Hartley, James, 165
Havelock, Eric, 21, 27, 165
Hawkes, Terence, 27, 165
Hayes, John R., 41–43, 48, 49, 163
Heath, Shirley Brice, 99, 165
Hemingway, Ernest, 67, 76, 165
Hendricks, John, 158
Herman, Gilbert, 165
Herrstrom, David Sten, 165
Hill, Adams Sherman, 34, 35, 46, 166
Hill, Forbes I., 26, 166
Hillocks, George, Jr., 156, 166
Hirsch, E. D., Jr., 48, 166
Holland, Norman, 64, 75, 166
Holtzman, Paul D., 12, 166
Holub, Robert C., 166
Horner, Winifred Bryan, 166
Hoy, David Couzens, 161, 165
Huckin, Thomas N., 130, 134, 135, 166, 171
Hughes, Richard E., 55, 61, 166

——— I ———

Ingham, Zita, 159
Inkster, Robert P., 45, 46, 157
Irmscher, William F., 55, 61, 166
Iser, Wolfgang, 64, 75, 76, 166

——— J ———

Jarratt, Susan C., 166
Jauss, Hans Robert, 64, 75, 122,
    166
Jenkins, Joseph R., 118, 166
Johannessen, Larry, 156
Johannessen, Richard L., 175
Johnson, Mark, 62, 125, 126, 168
Johnson, Michael L., 156
Johnson, Nan, 166
Johnstone, Henry W., Jr., 166
Journet, Debra, 134, 167
Juhl, P. D., 166
Jurkiewicz, Kenneth, 62, 166

——— K ———

Karlinsky, Stewart S., 166
Keene, Michael, 134, 156, 167
Kennedy, George, 27, 167
Kerferd, G. B., 167
Kifner, John, 70, 71, 76, 102, 167
Kinneavy, James L., 6, 52, 53,
    55–58, 59, 60, 61, 62, 76, 107,
    117, 167
Kirsch, Gesa, 13, 28, 45, 77, 97,
    118, 157, 159, 167, 171, 172,
    175
Kneupper, Charles, 45, 98, 117,
    160, 167, 168, 169
Knoblauch, C. H., 167
Koch, Bruce S., 166
Kogen, Myra, 135, 161, 164, 167
Kroll, Barry M., 13, 167
Kuhn, Thomas S., 88, 89, 95, 99,
    101, 107, 110, 117, 167

——— L ———

LaClau, Ernesto, 100, 168

Lakoff, George, 62, 125, 126, 168
Lamb, Catherine E., 168
Lanham, Richard A., 1, 2, 11, 168
Lauer, Janice, 2, 11, 55, 61, 77,
    142, 143, 168
LeFevre, Karen Burke, 83, 98, 168
Leggett, Glenn, 11, 168
Leitch, Vincent, 8, 9, 13, 68, 76,
    107, 112, 117, 118, 168
Lemert, Charles C., 14, 168
Lentricchia, Frank, 88, 99, 110,
    118, 168
Liebman-Kleine, Joanne, 157
Locker, Kitty, 168
Long, Russell C., 7, 12, 168
Lovejoy, Kim Brian, 98, 168
Luckmann, Thomas, 86, 99
Lundberg, Patricia Lorimer, 64,
    65, 75, 168
Lunsford, Andrea A., 6, 7, 11, 13,
    18, 19, 26, 27, 28, 61, 62, 63,
    73, 74, 77, 142, 160, 162, 164,
    168, 172
Lunsford, Ronald, 45, 60, 174
Lyotard, Jean-Francois, 101, 119,
    122, 125, 126, 168

——— M ———

Maccoby, Nathan, 164
Macdonald, Kathleen, 77, 169
MacDonald, Susan Peck, 83, 98,
    169
Macrorie, Ken, 31, 37, 38, 47, 169
Mailloux, Steven, 64, 74, 75, 169
Maimon, Elaine P., 76, 98, 99, 169
Makay, John J., 169
Matalene, Carolyn B., 163, 169
Mathes, J. C., 136, 169
Mathews, William, 169
McClaran, Jeanne L., 27, 162
McClearey, Keven E., 169
McConnell-Ginet, Sally, 169
McCrimmon, James M., 35, 37,
    46, 169
McDermott, Douglas, 169
McDonald, John C., 45, 169

McQuade, Donald, 60, 99, 117, 167, 169
Miller, Carolyn R., 25, 125, 169
Miller, James E., Jr., 31, 47, 170
Miller, Keith D., 170
Mills, Carl, 87, 88, 99, 170
Mills, C. B., 170
Minot, Walter, 170
Mitchell, Ruth, 170
Moffett, James, 170
Monahan, Brian D., 170
Montague, Gene, 2, 11, 61, 77, 142, 168
Moran, Michael G., 45, 60, 134, 167, 174
Mouffe, Chantal, 100, 168
Moxley, Joseph M., 170
Murphy, James J., 26, 27, 28, 47, 166, 170, 176
Murphy, John W., 82, 97, 112, 118, 170
Murray, Donald M., 31, 47, 170
Myers, Greg, 83, 98, 170

——— N ———

Najjar, Hazem, 98, 174
Neel, Jasper, 21, 23, 27, 28, 48, 170
Norris, Christopher, 170
Noujain, Elie Georges, 170
Nystrand, Martin, 99, 171

——— O ———

Odell, Lee, 45, 136, 162, 171, 176
Odom, Samuel L., 118, 166
Olbrechts-Tyteca, L., 51, 52, 53–55, 60, 61, 171
Olsen, Leslie, 134, 135, 171
Ong, Walter, S. J., 21, 27, 67, 75, 76, 171
Overington, Michael A., 171

——— P ———

Park, Douglas, 5, 6, 7, 11, 12, 61,
72, 76, 98, 108, 109, 107, 112, 117, 138, 142, 171
Pearce, W. Barnett, 158
Pearsall, Thomas, 134, 171
Perelman, Chaim, 6, 7, 51, 52, 53–55, 59, 60, 61, 62, 73, 76, 77, 83, 121, 122, 126, 171
Peterson, B. T., 174
Petrick, Joanne F., 171
Pfister, Fred R., 171
Phelps, Louise Wetherbee, 77, 97, 118, 125, 171
Piche, Gene L., 160, 173
Pike, Kenneth L., 2, 11, 55, 58, 59, 62, 72, 76, 77, 118, 176
Pirsig, Robert M., 171
Plato, 15, 17, 21, 24, 26, 171
Porter, James E., 26, 28, 76, 98, 99, 117, 136, 142, 145, 171, 172, 174
Porter, Jeffrey, 72, 76, 172
Pratt, Mary Louise, 172
Pressman, Rebecca, 135, 172
Purves, Alan C., 172

——— Q ———

Quintilian, 19–20, 47, 172

——— R ———

Rabinow, Paul, 14, 100, 101, 102, 117, 161, 164
Rabinowitz, Peter J., 12, 75, 76, 172
Rafoth, Bennett A., 172
Raymond, James C., 27, 172
Redish, Janice C., 131, 135, 136, 172, 173
Reising, Robert W., 161
Roberts, David D., 173
Rod, David K., 25, 173
Roen, Duane H., 13, 28, 45, 77, 97, 118, 157, 159, 167, 171, 172, 175
Romaine, Suzanne, 173
Ronald, Kate, 173

Rose, A., 136, 172
Rosenbaum, Stephanie, 173
Rosenblatt, Louise, 64, 173
Rosner, Mary, 173
Ross, William T., 72, 76, 173
Rossi, Michael J., 159
Roth, Robert G., 12, 173
Roundy, Nancy (*See also* Blyler) 173, 174
Rubin, Donald L., 173

——— S ———

Schenck, Eleanor M., 173
Schweickart, Patrocinio P., 75, 163, 173
Scott, Fred Newton, 35, 39, 40, 48, 173
Selden, Raman, 75, 173
Selzer, Jack, 76, 131, 135, 136, 165, 173
Shannon, Claude, 128, 129, 135, 173
Shoos, Diane, 75, 164
Sills, David, 165
Spellmeyer, Kurt, 94, 95, 96, 102, 118, 174
Speltz, Matthew L., 118, 166
Spilka, Rachel, 136, 174
Steinberg, Erwin, 49, 163
Stevenson, Dwight W., 136, 169
Stewart, Donald C., 45, 47, 60, 174
Stine, Donna, 162
Stock, Patricia, 166, 174
Street, Richard L., Jr., 27, 174
Strunk, William, Jr., 37, 45, 47, 174
Suchan, James, 12, 135, 174
Suleiman, Susan, 75, 174
Sullivan, Patricia A., 136, 173, 174
Swales, John, 98, 174

——— T ———

Tate, Gary, 76, 156, 167

Taylor, Mary, 170
Thomas, Gordon P., 174
Thralls, Charlotte, 135, 174
Tierney, Robert J., 174
Tompkins, Jane P., 75, 175
Toulmin, Stephen, 175
Trapp, Robert, 163
Treichler, Paula A., 169

——— V ———

Vande Kopple, William, 135, 175
Van Maannen, John, 99, 175
Vatz, Richard E., 60, 61, 175

——— W ———

Wagner, Carl G., 134, 156, 175
Wallace, Karl, 121, 175
Walters, R. Dennis, 173
Walzer, Arthur E., 12, 118, 175
Warren, Robert Penn, 33, 45, 158
Washington, Gene, 175
Weaver, Richard M., 52, 121, 124, 126, 175
Weaver, Warren, 128, 129, 135, 173
Welch, Kathleen Ethel, 13, 175
Wendell, Barrett, 34, 35, 46, 175
Wexler, Joyce, 47, 175
Whitburn, Merrill D., 158, 175
White, E. B., 29, 31, 37, 45, 47, 174
White, Edward M., 175
White, Hayden, 68, 175
Willard, Charles Arthur, 99, 175
Willard, Thomas, 28, 45, 159, 175
Williams, Joseph M., 111, 118, 135, 175, 176
Williamson, Michael M., 160
Wilson, W. Daniel, 11, 12, 65, 66, 68, 75, 76, 176
Winterowd, W. Ross, 55, 61, 176
Wolford, Chester L., 176
Woodson, Linda, 1, 2, 11, 176

——— Y ———

Youga, Jan, 62, 176
Young, Richard E., 2, 11, 30, 37,
    38, 45, 46, 47, 52, 55, 58, 59,
    62, 72, 76, 77, 118, 156, 176
Yule, George, 27, 159

——— Z ———

Zappen, James P., 176
Ziman, John Michael, 176
Zolten, J. Jerome, 176